METAHEURISTICS ALGORITHMS FOR MEDICAL APPLICATIONS

METAHEURISTICS ALGORITHMS FOR MEDICAL APPLICATIONS
Methods and Applications

MOHAMED ABDEL-BASSET
Faculty of Computers and Informatics, Zagazig University, Zagazig, Sharqiyah, Egypt

REDA MOHAMED
Faculty of Computers and Informatics, Zagazig University, Zagazig, Sharqiyah, Egypt

MOHAMED ELHOSENY
College of Computing and Informatics, University of Sharjah, Sharjah, United Arab Emirates

ACADEMIC PRESS
An imprint of Elsevier

ELSEVIER

Academic Press is an imprint of Elsevier
125 London Wall, London EC2Y 5AS, United Kingdom
525 B Street, Suite 1650, San Diego, CA 92101, United States
50 Hampshire Street, 5th Floor, Cambridge, MA 02139, United States
The Boulevard, Langford Lane, Kidlington, Oxford OX5 1GB, United Kingdom

Notices

Knowledge and best practice in this field are constantly changing. As new research and experience broaden our understanding, changes in research methods, professional practices, or medical treatment may become necessary.

Practitioners and researchers must always rely on their own experience and knowledge in evaluating and using any information, methods, compounds, or experiments described herein. In using such information or methods they should be mindful of their own safety and the safety of others, including parties for whom they have a professional responsibility.

To the fullest extent of the law, neither the Publisher nor the authors, contributors, or editors, assume any liability for any injury and/or damage to persons or property as a matter of products liability, negligence or otherwise, or from any use or operation of any methods, products, instructions, or ideas contained in the material herein.

ISBN: 978-0-443-13314-5

For Information on all Academic Press publications
visit our website at https://www.elsevier.com/books-and-journals

Publisher: Mara Conner
Acquisitions Editor: Chris Katsaropoulos
Editorial Project Manager: Toni Louise Jackson
Production Project Manager: Fahmida Sultana
Cover Designer: Vicky Pearson Esser

Typeset by MPS Limited, Chennai, India

Contents

Metaheuristic algorithms and medical applications

1.1 Introduction

What is optimization? What is the role of optimization in several real-world applications? Several questions like these might be in the heads of several students and researchers. Therefore herein, we will try to define it and clarify its role in several applications, including medical, industrial, engineering, and several others. Optimization is around us in several fields, even for those that you might expect would be unbeneficial. In general, the term *optimization* means minimizing or maximizing some criteria as much as possible with the purpose of finding solutions that could yield a better return. These criteria are known as optimization problems and could be classified into two categories: continuous and discrete, depending on the decision variables to be optimized. Many optimization strategies, broadly falling into two classes—deterministic and stochastic—have been presented over the past few decades to address these optimization problems. Algorithms are said to be deterministic if and only if they always return the same result given the same input. Unfortunately, when tackling optimization problems with several local minima, these approaches tend to get stuck in local minima. To this end, researchers have devised stochastic optimization strategies that can bring about substantial results in a reasonable amount of time for a variety of optimization problems.

In this chapter, we will start an exciting journey to determine the types of optimization problems and the stochastic optimization techniques that can solve these problems, in addition to the role of these techniques in medical applications, which consider the main topic of this book.

1.2 What is the optimization problem

These problems are known as optimization problems because their global minima are found within a predefined search space

Metaheuristics Algorithms for Medical Applications. DOI: https://doi.org/10.1016/B978-0-443-13314-5.00013-8

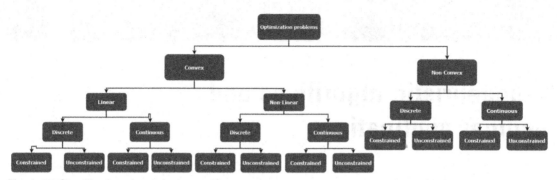

Figure 1.1 Classification of optimization problems.

that might have several local minima; hence, the solutions obtained for these problems might be local minima that need to be further optimized to reach the global minima. The optimization problems could be classified into two main categories: ***nonconvex*** and ***convex*** (See Fig. 1.1). The ***nonconvex*** problems have several local minima and are considered a challenge because most of the optimization techniques, especially traditional techniques, get caught in the local minima and could not get out to reach the global minima (see Fig. 1.2A). On the other hand, the convex problems are those that have one global minimum and no local minima, as depicted in Fig. 1.2B; so, they could be easily solved. The ***local minima*** are those solutions that have some of the properties of the global solution but do not consider the ***minimum*** of the optimization problem; this minimum is called the ***global minima***. Some of these optimization problems are solved in the presence of some constraints that have to be satisfied by the obtained solutions. These problems are called constrained optimization problems; while the others are directly solved without constraints.

The optimization problems might have single-, multi-, and many-objective functions that have to be accurately optimized for reaching their optimal solution. If you have a problem with only one objective function, finding the best possible solution is easy. In the case of a minimization problem, for instance, solution A is chosen if and only if it achieves a lower fitness value than the alternative solution B. Finding a solution that minimizes all objectives for multi- and many-objective problems is difficult since the objectives are in competition, and a solution that improves one objective may degrade the others. Thus in literature, the Pareto optimality theory has been employed to address this difficulty by creating a set of solutions known as ***nondominated solutions***, each of which could optimize at least one objective while maintaining the quality of the other

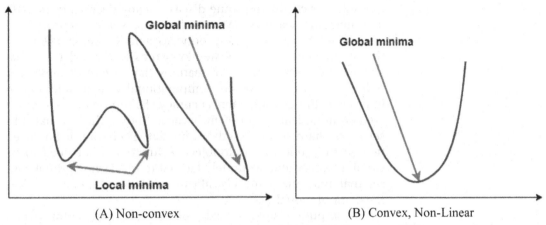

(A) Non-convex   (B) Convex, Non-Linear

Figure 1.2 Curves of nonconvex and convex optimization problems. (A) Nonconvex. (B) Convex, nonlinear.

objectives. Pareto-optimal solutions are those that, throughout the entirety of the search space, are unaffected by the dominance of any other feasible solution. An efficient front is the collection of Pareto-optimal solutions in the objective space [1]. In the following, to provide more clarity, a general mathematical model of a minimization-constrained problem is described:

$$\text{Minimize } f(\vec{X}) = \left\{ f_L(\vec{X}) \right\}, \qquad (1.1)$$

$$\text{Subject to } nq_i(\vec{X}) \geq 0, i = 1, 2, \ldots, z$$

$$q_i(\vec{X}) = 0, i = 1, 2, \ldots, k$$

In this model, $\vec{X}$ represents the estimated solution that is evaluated using a single objective function $f(\vec{X})$ if L is 1; otherwise, it is evaluated using multiobjectives when $L = 2$, or 3, and many objectives higher than 3. Although this solution might optimize the objectives, it might not be satisfied to some constraints that are classified into two categories: equality constraints (q_i) and inequality constraints (nq_i).

1.3   Optimization problems in medical applications

What is the relation between optimization problems and medical applications? There are a lot of applications in medical fields that need to be optimized to fulfill better findings. For example, for classifying some diseases using deep learning (DL) and machine learning (ML) techniques, some preprocessing steps need to be accurately done to achieve better accuracy; this step includes a crucial step known as feature selection that strives to extract a subset of features that is free of noise and redundant data to save on computational cost in addition to improving the classification accuracy. This problem is considered an optimization problem because finding the optimal subset is too hard to be exactly estimated. Therefore, it has been tackled by proposing multiobjective functions that need to be simultaneously and accurately tackled to reach the optimal subset that maximizes the classification accuracy and minimizes the computational cost.

In computer vision, several processes could be performed on the image for achieving better classification accuracy. For example, the image segmentation problem is considered a critical problem that aims to extract similar regions within an image to maximize the classification accuracy of the deep learning model [2]. This problem is modeled by three objective functions in literature, namely, Kapur's entropy [3], and Otsu function [4] that have to be accurately optimized for tackling this problem. Moreover, the biological images may have noise issues as well as other quality-related issues like poor contrast, blurring, and challenges with appropriate information extraction. Thus, it is essential to improve these images in a way that makes them suitable for further processing; this problem is called image enhancement. The field of medical imaging and processing faces the challenge of image corruption due to noise. There are a variety of noises that can contaminate images, each of which requires a unique denoising method. Denoising's primary principle is to clean up images by getting rid of the noise without damaging the edges. Processing models have difficulty when tasked with denoising while keeping edges because of the similarities between edge and noise components (high frequency and comparable properties) [5]. An important area of study in digital image processing is image registration (IR) [6]. It is utilized to align two or more images that were captured under various circumstances, including distinct times, sensors, views, or a combination of these. In IR, both the input and output images are present, but it is typically impossible to determine the precise transformation that resulted in the output image from the input image. In order to turn those separate images into a single common image, IR seeks to estimate the optimum geometric transformation that will produce the best potential overlap.

DNA is broken down into smaller parts called fragments or segments to make it easier to read when a huge DNA sequence is being read by the computer. There is a need for reassembly of the DNA fragments after reading because the order of the fragments is lost. This problem was known as the DNA Fragment Assembly Problem and is considered a hard optimization problem. This problem was solved in the literature based on two objectives: the first one is maximizing the overlap score, while the second one is minimizing the number of contigs to form a single strand of DNA.

Furthermore, ML and DL techniques are considered indispensable techniques in analyzing a huge amount of medical data for predicting and classifying various diseases [7]. Unfortunately, those techniques have some parameters that need to be carefully optimized for maximizing the classification and prediction accuracy. There are several techniques to estimate these parameters, which are divided into two categories: traditional and stochastic. The traditional techniques suffer from poor performance when those parameters are large-scale. Therefore, some scientists pay attention to the stochastic methods to solve this problem.

In general, to solve optimization problems in medical fields, there are two types of optimization techniques: deterministic and stochastic. The deterministic techniques suffer from poor performance when solving nonconvex optimization problems; on the contrary, the stochastic techniques, also referred to as metaheuristic algorithms, have strong performance for tackling those problems. As a result, metaheuristic techniques have indispensable roles in the medical field to aid in improving the quality of medical services. In the following section, the metaheuristics are discussed in more detail.

1.4 What is metaheuristics

Over the past few decades, many algorithms for solving optimization problems have been proposed. Each one of those tries to address the demerits of the previous algorithms in an attempt to overcome several optimization problems that are hard to be solved in polynomial time. Among those optimization algorithms, modern optimization algorithms known as metaheuristic algorithms or stochastic optimization algorithms, have been presented to solve the majority of the optimization problems, especially those on a large scale, in a considerable amount of time. These algorithms are not problem-specific; hence, they could be applied to solve several real-world optimization problems. For example, in the medical field, they have been employed to tackle multilevel thresholding image segmentation, medical feature selection, DNA fragment assembly problem, and image denoising. In addition, they could be employed to tackle several large-scale optimization problems at a reasonable time; some of them are scheduling problems, feature selection, UAV path planning, 0–1 knapsack problems, multidimensional knapsack problems, and several others. More than that, these algorithms could efficiently tackle several challenging continuous optimization problems with several local minima. Due to the significant success achieved by those algorithms for several optimization problems, in this book, we will analyze the performance of some recently proposed metaheuristic algorithms for solving optimization problems in the medical field. In this section, we will first discuss various categories of metaheuristics, followed by a description of the main stages of any metaheuristic. Finally, some of the recently-published and well-established algorithms are described in terms of their behavior and mathematical model. In the next chapters, those algorithms are either used as compared algorithms to show the effectiveness of the newly proposed algorithms or improved using a specific technique to maximize their performance for solving some optimization problems.

1.4.1 Metaheuristics classification

Over the last few decades, many different optimization strategies have been suggested as potential solutions to optimization problems. However, simultaneously, the complexity of optimization problems in the real world has dramatically increased as a result of the accelerated development of human society as well as modern industrial and technological processes. This presents a significant challenge for optimization techniques. Existing optimization methods can be broadly divided into main categories: deterministic and metaheuristic/Stochastic. Deterministic methods are mechanical and iterative, and have a precise mathematical formulation that does not involve random aspects. As their main advantage compared to stochastic optimization techniques, these methods may be able to converge to the near-optimal solution more quickly. This kind of optimization method is computationally expensive due to the need for gradient information. In addition, deterministic techniques are inherently single-objective. Certain components are required to initiate an optimization process, regardless of whether the approach is deterministic or stochastic [8]. Classic examples of deterministic methods are gradient descent and Newton's methods.

As a promising substitute for deterministic techniques, meta-heuristic algorithms (MAs), also known as stochastic optimization techniques, have been developed. MAs take their ideas from nature and use random search strategies to find near-optimal solutions in the search space. Unfortunately, due to the stochastic nature of these algorithms, the best possible solution cannot be discovered in each attempt. These algorithms have two main stages, namely exploration, and exploitation, which are followed within the whole optimization process without the need to use derivative informa-tion for reaching the desired solution. In the exploration stage, MAs try to explore all the regions in the search space in the hope of arriving at the promising region that may involve the desired solution. Afterward, this promising region is extensively explored in the exploitation stage for generating a better solution. Balancing between those two stages could aid in avoiding stagnation into local minima and moving quickly in the right direction of the global minima. Even now, no MH could achieve this balance. Over the last few years, researchers have paid attention to MAs because of the following merits:

- Easy to be understood and implemented.
- Able to reach the global optimum for complex optimization problems with several peaks.
- Able to be easily adapted for various fields, such as optimal control, image processing, energy, medicine, scheduling, finance, economy and trade, and engineering design applications.
- No need for the derivative information.

Nevertheless, the majority of MHs still suffer from the fol-lowing flaws that stand as strict obstacles in front of reaching the global minima of several optimization problems:

- Sensitivity to the controlling parameters.
- Entrapment into Local optimum.
- Population diversity's lack [9].

No free lunch (NFL) theorem has been presented to determine the relationship between effective optimization approaches and the addressed optimization problem [10]. According to NFL, the fact that an algorithm performs well for one class of optimization issues does not necessarily mean that it will perform as well when applied to other classes of optimization problems because of the variety of these problems' characteristics.

There are two primary classifications of metaheuristic algo-rithms: population-based and single solution-based algorithms [11]. The latter method takes into account only one solution for the entirety of the optimization stage, whereas the former method develops a population of solutions with each iteration of the process. For many different optimization problems, population-based metaheuristic algorithms, abbreviated as P-metaheuristics, can locate optimal or near-optimal solutions. These algorithms help avoid situations in which a locally optimal solution has been found because multiple solutions can support one another and result in a thorough investigation of the search space. In addition to this, they can go ahead to a potentially fruitful region of the search space. It is possible to divide P-metaheuristics into the following four categories: evolution-based, physics-based, swarm-based, and human-based algorithms that are described next in detail:

Evolution-based algorithms: these algorithms are inspired by the processes of natural evolution. These strategies begin their search with the generational evolution of a randomly generated population. The power of these methods lies in their consistent ability to bring together the fittest individuals to produce offspring using some operators like crossover and mutation borrowed from biology. Genetic Algorithm (GA), inspired by Darwinian evolution theory, is by far the most widely used algorithm with an evolutionary basis. To produce better offspring from some suitable parents, GA makes use of the concept of cross-over. Naturally occurring crossover keeps populations diverse so that several solutions can be covered in the search space for optimization problems. Changes brought about by mutations result in offspring that do not look or act like their parents. The purpose of this GA operator is to explore the solutions around a given parent. This operator is applied according to a probabilistic value, namely mutation probability, to prevent the randomized search. There are several other evolution-based algorithms, including Differential evolution (DE) [12], Evolution Strategy (ES) [12], Forest optimization algorithm [12], Gradient evolution algorithm (GEA) [12], Evolutionary programming (EP) [12], Biogeography-Based Optimizer (BBO) [12], Tree-seed algorithm (TSA) [12], and Genetic Programming (GP) [12].

Physics-based algorithms: These algorithms, which are drawn from physical laws of nature, frequently define how search agents interact in terms of governing laws derived from physical processes. Simulated annealing (SA), one of the most common algorithms in this category, was created by simulating the application of thermodynamic laws to the controlled heating and cooling of a material to enlarge the size of its crystals [10]. The Gravity Search Algorithm (GSA), which was based on the law of gravity and mass interactions to update the position towards the ideal point [10], is the second most well-known method in this class. There are several other physics-based techniques [12]: Big-Bang Big-Crunch (BBBC), Galaxy-based Search Algorithm (GbSA), Curved Space Optimization (CSO), Henry gas solubility optimization (HGSO) algorithm [13], Space Gravitational Algorithm (SGA), Ray Optimization (RO) algorithm, Black Hole (BH) algorithm, Artificial Chemical Reaction Optimization Algorithm (ACROA), Sine cosine algorithm (SCA), Multiverse Optimizer (MVO), Water cycle algorithm (WCA), Intelligent Water Drops (IWD) Algorithm, Gravitational Local Search Algorithm (GLSA), Integrated Radiation Algorithm (IRA), Central Force Optimization (CFO), Electromagnetism-Like Algorithm (EMA), Ion Motion Algorithm (IMA), River Formation Dynamics (RFD) Algorithm, Equilibrium Optimizer (EO), Artificial Physics Algorithm (APA), Charged System Search, and Archimedes optimization algorithm (AOA).

Swarm-based algorithms: These algorithms imitate how animals act in groups (i.e., flocks, herds, or schools). These algorithms' main trait is that they all share a common knowledge base while being optimized. Kennedy and Eberhart created the particle swarm optimization method, which is the most popular swarm-based algorithm [14]. This category includes several other optimization algorithms, including Duck Swarm Algorithm (DSA) [15], artificial hummingbird algorithm (AHA), chameleon Swarm Algorithm (CSA) [16], horse herd Optimization Algorithm (HOA) [17], slime mould algorithm (SMA) [16], bat algorithm (BA) [18], ant colony optimization (ACO) [19], wolf pack search algorithm (WPS) [20], firefly Algorithm (FA) [21], wasp swarm optimization (WSO) [16], grey wolf optimizer (GWO), red fox optimization algorithm (RFO), krill herd algorithm (KH), whale optimization algorithm (WOA) [16], Cuckoo Search Algorithm (CSA), Bee Collecting Pollen Algorithm (BCPA), salp swarm algorithm (SSA), donkey and smuggler optimization algorithm (DSA), marine predators algorithm (MPA) [16], cat optimization algorithm (COA), artificial gorilla troops Optimizer (GTO), hunting search (HUS), monkey search (MS) [16], chicken swarm optimization (CSO) [16], and butterfly optimization algorithm (BOA) [16].

Human-based algorithms: The human-based algorithms derive their inspiration from simulating human behaviors and social interactions. There are a number of algorithms in these areas, some of which are past-present future (PPF), exchange market algorithm (EMA), brainstorm optimization (BSO), harmony search (HS), political optimizer (PO), and soccer league competition (SLC) [16].

1.4.2 Main stages of a metaheuristic

The majority of the metaheuristics are compounded of three stages: initialization, evaluation, and optimization process. In the first stage, a number N of solutions will be randomly scattered within the search space of the optimization problem in an attempt to explore this space as possible for accelerating the convergence speed and avoiding being stuck in local optima. There are several ways to initialize these solutions, one of the most common ones is based on using the uniform distribution to distribute the solutions within the search space as formulated in the following formula:

$$\vec{X}_i = \vec{L} + (\vec{U} - \vec{L}) \cdot \vec{r} \tag{1.2}$$

where $\vec{L}$ represents the lower bound of the optimization problem, $\vec{U}$ represents the upper bound, and $\vec{r}$ stands for a vector including values generated randomly according to the uniform distribution. Afterward, the second stage called *evaluation* is executed to assess these solutions by the optimization problems, and the solution with the lowest objective value for the minimization problem is considered as the best-so-far solution. Following the evaluation stage, the optimization process of a MH is started to update the initialized solution for reaching better quality solutions. In this stage, the updated solutions are assessed and the best-so-far solution is replaced if there is a better solution. The optimization process is continued until the termination criteria are achieved. The termination condition is satisfied after reaching either the maximum number of function evaluations or the desired solutions. The main stages of any MH algorithm are summarized in Fig. 1.3.

1.4.3 Nutcracker optimization algorithm

Recently, the Nutcracker Optimization Algorithm (NOA) has been proposed as a new method for tackling global optimization and engineering optimization problems [12]. NOA simulates the foraging, storage, and pine seed retrieval behaviors of nutcrackers. In a general sense, nutcrackers exhibit two distinct behavioral patterns, each of which occurs at a different time. The first pattern of activity, prevalent during the warmer months of the year, indicates that the nutcracker is gathering seeds for winter storage. During the spring and winter, an alternative behavior is considered, which entails searching for concealed caches that have been marked at various angles using various reference points. If the nutcrackers are unable to access their stored food supply of seeds,

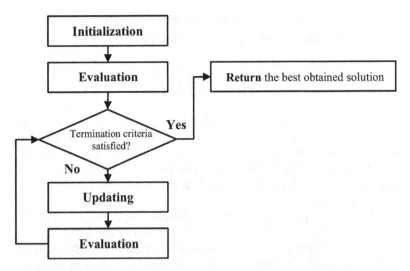

Figure 1.3 Main stages of MHs.

they will forage for food by randomly probing the search area. The mathematical model of NOA is based on two main strategies, which are extensively described next.

Strategy 1: Foraging and storage: This strategy can be divided into two primary phases, which are referred to as foraging and storing, and are described in greater detail below:

- Foraging stage

This stage is considered the first exploration stage in NOA. At this stage, the initial positions of the nutcrackers within the search space are chosen at random. Every nutcracker starts by exploring the initial positions of the cone which includes the seeds. If the nutcracker comes across any viable seeds, it will move them to a storage place and bury them in a cache. If it is unable to locate viable seeds, the nutcracker will hunt for another cone in a different region containing pine trees or other types of trees. The mathematical model of this behavior is as follows:

$$\vec{X}_i^{t+1} = \begin{cases} X_{i,j}^t & \text{if } \tau_1 < \tau_2 \\ \begin{cases} X_m^t + \gamma \cdot \left(X_{A,j}^t - X_{B,j}^t \right) + \mu \cdot (r^2 \cdot U_j - L_j), & \text{if } t \leq T_{max}/2.0 \\ X_{C,j}^t + \mu \cdot \left(X_{A,j}^t - X_{B,j}^t \right) + \mu \cdot (r_1 < \delta) \cdot (r^2 \cdot U_j - L_j), & \text{Otherwise} \end{cases} & \text{Otherwise} \end{cases}$$

$$(1.3)$$

where $\vec{X}_i^{t+1}$ represents the updated solution; $X_{i,j}^t$ refers to the current solution's jth dimension; γ is a numerical value chosen at random based on the levy flight; C, A, and B are the indices of three solutions chosen at random from the current population; τ_1, τ_2, r, and r_1 are numbers chosen at random in [0, 1];

$X_{m,j}^t$ represents the mean of the current population; and μ is a factor including a value generated as follows:

$$\mu = \begin{cases} \tau_3 & if\ r_1 < r \\ \tau_4 & if\ r < r_2 \\ \tau_5 & if\ r_1 < r_2 \end{cases} \qquad (1.4)$$

where r_2 is a numerical value selected at random in the interval (0, 1). τ_3 is a numerical value chosen at random between 0 and 1 based on the uniform distribution, τ_4 is a numerical value selected at random according to the normal distribution, and τ_5 is a numerical value chosen at random according to the levy flight.

• Storage stage

This stage represents the first exploitation operator in NOA. In this phase, the Nutcrackers transport the food they found in the former exploration phase to a temporary storage place. The mathematical expression for this behavior is as shown in the following:

$$\vec{X}_i^{t+1(new)} = \begin{cases} \vec{X}_i^t + \mu \cdot \left(\vec{X}^* - \vec{X}_i^t\right) \cdot |\lambda| + r_1 \cdot \left(\vec{X}_A^t - \vec{X}_B^t\right) & if\ \ \tau_1 < \tau_2 \\ \vec{X}^* + \mu \cdot \left(\vec{X}_A^t - \vec{X}_B^t\right) & if\ \ \tau_1 < \tau_3 \\ \vec{X}^* \cdot l & Otherwise \end{cases}$$
$$(1.5)$$

where λ is a numerical value chosen at random based on the lévy flight. $\vec{X}^*$ represents the best solution achieved yet. l is a factor decreasing linearly from 1 to 0. During the optimization process, the following formula directs the exchange between the exploitation and exploration phases to achieve equilibrium between them:

$$\vec{X}_i^{t+1} = \begin{cases} Eq.(1.3), & if\ \varphi < P_{a_1} \\ Eq.(1.5), & Otherwise \end{cases} \qquad (1.6)$$

where φ is a numerical value chosen in the interval (0, 1), and P_{a_1} is a value decreasing linearly from 1 to 0 as formulated in the following formula:

$$P_{a_1} = \frac{T_{max} - t}{T_{max}} \qquad (1.7)$$

Strategy 2: Cache-search and recovery strategy

This strategy may be broken down into two distinct parts: the cache-search phase and the recovery phase. Both of these phases are outlined in greater detail in the following two sections:

• Exploration phase 2

As soon as winter arrives, the trees lose their leaves, the nutcrackers start their search for their hidden caches. This phase represents the NOA's second exploration stage. The nutcrackers can locate their caches by employing a mechanism that relies on their spatial memories. There is a good chance that nutcrackers employ many objects as signals for a single cache. For the sake of simplicity, we will suppose that there are just two reference points as markers or signals for each cache. In NOA, each nutcracker employs two reference points (RPs) for each cache as signals, as shown in the matrix below:

$$
\text{RPs} = \begin{bmatrix} \overrightarrow{RP}_{1,1}^{\,t} & \overrightarrow{RP}_{1,2}^{\,t} \\ \vdots & \vdots \\ \overrightarrow{RP}_{i,1}^{\,t} & \overrightarrow{RP}_{i,2}^{\,t} \\ \vdots & \vdots \\ \overrightarrow{RP}_{N,1}^{\,t} & \overrightarrow{RP}_{N,1}^{\,t} \end{bmatrix} \tag{1.8}
$$

where $\overrightarrow{RP}_{i,1}^{\,t}$ represents the first RPs of the ith nutcracker, and $\overrightarrow{RP}_{i,2}^{\,t}$ represents the RPs. There are two distinct equations established to construct the two RPs, respectively, to improve the nutcracker exploring process during exploring the search space for reaching hidden caches. The first RP can be constructed according to Eq. (1.9), whereas the second RP is computed using Eq. (1.10):

$$
\overrightarrow{RP}_{i,1}^{\,t} = \begin{cases} \vec{X}_i^{\,t} + \alpha \cdot \cos(\theta) \cdot \left(\left(\vec{X}_A^{\,t} - \vec{X}_B^{\,t} \right) \right) + \alpha \cdot RP, \, if \, \theta = \pi/2 \\ \vec{X}_i^{\,t} + \alpha \cdot \cos(\theta) \cdot \left(\left(\vec{X}_A^{\,t} - \vec{X}_B^{\,t} \right) \right), \qquad \text{Otherwise} \end{cases}
$$

$$\tag{1.9}$$

$$
\overrightarrow{RP}_{i,2}^{\,t} = \begin{cases} \vec{X}_i^{\,t} + \left(\alpha \cdot \cos(\theta) \cdot \left(\left(\vec{U} - \vec{L} \right) \cdot \tau_3 + \vec{L} \right) + \alpha \cdot RP \right) \cdot \vec{U}_2, \, if \, \theta = \pi/2 \\ \vec{X}_i^{\,t} + \alpha \cdot \cos(\theta) \cdot \left(\left(\vec{U} - \vec{L} \right) \cdot \tau_3 + \vec{L} \right), \qquad \text{Otherwise} \end{cases}
$$

$$\tag{1.10}$$

$$
\vec{U}_1 = \begin{cases} 1 \, \vec{r}_2 < P_{rp} \\ 0 \, \text{Otherwise} \end{cases} \tag{1.11}
$$

where $\vec{r}_2$ is a vector chosen at random between 0 and 1; $\vec{X}_A^{\,t}$ is a solution chosen at random; θ is an angle chosen at random between 0 and π; and P_{rp} is a probability used to calculate the proportion of exploratory operators; and α can be estimated according to the following formula to ensure that the NOA converges regularly:

$$
\alpha = \begin{cases} \left(1 - \dfrac{t}{T_{\max}} \right)^{2 \frac{t}{T_{\max}}}, & \text{if } r_1 > r_2 \\ \left(\dfrac{t}{T_{\max}} \right)^{\frac{2}{t}}, & \text{Otherwise} \end{cases} \tag{1.12}
$$

where T_{max} indicates the maximum iteration and t represents the current iteration. In NOA, the following equation is used to adjust the position of a nutcracker based on the first RP:

$$\vec{X}_i^{t+1} = \begin{cases} \vec{X}_i^t, if\ f\left(\vec{X}_i^t\right) & < if(\overrightarrow{RP}_{i,1}^t) \\ \overrightarrow{RP}_{i,1}^t, & \text{Otherwise} \end{cases} \tag{1.13}$$

- Recovery stage: Exploitation phase 2

  The first scenario is that a nutcracker can reach the hidden cache's location using the first RP. This behavior is expressed using the following mathematical model:

$$X_{ij}^{t+1} = \begin{cases} X_{ij}^t, & if\ \tau_3 < \tau_4 \\ X_{ij}^t + r_1 \cdot \left(X_{best,j}^t - X_{ij}^t\right) + r_2 \cdot \left(\overrightarrow{RP}_{i,1}^t - X_{Cj}^t\right), & \text{Otherwise} \end{cases} \tag{1.14}$$

where C stands for the index of a solution chosen at random from the current population. The second scenario is that the nutcracker forgets where he concealed his food using the first RP, so it will activate its spatial memory to the second RP to search for its food. The mathematical formula given below describes how to activate the spatial memory of a nutcracker to the second RP:

$$\vec{X}_i^{t+1} = \begin{cases} \vec{X}_i^t, if\ f\left(\vec{X}_i^t\right) & < if(\overrightarrow{RP}_{i,2}^t) \\ \overrightarrow{RP}_{i,2}^t, & \text{Otherwise} \end{cases} \tag{1.15}$$

It is assumed in NOA that a nutcracker will use the second RP to locate its cache; hence, Eq. (1.14), which is based on the first RP, is modified to be based on the second RP:

$$X_{ij}^{t+1} = \begin{cases} X_{ij}^t, & if\ \tau_5 < \tau_6 \\ X_{ij}^t + r_1 \cdot \left(X_{best,j}^t - X_{ij}^t\right) + r_2 \cdot \left(\overrightarrow{RP}_{i,2}^t - X_{Cj}^t\right), & \text{Otherwise} \end{cases} \tag{1.16}$$

where τ_5, and τ_6 are numerical values chosen at random in the interval (0, 1). The following equation elaborates on how to trade-off between the first and second RPs within the recovery behavior:

$$\vec{X}_i^{t+1} = \begin{cases} \text{Eq.(1.14)}, & if\ \tau_5 < \tau_6 \\ \text{Eq.(1.16)}, & \text{Otherwise} \end{cases} \tag{1.17}$$

In the preceding equation, the first state simulates a nutcracker that could recall the secret store, whereas the second state simulates a nutcracker who forgets about the hidden store. The following equation describes how to activate the spatial memory between the first and second RPs, as well as the current solution, to search for the hidden cache:

$$\vec{X}_i^{t+1} = \begin{cases} \text{Eq.(1.13)}, & \text{if } f(\text{Eq.(1.13)}) < f(\text{Eq.(1.15)}) \\ \text{Eq.(1.15)}, & \text{Otherwise} \end{cases} \quad (1.18)$$

Lastly, the recovery and cache-search phases are randomly swapped based on the following equation to achieve a balance between exploitation and exploration operators:

$$\vec{X}_i^{t+1} = \begin{cases} \text{Eq.(1.17)}, & \text{if } \phi < P_{a_2} \\ \text{Eq.(1.18)}, & \text{Otherwise} \end{cases} \quad (1.19)$$

where P_{a_2} is a preset value between 0 and 1 that determines the probability of the exploitation phase of the optimization process. But, for each nutcracker, if the fitness value of the current position is better than that of the new position, its current position will be passed to the next generation for searching for a better position. In conclusion, this idea can be summed up by Eq. (1.20). Algorithm 1.1 provides a concise summary of the pseudo-code that constitutes NOA.

Algorithm 1.1 Steps of NOA

Input: population size N, $\vec{L}$, $\vec{U}$, and T_{max};
Output: $\vec{X}_{best}^t$
1 Initialize N solutions using Eq. (1.2);
2 Evaluation and estimating the best solution achieved yet.
3 $t = 1$; //the current evaluation//
4 **while** ($t < T_{max}$)
5   σ and σ_1: two numbers are chosen at random between 0 and 1.
6   φ is a numerical value selected at random in the intervals 0 and 1.
7   **If** $\sigma < \sigma_1$ //* ***Foraging and storage strategy****//
8   **for** $i = 1{:}N$
9   **if** $\varphi < P_{a_1}$ /* **Exploration phase1**/
10   Updating $\vec{X}_i^{t+1}$ using Eq. (1.3) and Eq. (1.20)
11   **else** /***Exploitation phase1**/
12   Updating $\vec{X}_i^{t+1}$ using Eq. (1.5) and Eq. (1.20)
13   **end if**
14    $t++$
15   **end for**
16 **else** //* ***Cache-search and recovery strategy*** *//
17   Compute RP matrix by Eq. (1.9), (1.10), and (1.11).
18   **for** $i = 1{:}N$
19   **if** $\phi < P_{a_2}$ /***Exploitation phase2**/
20   Updating $\vec{X}_i^{t+1}$ using Eq. (1.18) and Eq. (1.20)
21   **else** /***Exploration phase2**/
22   Updating $\vec{X}_i^{t+1}$ using Eq. (1.19) and Eq. (1.20)
23   **end if**
24    $t++$
25   **end for**
26 **end while**

$$\vec{X}_i^{t+1} = \begin{cases} \vec{X}_i^{t+1}, \ \textit{if } f\left(\vec{X}_i^{t+1}\right) \ < f\left(\vec{X}_i^{t}\right) \\ \vec{X}_i^{t}, \qquad\qquad\quad \text{Otherwise} \end{cases} \qquad (1.20)$$

1.4.4   Teaching-learning-based optimization

Hashim proposed a population-based metaheuristic algorithm, namely teaching-learning-based optimization (TLBO), for tackling global optimization and real-world optimization problems [22]. The TLBO algorithm was introduced with the specific aim of emulating the impact of a teacher on the performance of a group of students. The TLBO model includes two distinct phases, namely the teacher phase and the learner phase.

1.4.4.1   Teacher phase

During this phase, the educator who has been identified as the most proficient among the students will endeavor to enhance the average performance of the learners by imparting knowledge. The mean value of the learners in the class is calculated in the following manner:

$$\vec{X}_{mean} = \frac{1}{N}\sum_{i=1}^{N}\vec{X}_i \qquad (1.21)$$

Finally, the new solution for each learner could be generated using the following equation:

$$\vec{X}_i^{t+1} = \vec{X}_i^{t} + \vec{r}.(\vec{X}^* - T_F.\vec{X}_{mean}) \qquad (1.22)$$

where $\vec{X}^*$ represents the near-optimal solution achieved yet or the teacher vector, $\vec{r}$ is a vector assigning values chosen at random in the interval (0, 1) according to the uniform distribution, and T_F indicates a teaching factor and includes either 1 or 2. The fitness value of the new solution is computed and compared to that of the current solution. If the new solution is better, it is used in the next generation instead of the current solution.

1.4.4.2   Learner phase

Interactions and exchanges of ideas among students can facilitate the enhancement of their comprehension of the academic content. In this phase, every participant will choose a peer from the population to engage in a discussion with, to enhance their overall comprehension. The present stage is denoted mathematically by the subsequent expression:

$$\vec{X}_i(t+1) = \begin{cases} \vec{X}_i^t + \vec{r}.\left(\vec{X}_i^t - \vec{X}_j^t\right) & \text{if } f\left(\vec{X}_i^t\right) < f\left(\vec{X}_j^t\right) \\ \vec{X}_i^t + \vec{r}.\left(\vec{X}_j^t - \vec{X}_i^t\right) & \text{Otherwise} \end{cases} \quad (1.23)$$

where $f\left(\vec{X}_i^t\right)$ and $f\left(\vec{X}_j^t\right)$ represent the objective values of the ith and jth learners, respectively. j represents the index of a solution randomly chosen from the current population, such that $i \neq j$. The fitness value of the new solution is computed and compared to that of the current solution. If the new solution is better, it is used in the next generation instead of the current solution. T LBO's pseudocode is shown in Algorithm 1.2

Algorithm 1.2 TLBO.

Output: $\overrightarrow{X^*}$
1 Initialize N solutions $\vec{X}_i, (i = 1, 2, 3, \ldots\ldots\ldots N)$
2 Compute the fitness value for each $\vec{X}_i$.
3 Extract the near-optimal solutions achieved yet $\vec{X^*}$ to represent the teacher
4 $t = 0$
5 **While** $(t < T_{\max})$
6   Update $\vec{X}_{\text{mean}}$ using Eq. (1.21)
7   Increment the current iteration, $t = t + 1$;
8   ////teaching phase
9   **for** each i solution
10   Compute the new solution $\vec{X}_i^{t+1}$ according to Eq. (1.22)
11   If $f(\vec{X}_i^{t+1}) < f(\vec{X}_i^t)$
12             $\vec{X}_i^t = \vec{X}_i^{t+1}$
13   End if
14   **End for**
15   //learning phase
16   **for** each i solution
17   Compute the new solution $\vec{X}_i^{t+1}$ according to Eq. (1.23)
18   If $f(\vec{X}_i^{t+1}) < f(\vec{X}_i^t)$
19             $\vec{X}_i^t = \vec{X}_i^{t+1}$
20   End if
21   **End for**
22   Increment the current iteration, $t = t + 1$
23 **End while**

1.4.5 Differential evolution

Storn [23] proposed an evolution-based optimization algorithm called differential evolution for tackling optimization problems. This algorithm bears a resemblance to genetic algorithms in its utilization of selection operators, crossover, and mutation. Before beginning the optimization procedure, the DE algorithm generates a collection of individuals possessing d dimensions. These dimensions are distributed randomly throughout the optimization problem's search space. Subsequently, the crossover and mutation operators were employed to investigate the search space to discover superior solutions.

1.4.5.1 Mutation operator

By utilizing this particular operator, DE has successfully generated a mutant vector, denoted as, $\vec{v}_i^t$, for every member $\vec{X}_i$ present within the population. The creation of the mutant vector could be achieved through several mutation schemes defined below:

$$``\frac{DE}{\frac{rand}{1}}"\vec{v}_i^t = \vec{X}_a^t + F.\left(\vec{X}_k^t - \vec{X}_j^t\right) \tag{1.24}$$

$$``\frac{DE}{\frac{best}{1}}"\vec{v}_i^t = \vec{X}^* + F.\left(\vec{X}_k^t - \vec{X}_j^t\right) \tag{1.25}$$

$$``\frac{DE}{target} - to - \frac{best}{1}"\vec{v}_i^t = \vec{X}_i^t + F.\left(\vec{X}^* - \vec{X}_i^t\right) + F.\left(\vec{X}_a^t - \vec{X}_k^t\right) \tag{1.26}$$

$$``\frac{DE}{\frac{best}{1}}"\vec{v}_i^t = \vec{X}^* + F.\left(\vec{X}_j - \vec{X}_c^t\right) + F.\left(\vec{X}_a^t - \vec{X}_k^t\right) \tag{1.27}$$

where a, k, c, and j are the indices of four individuals chosen at random from the current population, such that $a \neq k \neq c \neq j \neq i$. F is a scaling factor, including a numerical value generated between 0 and 1 to determine the step size added to the new solutions.

1.4.5.2 Crossover operator

Afterward, the crossover operator was applied to build the trial vector $\vec{u}_i^t$ based on both the current position of the ith individual and the corresponding mutant vector. This operator uses a probability known as crossover probability (CR) to create this trial solution from the two solutions aforementioned. The following is the mathematical description of this crossover operation:

$$u_{i,j}^t = \begin{cases} v_{i,j}^t & if\ (r_1 \leq CR)||(j = j_r) \\ X_{i,j}^t & Otherwise \end{cases} \tag{1.28}$$

where j_r is an integer value chosen at random from the number of dimensions in the current solution, j is the current dimension, and CR is a predefined fixed value in the interval (0, 1).

1.4.5.3 Selection operator

Last but not least, the selection operator is used to contrast the trial vector $\vec{u}_i^t$ it and the present one $\vec{X}_i^t$. If the trial vector has a better objective value, it is integrated in place of the current solution within the current population. In general, the technique for selecting solutions for a minimization problem can be mathematically described as that.

$$\vec{X}_k^{t+1} = \begin{cases} \vec{u}_i^t & if\left(f\left(\vec{u}_i^t\right) < f\left(\vec{X}_i^t\right)\right) \\ \vec{X}_i^t & \text{Otherwise} \end{cases} \quad (1.29)$$

The DE's pseudocode is shown in Algorithm 1.3

Algorithm 1.3 DE's pseudocode.

1. Initialize N solutions $\vec{X}_i, (i = 1, 2, 3, \ldots \ldots N)$
2. Compute the objective value for each $\vec{X}_i$.
3. Extract the best-so-far solutions $\vec{X}^*$
4. $t = 0$
5. Set F and Cr
6. **while** $(t < T_{max})$
7.   **for** $i = 0$ to N
8.   **%%% Mutation Operator %%%**
9.   Create the mutant vector $\vec{v}_i^t$ according to Eq. (1.24)
10. **%%% Crossover Operator %%%**
11.   **for** $j = 0$ to d
12. r_1: is a numerical value selected at random in the intervals 0 and 1.
13.   **If**$(r_1 < Cr || j = j_r)$
14. $u_{i,j}^t = v_{i,j}^t$
15.   **Else**
16. $u_{i,j}^t = x_{i,j}^t$
17.   **End if**
18.   **end for**
19. **%%% Selection Operator %%%**
20.   **if** $\left(f\left(\vec{u}_i^t\right) < f\left(\vec{x}_i^t\right)\right)$
21. $\vec{x}_i^t = \vec{u}_i^t$
22.   **end if**
23.   **If** $\vec{u}_i^t$ is better than $\vec{X}_i^*$, $\vec{X}_i^* = \vec{u}_i^t$
24.   **end for**
25. $t++$
26. **end while**
Return $\vec{X}_i^*$

1.4.6   Light spectrum optimizer

The light spectrum optimizer (LSO) algorithm was presented as a new meta-heuristic approach to address global optimization and some real-world optimization problems [24]. The LSO has drawn inspiration from a meteorological phenomenon whereby the reflection, refraction, and dispersion of light rays at varying angles through raindrops result in the emergence of a colorful spectrum of rainbow rays. These rays exhibit a reflective index that ranges between 1.331 as k^{red} and 1.344 as k^{violet}. During the optimization process, it can be observed that every ray that is generated represents a candidate solution to the tackled problem. The optimization process of LSO can be divided into two stages, similar to metaheuristic algorithms. The first stage involves generating new colorful rays for exploration, while the second stage involves exploitation through scattering the colorful rays. These stages are extensively explained in the subsequent sections.

1.4.7   Exploration mechanism

The first step in the process of optimization using LSO will be to perform an update on the reflective index between k^{red} and k^{violet} as that:

$$k^r = k^{red} + r_1 \times \left(k^{violet} - k^{red} \right) \qquad (1.30)$$

The variable r_1 is a uniformly distributed random variable with a range of values between 0 and 1. To regulate the behavior of light rays about reflection and refraction, a probability variable denoted as p is employed, with a designated range of values between 0 and 1. The original paper recommended a value of 0.8 for this parameter. On the other hand, To regulate the scattering of the colorful rainbow curve, a likelihood called q that is randomly produced between 0 and 1 is utilized. During the search process, the directions of the rainbow spectrums are established based on the normal vector of inner reflection $\overrightarrow{x_{nB}}$, inner refraction $\overrightarrow{x_{nA}}$, and outer refraction $\overrightarrow{x_{nC}}$, which are sequentially generated using the equations provided:

$$\overrightarrow{x_{nA}} = \frac{\vec{X}_r^t}{norm\left(\vec{X}_r^t\right)} \qquad (1.31)$$

$$\vec{x_{nB}} = \frac{\vec{X}_p^t}{norm\left(\vec{X}_p^t\right)} \tag{1.32}$$

$$\vec{x_{nC}} = \frac{\vec{X^*}}{norm\left(\vec{X^*}\right)} \tag{1.33}$$

where $\vec{X}_r^t$ is a solution selected randomly from the individuals in the current population at time t, $\vec{X}_p^t$ is the solution of the current ray, $\vec{X^*}$ is the optimal solution, and $norm(.)$ is the normalized vector. The incident light ray $\vec{x_{L0}}$ could be computed using the following formula:

$$X_{mean} = \frac{\sum_i^N \vec{x_i}}{N} \tag{1.34}$$

$$\vec{x_{L0}} = \frac{X_{mean}}{norm\left(X_{mean}\right)} \tag{1.35}$$

The symbol X_{mean} represents the population's mean value during the current iteration. The computation of the vectors of refracted and reflected light rays, both inside and outside, is performed as follows:

$$\vec{x_{L1}} = \frac{1}{k^r}\left[\vec{x_{L0}} - \vec{x_{nA}}\left(\vec{x_{nA}} \cdot \vec{x_{L0}}\right)\right] - \vec{x_{nA}}\left|1 - \frac{1}{(k^r)^2} + \frac{1}{(k^r)^2}\left(\vec{x_{nA}} \cdot \vec{x_{L0}}\right)^2\right|^{\frac{1}{2}} \tag{1.36}$$

$$\vec{x_{L2}} = \vec{x_{L1}} - 2\vec{x_{nB}}\left(\vec{x_{L1}} \cdot \vec{x_{nB}}\right) \tag{1.37}$$

$$\vec{x_{L3}} = k^r\left[\vec{x_{L2}} - \vec{x_{nC}}\left(\vec{x_{nC}} \cdot \vec{x_{L2}}\right)\right] + \vec{x_{nC}}\left|1 - (k^r)^2 + (k^r)^2\left(\vec{x_{nC}} \cdot \vec{x_{L2}}\right)^2\right|^{\frac{1}{2}} \tag{1.38}$$

The vectors $\vec{x_{L2}}$, $\vec{x_{L1}}$, and $\vec{x_{L3}}$ correspond to the inner reflected, inner refracted, and outer refracted light rays, respectively.

After computing the directions of the rays, the potential solutions are computed according to a probability p that is randomly generated in the range (0, 1). To be more specific, the newly-generated solution is computed using the following mathematical equation if the value of p is less than a value that was produced at random in the range (0, 1):

$$\overrightarrow{X^{t+1}} = \overrightarrow{X^t} + \epsilon RV_1^n GI\left(\overrightarrow{x_{L1}} - \overrightarrow{x_{L3}}\right) \times \left(\overrightarrow{X_{r1}^t} - \overrightarrow{X_{r2}^t}\right) \qquad (1.39)$$

Otherwise, this solution is generated using the following equation:

$$\overrightarrow{X^{t+1}} = \overrightarrow{X^t} + \epsilon RV_2^n GI\left(\overrightarrow{x_{L2}} - \overrightarrow{x_{L3}}\right) \times \left(\overrightarrow{X_{r3}^t} - \overrightarrow{X_{r4}^t}\right) \qquad (1.40)$$

where $\overrightarrow{X_{t+1}}$ represents the updated solution. $r1$, $r2$, $r3$, and $r4$ are four solutions selected at random from the individuals in the current population. The vectors RV_1^n and RV_2^n are generated uniformly. The scaling factor ϵ is computed based on a specific formula described below:

$$\epsilon = a \times RV_3^n \qquad (1.41)$$

where RV_3^n is a random vector including values generated according to the normal distribution. a is an adaptive controlling parameter discussed later. The adaptive control factor GI is determined by utilizing the inverse incomplete gamma function and can be computed using the following formula:

$$GI = a \times r^{-1} \times P^{-1}(a, 1) \qquad (1.42)$$

where r is a number chosen at random between 0 and 1 that is inversed to strengthen the exploration operator. P^{-1} represents the inverse incomplete gamma function with respect to a.

$$a = RV_2\left(1 - \left(\frac{t}{T_{\max}}\right)\right) \qquad (1.43)$$

where RV_2 is a numerical quantity that is uniformly generated within the range of 0 to 1.

1.4.7.1 Exploitation mechanism

This stage aims to facilitate the dispersion of light towards the present solution, the most optimal solution thus far, and a randomly selected solution from the current population, thereby augmenting the exploitation capability. The subsequent expression denotes the mathematical depiction of scattering in proximity to the current solution:

$$\overrightarrow{X^{t+1}} = \overrightarrow{X^t} + RV_3 \times \left(\overrightarrow{X_{r1}^t} - \overrightarrow{X_{r2}^t} \right) + RV_4^n \times (R < \beta) \times \left(\overrightarrow{X^*} - \overrightarrow{X^t} \right) \quad (1.44)$$

where RV_3 contains a number that is arbitrarily created between 0 and 1. RV_4^n is a vector that has a numerical value chosen randomly in the range (0, 1). For the second phase of scattering, we apply the following formula to create rays at a new location based on the near-optimal solution achieved yet:

$$\overrightarrow{X^{t+1}} = 2\cos{(\pi \times r_1)} \left(\overrightarrow{X^*} \right) \left(\overrightarrow{X^t} \right) \quad (1.45)$$

where r_1 is a numerical value randomly chosen in the range (0, 1). The transition between the first and second scattering phases can be achieved using the following formula, where P_e is a fixed probability.

$$\overrightarrow{X^{t+1}} = \begin{cases} \text{Eq.(1.43)} & \text{if } R < P_e \\ \text{Eq.(1.44)} & \text{Otherwise} \end{cases} \quad (1.46)$$

where R is a number chosen randomly in the range (0, 1). The formula for the final scattering phase involves combining the current solution with a randomly selected solution from the population.

$$\overrightarrow{X^{t+1}} = \left(\overrightarrow{X_{r1}^t} + |RV_5| \times \left(\overrightarrow{X_{r2}^t} - \overrightarrow{X_{r3}^t} \right) \right) \times \overrightarrow{U} + \left(1 - \overrightarrow{U} \right) \times \overrightarrow{X^t}$$

$$(1.47)$$

where RV_5 is a normal-distributed random number and U is a vector including binary values generated randomly. In order to swap out Eqs. (1.46) and (1.47), we first calculate the fitness value difference between each solution and the near-optimal solution achieved yet and then normalize this difference between 0 and 1 using Eq. (1.48). If the difference is less than a random threshold value R_1 between 0 and 1, then Eq. (1.46) is applied; otherwise, Eq. (1.47) is carried out. This is mathematically clarified in Eq. (1.49).

$$F' = \left| \frac{F - F_b}{F_b - F_w} \right| \quad (1.48)$$

$$\overrightarrow{X^{t+1}} = \begin{cases} \text{Eq.(1.46)} & \text{if } R < P_s | F' < R_1 \\ \text{Eq.(1.47)} & \text{Otherwise} \end{cases} \quad (1.49)$$

The LSO's pseudocode is shown in Algorithm 1.4

Algorithm 1.4 LSO's pseudocode.

Input: Population size of N rays, T_{max}

1. Initialization
2. ***While*** $(t < T_{\max})$
3.   *for each i ray*
4.   Evaluate the fitness value for each solution
5.   update $\vec{X}^{*}$ if there is better
6.   Compute the normal lines $\overrightarrow{x_{nA}}, \overrightarrow{x_{nB}},$ & $\overrightarrow{x_{nC}}$
7.   Compute the direction vectors $\overrightarrow{x_{L0}}, \overrightarrow{x_{L1}}, \overrightarrow{x_{L2}}$ & $\overrightarrow{x_{L3}}$
8.   Update k^r
9.   Update $a, \epsilon,$ & GI
10.   Create two numerical values randomly: p, q between 0 and 1

        %%%% Generating new ColorFul ray: Exploration phase
11.   ***if*** $p \leq q$
12.   Update the current solution using Eq. (1.39)
13.   ***Else***
14.   Update the current solution using Eq. (1.40)
15.   ***end if***
16.   Evaluate the fitness value for each solution
17.   update $\overrightarrow{X}^{*}$ if there is a better

        %%%Scattering phase: exploitation phase
18.   Update the current solution using Eq. (1.49)
19.   ***end for***
20. ***end while***
Return *the best-so-far solution:* $\overrightarrow{X}^{*}$

1.5 Chapter summary

In this chapter, we described the types of optimization problems as well as the optimization techniques that could be used to tackle those problems. As aforementioned, there are two types of optimization techniques: gradient-based and Gradient-Free. The gradient-based techniques use the derivative to update the current solution for reaching the near-optimal solution to the tackled problem. On the other side, the Gradient-Free methods, also known as stochastic or metaheuristic algorithms employ the randomization process to explore the search space for finding the near-optimal solution. In addition, we clarified various categories of metaheuristics, including evolution-based, swarm-based, human-based, and physics-based. Metaheuristics play a crucial role in medical applications, where they can be used to discover near-optimal solutions to a variety of medical optimization problems for the early detection of several diseases, as well as enhancing medical care services. Finally, the behaviors and mathematical models for four metaheuristic algorithms: NOA, LSO, DE, and TLBO that belong to different categories were reviewed.

References

[1] M. Abdel-Basset, R. Mohamed, S. Mirjalili, A novel whale optimization algorithm integrated with Nelder–Mead simplex for multi-objective optimization problems, Knowledge-Based Systems 212 (2021) 106619.

[2] P. Ghamisi, et al., Multilevel image segmentation based on fractional-order Darwinian particle swarm optimization, IEEE Transactions on Geoscience and Remote sensing 52 (5) (2013) 2382–2394.

[3] J.N. Kapur, P.K. Sahoo, A.K. Wong, A new method for gray-level picture thresholding using the entropy of the histogram, Computer Vision, Graphics, and Image Processing 29 (3) (1985) 273–285.

[4] N. Otsu, A threshold selection method from gray-level histograms, IEEE Transactions on Systems, Man, and Cybernetics 9 (1) (1979) 62–66.

[5] P. Vineeth, S. Suresh, Performance evaluation and analysis of population-based metaheuristics for denoising of biomedical images, Research on Biomedical Engineering 37 (2021) 111–133.

[6] B. Zitova, J. Flusser, Image registration methods: a survey, Image and Vision Computing 21 (11) (2003) 977–1000.

[7] M. Shehab, et al., Machine learning in medical applications: a review of state-of-the-art methods, Computers in Biology and Medicine 145 (2022) 105458.

[8] W. Zhao, L. Wang, S. Mirjalili, Artificial hummingbird algorithm: a new bio-inspired optimizer with its engineering applications, Computer Methods in Applied Mechanics and Engineering 388 (2022) 114194.

[9] J. Dréo, A. Pétrowski, P. Siarry, and E. Taillard, Metaheuristics for hard optimization: methods and case studies. Springer Science & Business Media, 2006.

[10] D.H. Wolpert, W.G. Macready, No free lunch theorems for optimization, IEEE Transactions on Evolutionary Computation 1 (1) (1997) 67–82.

[11] Z. Beheshti, S.M.H. Shamsuddin, A review of population-based meta-heuristic algorithms, International Journal of Advances in Soft Computing 5 (1) (2013) 1–35.

[12] M. Abdel-Basset, R. Mohamed, M. Jameel, M. Abouhawwash, Nutcracker optimizer: a novel nature-inspired metaheuristic algorithm for global optimization and engineering design problems, Knowledge-Based Systems 262 (2023) 110248.

[13] F.A. Hashim, E.H. Houssein, M.S. Mabrouk, W. Al-Atabany, S. Mirjalili, Henry gas solubility optimization: a novel physics-based algorithm,", Future Generation Computer Systems 101 (2019) 646–667.

[14] J. Kennedy, R. Eberhart, Particle swarm optimization, Proceedings of ICNN'95-International Conference on Neural Networks 4 (1995) 1942–1948. IEEE.

[15] Zhang, M., G. Wen, and J. Yang. Duck Swarm Algorithm: A Novel Swarm Intelligence Algorithm. arXiv:2112.13508, 2021.

[16] M. Abdel-Basset, R. Mohamed, S.A.A. Azeem, M. Jameel, M. Abouhawwash, Kepler optimization algorithm: a new metaheuristic algorithm inspired by Kepler's laws of planetary motion, Knowledge-Based Systems 268 (2023) 110454.

[17] F. MiarNaeimi, G. Azizyan, M. Rashki, Horse herd optimization algorithm: a nature-inspired algorithm for high-dimensional optimization problems, Knowledge-Based Systems 213 (2021) 106711.

[18] X.-S. Yang, A.H. Gandomi, Bat algorithm: a novel approach for global engineering optimization, Engineering Computations 29 (2012) 464–483.

[19] M. Dorigo, M. Birattari, T. Stutzle, Ant colony optimization, IEEE Computational Intelligence Magazine 1 (4) (2006) 28–39.

[20] C. Yang, X. Tu, and J. Chen, "Algorithm of marriage in honey bees optimization based on the wolf pack search," in Proceedings of the International Conference on Intelligent Pervasive Computing (IPC 2007), 2007, pp. 462–467: IEEE.

[21] X.-S. Yang, Firefly algorithm, stochastic test functions and design optimisation, International Journal of Bio-Inspired Computation 2 (2) (2010) 78–84.

[22] R. Rao, V.J. Venkata, Savsani, D.P. Vakharia, Teaching–learning-based optimization: a novel method for constrained mechanical design optimization problems, Computer-Aided Design 43 (3) (2011) 303–315.

[23] R. Storn, Differrential evolution-a simple and efficient adaptive scheme for global optimization over continuous spaces, Technical Report, International Computer Science Institute 11 (1995).

[24] M. Abdel-Basset, et al., Light spectrum optimizer: a novel physics-inspired metaheuristic optimization algorithm, Mathematics 10 (19) (2022) 3466.

Wavelet-based image denoising using improved artificial jellyfish search optimizer

2.1 Introduction

Images are pictorial representations of the attributes of the observed scene. The use of an image processing system allows for the efficient capture and processing of images. Acquisition, storage, transmission, processing, and display are the five steps that make up digital image processing systems [1]. However, at each stage, the overall quality of the images might be significantly degraded because of the added noise. The noise might cause the loss of some information that is so essential in medical and satellite images. For example, the information on a potentially cancerous growth that is about to emerge may be distorted by noise. This demonstrates the importance of properly processing and eliminating noise from these images. There are several noise removal methods that have been proposed to eliminate the noise of the images, especially those that are sensitive to information. Imaging modalities in medicine that rely on image processing principles include computed tomography (CT), magnetic resonance imaging (MRI), x-ray, ultrasound, positron emission tomography (PET), optical coherence tomography (OCT), and single photon emission tomography (SPECT). Noise is introduced during the acquiring and transforming processes of all these image modalities. Depending on the type of corruption and the source of the noise, different types of noise can be introduced into the images. There is a wide variety of noise, each with its unique properties and distribution, and each capable of altering the pixel intensity values in unique ways. Some of these types of noise are presented in the following list:

- Gaussian noise: It is a statistical noise that is created by adding noise to each pixel, and is hence referred to as additive noise.
- Salt and pepper: It appears as white and black pixels appearing at random intervals.

Metaheuristics Algorithms for Medical Applications. DOI: https://doi.org/10.1016/B978-0-443-13314-5.00012-6

- Speckle noise: In contrast to Gaussian and Salt and Pepper noises, this noise is multiplicative due to being multiplied by each pixel.
- Periodic noise: it manifests as repeating patterns because of electric and magnetic interference during the photographing process.
- Film grain: it is a type of noise that emerges as texture in the processed image due to the existence of the silver halide crystals.
- Quantization noise: This noise is the result of quantizing the pixels of a perceived image to a discrete number of levels.

The denoising process is a crucial step to eliminate the noise of the images and extract the useful information needed to make the right decision in different fields. Several denoising techniques have been developed over time, which could be divided into three kinds [2]:

- Spatial domain denoising: Those methods directly manipulate the pixels for getting rid of the noisy data.
- Frequency-domain filtering: In those methods, the Fourier transform is used to convert the images into a frequency-domain that is manipulated using certain operations to remove the noisy data.
- Optimal linear filtering methods: These methods attempt to create an ideal filter according to a given criterion in order to remove noisy data from the original image.

This variation in the denoising techniques is due to various types of noise with different characteristics that cannot all be extracted with a single technique. For example, low-pass filtering regards one of the fundamental or early techniques for eliminating noise. As there are frequent abrupt changes, noise is a high-frequency component, that could be removed from the images by a low-pass filter. Yet, in some images, such as those used in biomedicine, the edges may also include information. As a result, filtering should not only be a low pass but also adaptive to the edges, which are high-frequency and may also contain useful information.

Over the last few years, image denoising using the wavelet concept has significant interest from researchers due to its capacity to maintain both time-domain frequency and frequency-domain information. Because of its superior localization property, the wavelet transform has quickly emerged as a crucial component in signal and image processing. The goal of wavelet denoising is to eliminate noise from a signal while maintaining its original properties, regardless of the signal's frequency content [3]. However, the wavelet transform has some parameters, like the wavelet type and the threshold values that need to be accurately optimized for getting rid of different noises. Finding the optimal threshold values is the most effective thing on the performance of the wavelet function for denoising an image [2]. This problem is classified as NP-hard because it could not be solved in polynomial time, so it could not be accurately tackled using the traditional techniques. Therefore, the researchers pay attention to the metaheuristics that could solve several optimization problems with various complexities in a reasonable amount of time [2]. For example, in [2], an adaptive self-organizing migration algorithm (ASOMA) was suggested for estimating the near-optimal parameters for the wavelet functions to get rid of the noisy data of the images. This variant was applied to find the optimal threshold values of the wavelet transformation for denoising a collection of images and compared to the classical SOMA and some of its other variants to show its effectiveness. In addition, differential evolution (DE) was applied to identify the near-optimal values for the parameters of the wavelet shrinkage denoising [4]. Alyasseri [5] adapted the β-hill climbing for estimating the near-optimal parameters of the wavelet transform with the purpose of minimizing the mean square error (MSE) between the original and denoised electrocardiogram (ECG) signals. Furthermore, the Harris hawk optimization (HHO) was applied for estimating the optimal values for the wavelet coefficients [2].

In this chapter, we will investigate the performance of five metaheuristics for revealing their capabilities to estimate the near-optimal values for the wavelets parameters. In addition, two different updating schemes are effectively integrated with one of those algorithms, namely Jellyfish Search Optimizer, to estimate the unknown parameters of the wavelet denoising more accurately. Finally, the chapter summary is presented.

2.2 Wavelet denoising

2.2.1 Wavelet transform

The Wavelet transform was developed as an alternative to the Fourier transform since the Fourier transform is unable to simultaneously assess both the frequency and time of a signal. In contrast, the Wavelet transform is able to do so. Using the scale to analyze signal and using shifting and extending the wavelet foundation to analyze the correlation between the wavelet and the signal are the two primary components that make up the essence of wavelet analysis. The wavelet transform expression could be expressed as follows [2]:

$$WT(\alpha, \tau) = \frac{1}{\sqrt{\alpha}} \int_{-\infty}^{\infty} f(t) \times \varphi\left(\frac{t - \tau}{\alpha}\right) \qquad (2.1)$$

where φ is the wavelet function, τ refers to the factor of translation, and α is the scale factor. From the previous equation, we can observe that the wavelet transform is similar to the Fourier transform in terms of the integral transform. However, the wavelet transform has a clear difference from the Fourier transform, where the latter has only one variable to represent the frequency. On the contrary, the wavelet transform has two different factors: the factor α represents the frequency, and τ represents the time. There are several wavelet functions, like symlets, biorthogonal, haar, Daubechies, Mexican, morlet, hat, coiflets, and Meyer [6].

2.2.2 Principle of wavelet denoising

Weaver et al. [7] was the first to propose the wavelet threshold for denoising images. The basic goal is to identify the wavelet function that could produce the most accurate mapping of the actual signal. Through a process known as wavelet transform, the signal is broken down into low-frequency and high-frequency components. The high-frequency component represents the image's finer details, while the low-frequency component represents the approximate coefficient. Following the initial decomposition, the low-frequency signal that was obtained is further decomposed into both the high-frequency and low-frequency signals for the second layer. The decomposition for the low-frequency signal is then continued until the necessary number of decomposition layers has been attained. In a nutshell, the denoising process can be broken down into the three parts listed below [2,5]:

- Decomposition: the noised images are divided into a number of levels L, and each level decomposes the input signal into two coefficients: approximation coefficient (cA) and detail coefficient (cD). The latter is processed by a high pass filter, while the former is decomposed into two coefficients at the next level. This process is then continued until the necessary number of decomposition layers has been attained. In this phase, the appropriate wavelet function in addition to the maximum number of layers used in decomposing the noised images have to be accurately selected to maximize the performance of the wavelet denoising. In this chapter, we will investigate the performance of metaheuristics for selecting the near-optimal values for those parameters.

- Thresholding: In which, the resulting wavelet coefficients must be fine-tuned using a suitable threshold value to preserve the important feature of the image while omitting the superfluous elements; these coefficients are referred to as thresholded wavelet coefficients. There are two standard thresholding functions, namely hard and soft functions. In the hard thresholding function, all the wavelet coefficients with absolute values smaller than a threshold value, th, are deleted, whereas the other coefficients are kept without any changing. The soft thresholding function is similar to the hard function in terms of deleting the coefficients with absolute values smaller than th, but the coefficients that are greater than th are reduced toward zero.
- Reconstruction: The thresholded wavelet coefficients need to be subjected to an inverse wavelet transform to retrieve the de-noised image

As indicated in Fig. 2.1, the aforementioned processes are called decomposition tree operations.

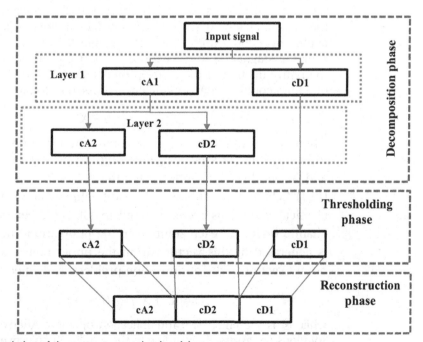

Figure 2.1 Depiction of three stages wavelet denoising process.

2.3 Artificial jellyfish search optimizer

Recently, a swarm-based optimization algorithm called artificial jellyfish search optimizer (JS) was proposed for solving global optimization and engineering problems [8]. This algorithm was developed by trying to replicate the actions taken by jellyfish in the ocean when they are looking for food. Those behaviors include the ocean current, or movements in the swarm, which are discussed in the next subsections for more clarification. JS has been applied to several real-world optimization problems and could achieve significant success in comparison to several other metaheuristic algorithms [9]. This success motivates us in this chapter to investigate its performance in searching for the near-optimal parameters of the wavelet transformation for accurately denoising the medical images. The main stages of the classical JS are as follows:

- Initialization using chaotic maps
- Mathematical model of ocean current
- Mathematical model of movement inside the swarm

Similar to the other metaheuristics, JS starts with distributing a number of solutions within the search space to be optimized during the search space for reaching better solutions. The majority of the metaheuristics employ uniform distribution within the optimization process. On the contrary, the JS optimizer employs the logistic chaotic map to distribute the solutions in a way that could cover the search space as possible for two purposes: (1) avoiding stagnation into local optima and (2) moving quickly in the right direction of the near-optimal solution. The logistic chaotic map could be mathematically expressed as follows [10]:

$$\overrightarrow{X''_{i+1}} = \eta \overrightarrow{X''_i}(1 - \overrightarrow{X''_i}), 0 \le \overrightarrow{X''_0} \le 1 \tag{2.2}$$

where $\overrightarrow{X''_0}$ is a vector generated at random at the interval [0, 1] to be used as the seed for generating the next chaotic vectors, and $\overrightarrow{X''_i}$ is the ith chaotic vector that is used to generate the $(i+1)^{th}$ chaotic vector, η is a constant value, which is set in the classical JS to 4 as recommended in [8]. After generating the chaotic vector for each solution in the population, the solution is generated by this vector within the upper bound and lower bound vectors of the optimization problem as defined below:

$$\vec{X}_i = \vec{L} + \overrightarrow{X''_i} \otimes (\vec{U} - \vec{L}) \tag{2.3}$$

while $\otimes$ is the entry-wise multiplication operator. Afterward, those solutions are assessed according to the employed objective function, and the solution with the lowest objective value for the minimization problem is considered the best solution obtained even now $\vec{X}^*$. This solution is later used in the optimization process for finding better solutions. Following that, the JS starts with updating the current population either toward the ocean current or the movements inside the population based on the time-controlling mechanism described later. The following formula could be used to update the jellyfish toward the ocean current:

$$\vec{X}_i(t+1) = \vec{X}_i(t) + \vec{r} * (\vec{X}^* - \beta * r_1 * \mu) \qquad (2.4)$$

where $\vec{r}$ is a vector assigned at random between 0 and 1 according to the uniform distribution, β is a constant value to represent the distribution coefficient (set to 3 in the classical JS), r_1 is a randomly-generated numerical value between 0 and 1. μ is the mean of all the solutions in the current population, which could be computed according to the following formula:

$$\mu = \frac{1}{N} \sum_{i=0}^{N} \vec{X}_i^t \qquad (2.5)$$

where N represents the population size. Regarding the behavior of the motions inside the population, it is divided into two motions: active and passive. In passive motion, the JS explores the solutions around current solutions in an attempt to find better solutions. The mathematical expression of this motion could be as shown in the following formula:

$$\vec{X}_i^{t+1} = \vec{X}_i^t + r_3 * \gamma * (\vec{U} - \vec{L}) \qquad (2.6)$$

where r_3 is a numerical value chosen at random between 0 and 1, and γ represents the length of the motion around the current solution. In the active motion, the jellyfish is updated in the direction of the fittest solution between two solutions: the current solution and a randomly-selected solution. The mathematical expression of this motion is described as follows:

$$\vec{X'}_i(t+1) = \vec{X}_i^t + \vec{r} * \vec{D} \qquad (2.7)$$

$$\vec{D} = \begin{cases} \vec{X}_i^t - \vec{X}_j^t, & \text{if } f(\vec{X}_i) < f(\vec{X}_j) \\ \vec{X}_j^t - \vec{X}_i^t, & \text{otherwise} \end{cases} \qquad (2.8)$$

where f represents the objective function, and $\vec{X}_j$ is a jellyfish selected at random from the current solution. The time-controlling mechanism is used to select the behavior that is applied to the current solution for generating the updated solution, as depicted in

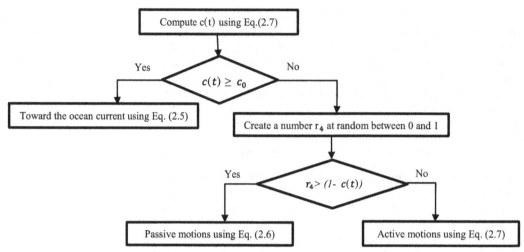

Figure 2.2 Flowchart of the time control mechanism.

Fig. 2.2. This mechanism utilizes a predefined threshold value c_0 to assist in selecting suitable behavior. This mechanism could be mathematically expressed as follows:

$$c(t) = \left(1 - \frac{t}{T_{max}}\right) * (2 * r - 1) \tag{2.9}$$

2.4   How to estimate the wavelet coefficients

The wavelet transform has six unknown parameters that need to be optimized for improving its performance when denoising the images. Those parameters are the decomposition layer, threshold, and wavelet type. In this chapter, we will investigate the performance of the classical JS, NOA, TLBO, DE, and LSO to analyze their performance for showing the best algorithm, which can estimate the near-optimal values for those parameters. In addition, the classical JS is improved using an effective strategy to enhance its exploitation operator for reaching better coefficients for the wavelet transform. The main steps of the proposed improved JS for denoising an image are as follows: Initialization, evaluation, improvement schemes, and pseudocode of the improved JS (IJS).

2.4.1   Initialization

The wavelet transform has six parameters that need to be accurately identified for denoising the images well. Those parameters include four threshold values (thr1, thr2, thr3, and thr4), the wavelet type (ty), and the decomposition level (L). Those parameters represent the number of dimensions for each solution in the population created later. In each solution, those parameters are represented in the same order shown in Table 2.1. Each metaheuristic algorithm employed in this study starts with generating a two-dimensional array of $N*D$, where N represents the population size, and D is set to 6 to represent the number of dimensions of the tackled optimization problem. Following that, this array is randomly initialized within the search space of each parameter to generate N candidate solutions, where each solution includes different parameter values for the wavelet coefficient. However, the last two dimensions in each solution have to be rounded because the decomposition level and wavelet type selection must be an integer. For example, assuming that the initialized values for the ith solution are represented in Table 2.2. The last two dimensions in this table include two decimal values of 5.2 and 6.5 that could not be used to represent the values of both the decomposition layer and wavelet type selection for the wavelet transform. Therefore, those values are rounded to become applicable to the previously-mentioned parameters. There are nine wavelet types that are selected among them during the optimization process in the hope of reaching the optimal selection that could improve the performance of the wavelet transform for denoising the medical images. Therefore, the upper bound of the wavelet types in each solution is limited to 9. The wavelet types in addition to some of the other parameters are described in Table 2.3. Finally, each initial solution in the population is evaluated to determine its fitness value. Based on their fitness values, we can determine the best-so-far solution. However, what is the objective

Table 2.1 Order of the wavelet transform's parameters in each solution.

Parameters	Threshold 1	Threshold 2	Threshold 3	Threshold 4	Level	Type
Abbreviation	Thr1	Thr1	Thr1	Thr1	L	T

Table 2.2 The wavelet transform's parameters by the ith solution.

Parameters	Thr1	Thr1	Thr1	Thr1	L	T
Values	0.7	1.2	1.4	1.5	5.2	6.3

Table 2.3 Characteristics of wavelet types.

Wavelet types	Symmetry	Orthogonality	Filter length	Biorthogonality	Support length
sym4	Approximately symmetric	Yes	2	Yes	1–2
sym6	Approximately symmetric	Yes	2	Yes	1–2
sym8	Approximately symmetric	Yes	2	Yes	1–2
sym10	Approximately symmetric	Yes	2	Yes	1–2
db4	Approximately symmetric	Yes	2	Yes	1–2
db6	Approximately symmetric	Yes	2	Yes	1–2
db8	Approximately symmetric	Yes	2	Yes	1–2
coif2	Approximately symmetric	Yes	6	Yes	1–6
coif4	Approximately symmetric	Yes	6	Yes	1–6

function that could be employed with the metaheuristics for estimating those parameters? This question is answered in the next section.

2.4.2 Objective function

In [2], the authors proposed a fitness function composed of two metrics: peak signal-to-noise ratio (PSNR), and the structured similarity index metric (SSIM). They employed those two metrics due to the different functions of each one. For example, PSNR is based on computing the error ratio between the original image and the denoised image while disregarding the image's structure; on the contrary, SSIM considers the similarity, contrast distortion, and brightness of two images. To relate those two metrics together in a single objective function, a weighting variable is employed to determine the significance of each objective. In general, the objective function employed in this study is mathematically defined as follows:

$$f\left(\vec{X}_i(t)\right) = PSNR\left(\vec{X}_i(t)\right) * \beta_1 + SSIM\left(\vec{X}_i(t)\right) * \beta_2 \qquad (2.10)$$

where β_1 and β_2 are two weighting variables to determine the significance of both PSNR and SSIM metrics in the objective function. In this chapter, due to the significance of the SSIM metric over the PSNR, β_1 is set to 0.002 and β_2 is set to 0.5.

2.4.3 Improved JS

The classical JS optimizer has a poor exploitation operator that makes it converge slowly toward the near-optimal solution achieved even now algorithm. Therefore in this chapter, we try to improve this shortcoming using two updating schemes. The first scheme is based on updating the near-optimal solution achieved yet with a step size created by computing the difference between the current solution and a solution selected randomly from the current population, while the second is based on a step size created by computing the difference between the near-optimal solution obtained even now and the mean of the population. The mathematical expression of the first scheme is as follows:

$$\vec{X}_i^{t+1} = \vec{X}^* + r_1 * \left(\vec{X}_i^t - \vec{X}_a^t \right) \tag{2.11}$$

where r_1 is a numerical value chosen at random between 0 and 1, and $\vec{X}_a$ is a solution selected at random from the current population. The mathematical expression of the second scheme is as follows:

$$\vec{X}_i^{t+1} = \vec{X}^* + r_2 * \left(2 * r_3 * \vec{X}^* - \mu \right) \tag{2.12}$$

where r_2 and r_3 are numerical values chosen at random between 0 and 1. The tradeoff between the first and second updating schemes is randomly achieved, as mathematically defined in the following equation:

$$\vec{X}_i(t+1) = \begin{cases} \text{Applying Eq. (2.11) } r_4 < r_5 \\ \text{Applying Eq. (2.12) } r_4 \geq r_5 \end{cases} \tag{2.13}$$

where r_4 and r_5 are two random values generated between 0 and 1. Those schemes are effectively integrated with the JS to propose a new strong variant with a better exploitation operator to estimate the wavelet parameters for effective denoising the medical images. This variant is called IJS. Finally, the steps of this variant are listed in Algorithm 2.1.

Algorithm 2.1 The steps of IJSO

Input: N and t_{max}
Output: $\vec{X}^*$

1. Initialize N solutions, $\vec{X}_i(i = 1, 2, \ldots\ldots, N)$
2. Rounding the last two dimensions in each solution
3. Evaluate each X_i using Eq. (2.10)
4. Identifying the solution with the fittest as the best solution achieved yet $\vec{X}^*$
5. $t = 1$;
6. **while** $t < t_{max}$
7.   **for** $i = 1$: N
8.   Compute c(t) according to Eq. (2.9)
9.   **If** $c(t) \geq c_0$ %% Ocean current
10.   Applying Eq. (2.4)
11.   **Else** %% Movements inside the population
12.   **If** $r_4 > (1 - c(t))$ %% Passive motion
13.   Applying Eq. (2.6)
14.   **Else** %% Active motion
15.   Applying Eq. (2.7)
16.   **End**
17.   Evaluate the new solution and update the previous solution if the new solution is better
18.   Update the best-so-far solution if there is better
19.   **End for**
20. $t = t + 1$;
21.   %% Applying the improvement mechanism
22.   **for** $i = 1$: N
23.   Applying Eq. (2.13)
24.   Evaluate the new solution and update the previous solution if the new solution is better
25.   Update the best-so-far solution if there is better
26.   **End for**
27. $t++$;
28. **End while**

2.5 Experimental settings

This section investigates the performance of the studied algorithms to show their ability to denoise medical images. Six different medical images, including teeth and brain tumors, are noised with four different types of noises: salt and pepper noise, speckle noise, Poisson noise, and Gaussian noise. The teeth images are taken from [11], and the brain tumor images are available in [12]. Those noises are added to the test images using the built-in imnoise function in MATLAB under the following parameters:

- Gaussian noise with a variance of 0.01 and a mean value of 0
- Salt and pepper noise with a noise density of 0.3

- Speckle noise employs the following formula to add noise to the test images:

$$J = I + n * I \qquad (2.14)$$

where I is the original image, J is the noised image, and n is random noise that is uniformly distributed with 0.05 as variance and a mean value of 0.

All algorithms are implemented using MATLAB® R2019a and executed 30 independent times to avoid their stochastic nature. For all the algorithms, the population size and maximum iteration are set to 20 and 10, respectively, to ensure a fair comparison. Those algorithms are implemented on a device with the following characteristics: 32 gigabytes of random access memory (RAM), a Core i7 processor, and a Windows 10 operating system.

2.6 Performance metrics

Several performance measures have been developed to show the quality of the denoised images contrasted to the original images; these metrics are the peak signal-to-noise ratio (PSNR), the feature similarity index (FSIM), and the structured similarity index metric (SSIM):

- PSNR metric: PSNR [13] is a performance indicator based on calculating the error ratio between the original and denoised images. The mathematical expression of this metric is as follows:

$$\text{PSNR} = 10 \left(\frac{255^2}{\text{MSE}} \right) \qquad (2.15)$$

MSE is synonymous of the MSE that computes the average of the squared errors between the original and modified image:

$$\text{MSE} = \frac{\sum_{i=1}^{M} \sum_{j=1}^{N} |A(i,j) - S(i,j)|}{M * N} \qquad (2.16)$$

where $A(i,j)$ represents the intensity of the pixel in the ith row and jth column in the original image, and $S(i,j)$ represents the denoised image. M and N refer to the numbers of columns and rows in the given image, respectively.

- Structural similarity index (SSIM): PSNR disregards the image's structure because it computes the error ratio between the denoised image and the original image. SSIM

[13] is a mathematical formula intended to consider the contrast distortion, similarity, and brightness of two images:

$$SSIM(O, S) = \frac{(2\mu_o\mu_s + a)(2\sigma_{os} + b)}{(\mu_o{}^2 + \mu_s{}^2 + a)(\sigma_o{}^2 + \sigma_s{}^2 + b)} \tag{2.17}$$

where μ_o represents the average intensities of the original image and μ_s represents the average intensities of the denoised image. μ_o and μ_s represent the standard deviations of the denoised and original images, respectively. μ_{os} represents the covariance between two images, whereas a and b are constants with values of 0.001 and 0.003, respectively. The best method is the one that returns the highest SSIM value.

• Features similarity index (FSIM): FSIM [14] is a statistic for determining the similarity of features between the segmented and original images. FSIM could be expressed mathematically as follows:

$$FSIM(O, S) = \frac{\sum_{X \in \Omega} S_T(X) * PC_m(X)}{\sum_{X \in \Omega} PC_m(X)} \tag{2.18}$$

where Ω represents the entire pixel domain of an image. $S_T(X)$ defines a similarity score. The phase consistency measure is denoted by $PC_m(X)$, which is expressed as:

$$PC_m(X) = \max(PC_1(X), PC_2(X)) \tag{2.19}$$

where $PC_1(X)$ and $PC_2(X)$ describe the phase consistency of the two blocks, respectively:

$$S_T(X) = [S_{PC}(X)]^\alpha \cdot [S_G(X)]^\beta \tag{2.20}$$

$$S_{PC}(X) = \frac{2PC_1(X) \times PC_2(X) + T_1}{PC_1^2(X) \times PC_2^2(X) + T_1} \tag{2.21}$$

$$S_G(X) = \frac{2G_1(X) \times G_2(X) + T_2}{G_1^2(X) \times G_2^2(X) + T_2} \tag{2.22}$$

where the similarity measure of phase consistency is denoted by $S_{PC}(X)$. The gradient magnitude of the two areas $G_1(X)$ and $G_2(X)$ is denoted by $S_G(X)$. The constants, T_1, and T_2 are all present. The value of FSIM is ranged between 0 and 1, and indicates that the segmented image quality is greater when the value is higher.

2.7 Practical analysis

This section reports the results obtained by each algorithm on each type of noise added to the medical test images. All the algorithms were executed 30 independent times on the images with salt and pepper noise. Then, the average fitness (F-value), PSNR, SSIM, and FSIM values were calculated and reported in Fig. 2.3. Inspecting this figure shows that IJS is better than all algorithms for all the employed performance metrics, followed by TLBO as the second-best and JS as the third-best, while DE is the worst algorithm. From that, we can conclude that IJS is the best alternative for removing the salt and pepper noise from the medical images. In addition, we added the Gaussian noise to the medical images and ran the studied algorithms to test their ability to estimate the wavelet coefficients that could remove this type of noise.

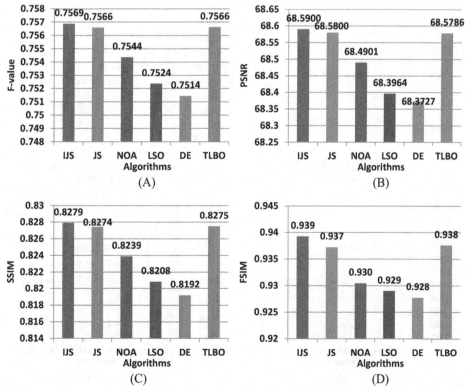

Figure 2.3 Comparison among algorithms over the salt and pepper noise: (A) Comparison in terms of fitness value; (B) Comparison in terms of PSNR values; (C) Comparison in terms of SSIM values; (D) Comparison in terms of FSIM.

Under the Gaussian noise, all the algorithms were executed 30 independent times. The average values of various performance metrics are computed and reported in Fig. 2.4. This figure illustrates that IJS is the best for all performance metrics, followed by TLBO as the second-best, while DE is the worst algorithm. This confirms that IJS is a strong alternative for removing various types of noise from medical images. Furthermore, two additional types of noise, namely Poisson and speckle noises, are added to the medical images to further investigate the ability of IJS for reaching the near-optimal values of the wavelet coefficients. The findings of the algorithms under those types of noise are reported in Figs. 2.5 and 2.6 for both Poisson and speckle noises, respectively. Those findings show that the performance of IJS deteriorates slightly when denoising the medical images with the Poisson noises, while its performance for the speckle noise is superior to all the other algorithms. As a result, IJS is considered a

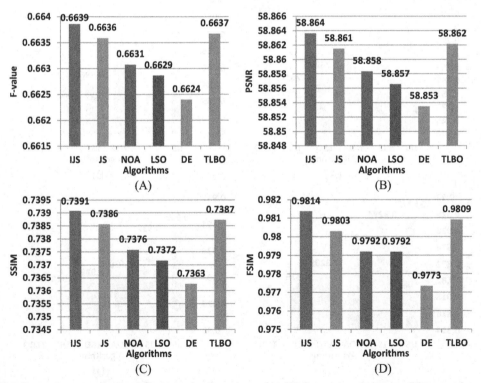

Figure 2.4 Comparison among algorithms over the Gaussian noise: (A) Comparison in terms of fitness value; (B) Comparison in terms of PSNR values; (C) Comparison in terms of SSIM values; (D) Comparison in terms of FSIM.

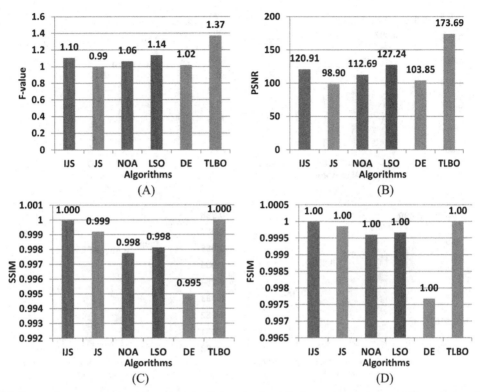

Figure 2.5 Comparison among algorithms over the Poisson noise: (A) Comparison in terms of fitness value; (B) Comparison in terms of PSNR values; (C) Comparison in terms of SSIM values; (D) Comparison in terms of FSIM.

strong alternative for removing various types of noises from medical images, followed by TLBO as the second-best one and classical JS as the third-best algorithm.

2.8 Chapter summary

This chapter investigates the performance of five meta-heuristic algorithms, namely NOA, JS, LSO, TLBO, and DE, for estimating the near-optimal values of the wavelet parameters for improving the wavelet transform's performance when denoising the medical images. Those parameters include the decomposition layer, the wavelet type selection, and four threshold values. To assist in reaching better coefficients, the classical JS is improved with two updating schemes to improve its exploitation operator for reaching better outcomes in a smaller number of iterations; this improved

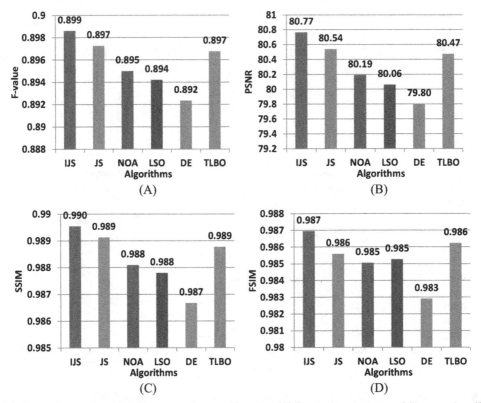

Figure 2.6 Comparison among algorithms over the speckle noise: (A) Comparison in terms of fitness value; (B) Comparison in terms of PSNR values; (C) Comparison in terms of SSIM values; (D) Comparison in terms of FSIM.

variant is called IJS. To observe the effectiveness of those studied algorithms, four different types of noises are added to six medical images, and the different algorithms with the wavelet transform are executed on those images to reveal their ability to remove those noises. The experimental findings show the superiority of IJS because it could achieve outstanding results for three different types of noise, while its performance for the other type is poor compared to TLBO.

References

[1] P. Vineeth, S. Suresh, Performance evaluation and analysis of population-based metaheuristics for denoising of biomedical images, Research on Biomedical Engineering 37 (2021) 111–133.

[2] Z. Cao, H. Jia, T. Zhao, Y. Fu, Z. Wang, An adaptive self-organizing migration algorithm for parameter optimization of wavelet transformation, Mathematical Problems in Engineering 2022 (2022).

[3] M. Shahid, J.P. Li, N.A. Golilarz, A. Addeh, J. Khan, and A.U. Haq, Wavelet based image de-noising with optimized thresholding using HHO algorithm, in *Proceedings of the Sixteenth International Computer Conference on Wavelet Active Media Technology and Information Processing*, 2019, pp. 6–12: IEEE.

[4] V. Gupta, E. Lim, C.-L. Poh, and C.C. Chan, An evolutionary algorithm to automate noise reduction in MR images, in *Proceedings of the International Conference on Information Technology and Applications in Biomedicine*, 2008, pp. 148–151: IEEE.

[5] Z.A.A. Alyasseri, A.T. Khader, M.A. Al-Betar, M.A. Awadallah, Hybridizing β-hill climbing with wavelet transform for denoising ECG signals, Information Sciences 429 (2018) 229–246.

[6] D.T. Lee, A. Yamamoto, Wavelet analysis: theory and applications, Hewlett Packard journal 45 (1994) 44.

[7] J. Weaver, Y. Xu, D. Healy, J. Driscoll, Filtering MR images in the wavelet transform domain, Magnetic Resonance in Medicine: Official Journal of the Society of Magnetic Resonance in Medicine/Society of Magnetic Resonance in Medicine 21 (3) (1991) 288–295.

[8] J.-S. Chou and D.-N. Truong, A novel metaheuristic optimizer inspired by behavior of jellyfish in ocean, *Applied Mathematics and Computation*, 389, 2021, p. 125535.

[9] M. Abdel-Basset, R. Mohamed, M. Abouhawwash, R.K. Chakrabortty, M.J. Ryan, Y. Nam, An improved jellyfish algorithm for multilevel thresholding of magnetic resonance brain image segmentations, Computers, Materials & Continua 68 (3) (2021) 2961–2977.

[10] A.H. Gandomi, X.-S. Yang, S. Talatahari, A.H. Alavi, Firefly algorithm with chaos, Communications in Nonlinear Science and Numerical Simulation 18 (1) (2013) 89–98.

[11] https://www.kaggle.com/datasets/pushkar34/teeth-dataset (accessed 25.02.2023).

[12] https://www.kaggle.com/datasets/masoudnickparvar/brain-tumor-mri-dataset (accessed 25.02.2023).

[13] A. Hore and D. Ziou, Image quality metrics: PSNR vs. SSIM, in *Proceedings of the Twentieth International Conference on Pattern Recognition*, 2010, pp. 2366–2369: IEEE.

[14] L. Zhang, L. Zhang, X. Mou, D. Zhang, FSIM: a feature similarity index for image quality assessment, IEEE transactions on Image Processing 20 (8) (2011) 2378–2386.

3

Artificial gorilla troops optimizer for human activity recognition in IoT-based medical applications

3.1 Introduction

At present, the Internet of Things (IoT) enables the interconnection of various smart objects through the internet to present high-quality services in the medical field. Wearable devices have the potential to monitor various physiological parameters within the human body. Some can be implanted to monitor various functions of the body in order to guarantee that the medical services provided to such individuals are effective. The information that is gathered in this way can be analyzed, aggregated, and mined in order to perform early illness prediction [1]. In addition, with the aid of IoT, doctors or healthcare centers could monitor the clinical data for a patient at home to take the emergency medical decision remotely and easily without needing to visit the patient. This will help rescue several patients because the medical decision can be made quickly and at a lower cost. Furthermore, several medical analytics, like measuring blood glucose level, blood pressure, and pO2 level, can be conducted at home without going the patients to healthcare centers. Therefore, IoT enables the transformation of a healthcare system that is hospital-centric into a system that is patient-centric [2]. One of the most common applications of IoT in medical systems is human activity recognition (HAR), which enables the monitoring of daily human activities in real-time for improving medical care services like old-age care services, personal health care assistants, and keeping patient records to be aided in future [3]. The utilization of HAR in the public health care sector has proven to be highly advantageous in the monitoring and regulation of daily physical activities, which can aid in mitigating the risk of various diseases such as diabetes, obesity, and cardio and neuro-related diseases [4]. In a broad sense, wearable sensors over the IoT monitor various

Metaheuristics Algorithms for Medical Applications. DOI: https://doi.org/10.1016/B978-0-443-13314-5.00002-3

human activities and submit the collected data into the HAR models to guess the types of these activities performed by humans. These models are based on machine learning and deep learning models that have high abilities to analyze a huge amount of data for reaching the right prediction. In literature, several machine learning and deep learning based HAR models have been proposed to improve the quality of services presented in the medical systems. For example, in [5], a new video-based HAR model was presented based on using multifeatures and embedded Hidden Markov Models to recognize the everyday life activities of elderly people who live alone in an indoor environment such as smart homes. There are several other HAR models proposed in the healthcare to monitor various activities performing by humans to improve the medical care services.

However, the deep learning techniques as processing algorithms for analyzing the data collected by the smart sensors have some hyperparameters that have to be accurately optimized to improve recognition accuracy. For example, convolutional neural networks (CNN) have a large number of hyperparameters that need to be accurately tuned to maximize their performance for several medical instances. Estimating the hyperparameters of the deep learning and machine learning techniques using traditional methods like exhaustive grid search and guestimating method is hard to be achieved due to the high complexity level of this optimization problem. Therefore, scientists pay attention to applying metaheuristic algorithms, which could achieve outstanding outcomes for several applications in a reasonable amount of time, to solve this problem [6]. Furthermore, the gradient-based optimizers might fall into local minima solution during searching for the near-optimal weights that could attain better classification accuracy. The metaheuristic algorithms have two strong characteristics: Exploration and exploitation, which make them able to escape from the local minima and achieve strong outcomes for several optimization problems, especially those on a large scale. Therefore, scientists, over the last few years, have applied those algorithms as optimizers to find the near-optimal weights that could achieve better classification and clustering accuracy.

In this chapter, we will investigate the role of the metaheuristics algorithms in helping the deep learning models accurately estimate human activities for improving medical care services. In general, this chapter is organized as follows. In the beginning, the deep neural network used to analyze the data collected from the sensors will be described to illustrate its hyperparameters that need to be estimated. Then, one of the recently-published metaheuristic algorithms, named artificial gorilla troops optimizer (GTO), is discussed to elaborate its mathematical model and search behaviors. Following that, the steps of the metaheuristics-based HAR model are described in detail to elaborate on how to employ the metaheuristics with the deep learning model to improve medical care services. Some experiments are conducted in the next section to illustrate the performance of various metaheuristics algorithms for estimating the hyperparameters of deep neural networks. Finally, the last section presents the chapter summary.

3.2 Methods

In this section, the deep neural network (DNN) is described in detail to illustrate the role of metaheuristics in improving its performance. Following that, the newly-proposed metaheuristic algorithm known as GTO in addition to the well-established algorithm known as the grey wolf optimizer (GWO) are described in detail to illustrate its behaviors used to estimate the hyperparameters of DNN for analyzing data gathered by IoT devices.

3.2.1 Deep neural network

The DNN is considered a fully-connected feed-forward neural network with multiple hidden layers. These layers are added with the purpose of automatically extracting the relevant features from the input data for achieving better accuracy. Generally, DNN consists of three different types of layers, including hidden, input, and output layers. The input layer receives a dataset, which is comprised of M samples, where each sample belongs to a specific class and is comprised of d features. Following that, the hidden layers are set to receive the output of the input layer for performing further processing for extracting the most relevant features from the input data in an attempt to learn its characteristics for reaching better classification accuracy. The output from the hidden layers is taken as input to the output layer for estimating the final class. Each layer from those is comprised of a number of nodes known as neurons where their output is based on the output of all the neurons in the previous layers and the connection weights, as defined in the following formula:

$$O_j^{i+1} = \left(\sum_{k=1}^{n} w_{kj}^{i+1} \cdot o_j^i \right) + \theta_j^{i+1} \tag{3.1}$$

where O_j^{i+1} represents the computed output of the jth neuron in the $(i+1)^{\text{th}}$ layer, n refers to the number of neurons in the previous layers, w_{kj}^{i+1} is the weight parameter between the kth neuron in the ith layer and the jth neuron in the $(i+1)^{th}$ layer, θ_j is the jth hidden neuron's bias in the $(i+1)^{th}$ layer, and o_j^i stands for the jth neuron's outputs in the ith layer. O_j^{i+1} is passed to an activation function f for computing the output of the j neuron in the $(i+1)^{th}$ layer, as defined in the following formula:

$$o_j^{i+1} = f(s_j) \tag{3.2}$$

Various activation functions have been suggested to enhance the precision of predicted labels by the deep learning model. Those functions will be further deliberated in the next chapters. DNN starts with randomly initializing the weights of each connection between every two neurons, then seeks to accurately update these weights within the optimization process to effectively estimate the optimal label of every input record present in the dataset. This process is considered an optimization process, so there is a need for an objective function, also referred to as a loss function, to show the accuracy of the obtained weights during the optimization process. The most common loss function is the Categorical Cross Entropy (CCE), which is mathematically formulated as follows:

$$\text{Minimize } loss\,(CCE) = -\sum_{i=1}^{M} y_i \cdot \log \breve{y}_i \tag{3.3}$$

The notation $\breve{y}_i$ refers to a vector that encompasses the anticipated outputs of the training samples. As aforementioned that the metaheuristic could be used to search for the near-optimal weights that could minimize this loss function for achieving better classification accuracy. However, the main drawback of these techniques is that they need several function evaluations till reaching the near-optimal weights. Therefore they are not preferred for solving this problem. As a strong alternative, Gradient-based algorithms are commonly favored for minimizing loss functions in order to achieve universal approximation. This is due to their ability to quickly reach near-optimal weights that minimize the loss function, while also requiring fewer computational resources. However, these methods are prone to fall into local minima because the gradient when the local minima solutions are 0, and hence the current weights could not be updated. There are several gradient-based optimizers like the stochastic gradient descent (SGD) algorithm, momentum gradient descent (MGD), Adam optimizer, and adaptive gradient (AdaGrad) algorithm.

3.2.2 Artificial gorilla troops optimizer

Recently, Abdollahzadeh proposed a new population-based optimization technique named GTO for solving global optimization and engineering design optimization problems [7]. GTO mimicked the social intelligence of the gorilla troops, which are divided into two main operators known as exploration and exploitation. In the former, GTO tries to explore the majority of regions within the search space as much as possible in the hope of finding the promising regions. Within the optimization process, those regions are exploited using the latter operator to improve the convergence rate toward the near-optimal solution. The mathematical model of GTO is described in the following sections, and its pseudocode is presented in Algorithm 3.1.

Algorithm 3.1 The steps of GTO

Output: X^*
1. Initializes randomly N individuals, $\vec{X_i}(i \in N)$.
2. Set β_1, W, and p.
3. Evaluate each $\vec{X_i}$
4. Identify the near-optimal solution achieved yet, X^*
5. t = 0; %% Initialize the current iteration
6. **while** (t $<$ t_{max})
7.   **Update** C and L according to (3.5) and (3.7), respectively.
8.   // **Exploration**
9. r: a numerical value selected at random in the interval (0, 1)
10.   *for* each i solution
11.   Update X_i using Eq. (3.4)
12.   Replace X_i with G_i if the objective value of the latter is better
13.   Update X^* if there is better
14. $t++$;
15.   *End*
16.   // **Exploitation**
17.   *for* each i solution
18.   update X_i using (3.16)
19.   Replace X_i with G_i if the objective value of the latter is better
20.   Update X^* if there is better
21. $t++$;
22.   *fEnd*
23.   *End while*

Phase 1: Exploration operator

This operator encourages exploring the search space as possible for reaching the most promising regions that might involve near-optimal solutions. The weakness of this operator might cause falling into local minima and hence the algorithm could not reach these promising regions. Therefore the authors tried to design GTO with a strong exploration operator by diversifying the search process to attack the most possible regions within the search space. This operator is mathematically described using the following formula:

$$\vec{G_i}(t+1) = \begin{cases} \vec{lb} + \left(\vec{ub} - \vec{lb}\right) * r & r_1 < p \\ (r_2 - C) \times \left(\vec{X_r}(t)\right) + \vec{H} \times L & r_1 \geq 0.5 \\ \vec{X_i^t} - L \times \left(L \times \left(\vec{X_i^t} - \vec{G_r}(t)\right), + r_3, \times \left(\vec{X_i^t} - \vec{G_r^t}\right)\right) & r_1 < 0.5 \end{cases}$$

(3.4)

$$C = F \times \left(1 - \frac{t}{T_{\max}}\right)$$

(3.5)

$$F = \cos(2 \times r_4) + 1$$

(3.6)

$$L = C \times l$$

(3.7)

$$\vec{H} = \vec{Z} \times \vec{X_i}(t) | Z = [-C, C]$$

(3.8)

where l is a controlling factor that includes numerical data generated randomly in the range (1, -1), $\vec{G_i}$ is a vector to include the newly-generated positions of the ith solution, while $\vec{X_i^t}$ are a vector containing the current position of the same solution. $\vec{G_r}$ is a vector including the positions of a solution chosen at random from the newly-generated solutions, and $\vec{X_r^t}$ is a vector storing a solution chosen at random from the individuals in the current population. p is a predefined controlling parameter at the interval of (0, 1). $\vec{Z}$ is a vector including numerical data generated at random in the range (-C, C). After that, $\vec{X_i}(t)$ is compared with the newly-generated $\vec{G_i}(t+1)$, if the latter is better, it is set in the current population instead of the former.

Phase 2: Exploitation operator

In this operator, GTO simulates two behaviors: Following the best-so-far solution and competing for adult females. The first behavior in GTO is mathematically formulated as follows:

$$\vec{G}_i(t+1) = L \times M \times \left(\vec{X}_i^t - \vec{X}^*\right) + \vec{X}_i^t \qquad (3.9)$$

$$\vec{M} = \left(\left|\frac{1}{N}\sum_{i=0}^{N}\vec{G}_i(t)\right|^g\right)^{\frac{1}{g}} \qquad (3.10)$$

$$g = 2^L \qquad (3.11)$$

The second behavior is mathematically defined as follows:

$$\vec{G}_i(t+1) = -\left(Q \times \vec{X}_i^t - Q \times \vec{X}^*\right) \times A + \vec{X}^* \qquad (3.12)$$

$$Q = 2 \times r_5 - 1 \qquad (3.13)$$

$$A = E \times \beta_1 \qquad (3.14)$$

$$\vec{E} = \begin{cases} \vec{N_1}, r_6 \geq 0.5 \\ \vec{N_2}, r_6 < 0.5 \end{cases} \qquad (3.15)$$

The variables r_5 and r_6 were selected randomly from the interval between 0 and 1. The value of β_1 is predetermined prior to commencing the search process. Vector $\vec{N_1}$ comprises randomly generated values following the normal distribution, whereas $\vec{N_2}$ denotes a randomly assigned number conforming to the normal distribution. To alternate between the aforementioned behaviors, GTO utilizes a predetermined controlling parameter known as W and a factor denoted as C, as presented in the following equation:

$$\vec{G}_i(t+1) = \begin{cases} \text{Eq(3.9) } if\ C \geq w \\ \text{Eq(3.12) } if\ C < w \end{cases} \qquad (3.16)$$

3.2.3 Grey wolf optimizer

In [8], the authors presented a population-based metaheuristic algorithm termed the grey wolf optimizer (GWO). This algorithm emulated the behavior of grey wolves when they are hunting for, encircling, and catching their prey. In GWO, grey wolves are separated into four varieties based on their dominance and leadership: alpha, beta, delta, and omega. The alpha wolf symbolized as α is regarded as the best solution discovered thus far, the beta wolf symbolized β is regarded as the second best solution, and the delta wolf symbolized as δ is regarded as the third best solution, while the omega wolf symbolized as ω represents the rest of the wolves. During the chase, the wolves can geometrically encircle the prey they are hunting by employing the model below:

$$\vec{D} = \left| \vec{C}.\vec{X}_{p}^{t}, - \vec{X}_i^t \right| \tag{3.17}$$

$$\vec{X}_i^{t+1} = \vec{X}_p^t - \vec{D}.\vec{A} \tag{3.18}$$

where $\vec{X}_i^t$ is a vector including the solution of the ith grey wolf, and $\vec{X}_p$ represents a vector storing the location of the prey. $\vec{C}$ is a vector generated according to the following equation:

$$\vec{C} = 2 * \vec{r}_1 \tag{3.19}$$

where $\vec{r}_1$ is a vector assigned numerical data at random in the interval (0, 1). $\vec{A}$ is a controlling factor utilized to control the exploration and exploitation capabilities of GWO through the optimization process. The mathematical expression that could be used to compute the values of this factor during the optimization process is formulated as defined below:

$$\vec{A} = 2 * \vec{a} * \vec{r}_2 - \vec{a} \tag{3.20}$$

The $\vec{r}_2$ represents a vector storing numerical data chosen at random in the interval (0, 1). $\vec{a}$ is a linearly-decreased factor from 2 to 0 to control the exploration and exploitation. This factor is represented according to the following mathematical model:

$$\vec{a} = 2 - 2 * \frac{t}{T_{\max}} \tag{3.21}$$

The previous mathematical model mimics the behavior of grey wolves when surrounding prey. It was proposed by GWO that the three best grey wolves (α, β, and δ) should have knowledge of the possible location of the prey and that the other grey wolves should adjust their position based on the information provided by the top three grey wolves. The method by which grey wolves go about their hunting can be expressed in mathematical terms as follows:

$$\vec{X}_i^t = \left(\vec{X}_1^t + \vec{X}_2^t + \vec{X}_3^t \right)/3.0 \tag{3.22}$$

$$\vec{X}_1^t = \vec{X}_\alpha^t - \vec{A}_1.\vec{D}_\alpha^t, \quad \vec{D}_\alpha^t = \left| \vec{C}_1.\vec{X}_\alpha^t - \vec{X}_i^t \right| \tag{3.23}$$

$$\vec{X}_2^t = \vec{X}_\delta^t - \vec{A}_2.\vec{D}_\beta^t, \quad \vec{D}_\beta^t = \left| \vec{C}_2.\vec{X}_\beta^t - \vec{X}_i^t \right| \tag{3.24}$$

$$\vec{X}_3^t = \vec{X}_\delta^t - \vec{A}_3.\vec{D}_\delta^t, \quad \vec{D}_\delta^t = \left| \vec{C}_3.\vec{X}_\delta^t - \vec{X}_i^t \right| \tag{3.25}$$

When $\vec{A}$ are in the interval of 1 and -1, the next position that a grey wolf will take could be in any position in the interval of its current position and the prey's position. On the other hand, when $\vec{A} > 1$ and $\vec{A} < -1$, the grey wolves are compelled to separate themselves from the prey and travel to new areas in the hope of locating more suitable prey. Finally, the GWO's pseudocode is presented in Algorithm 3.2.

Algorithm 3.2 Grey wolf optimizer (GWO)

24. Initialization.
25. Evaluate each grey wolf by computing he fitness value for each one
26. Identify X_α, X_β, and X_δ.
27. t = 0; %% Initialize the current iteration
28. **while** (t < t_{max})
29. update the current position according to Eq. (3.22)
30. Compute the fitness value for each updated solution.
31. Update A, a, and C
32. Update the X_β, X_α, and X_δ
33. t++
34. **end**
   Output: return X_α.

3.3 Metaheuristics-based DNN's hyperparameters tuning

In this chapter, we will investigate the performance of GTO, DE, TLBO, and GWO for constructing the optimal architecture of the DNN for recognizing the human activities collected from IoT devices. The architecture of DNN is comprised of the number of layers and the number of neurons that have to be accurately estimated to avoid the overfitting problem. Furthermore, the gradient-based optimizers have a controlling factor known as learning rate (γ) that has to also be estimated to optimize the performance of the gradient-based optimizers. In this study, we will investigate the performance of the previously-stated metaheuristics for estimating the optimal values for those parameters to maximize the performance of the DNN. The main steps of adapting a metaheuristic for hyperparameters tuning of DNN are initialization, Constructing DNN, and evaluation.

3.3.1 Initialization

In the beginning, the metaheuristic algorithms take the initial values for the following parameters: the number of population (N), number of dimensions (d), and lower bound and upper bound for each dimension. Since the number of dimensions is based on the number of layers estimated in each iteration by each solution, the length of each solution, known as the number of dimensions, is dynamically changed. This dynamic change is due to the number of dimensions being dependent on the number of layers that is updated in each iteration. In general, the dimension size is based on three factors: the number of layers, the number of neurons for each layer, and the learning rate. Based on that, the number of dimensions (d) could be computed as follows:

$$d = 2 + \mu \tag{3.26}$$

where μ represents the estimated number of layers, while the number 2 in this equation represents two dimensions used to store the number of layers and γ. Following computing the number of dimensions, it is imperative to explicate the process of initializing these dimensions within the search space of each respective dimension. Initially, it is imperative to determine the upper and lower values for each dimension. Comprehensively, it can be stated that the learning rate possesses an upper limit of 1 and a lower limit of 0. Nevertheless, it is not feasible for the upper limit of the learning rate to be 1 and the lower limit to be 0. Moreover, as the learning rate approaches 1, the updated steps become excessively large, causing the omission of the near-optimal solution. Conversely, if the learning rate is closer to 0, the near-optimal solutions may require a significant number of epochs and might potentially become intractable. Hence, in our experimental setup, we set the lower and upper bounds for the learning rate as 0.00001 and 0.1, respectively, to circumvent the aforementioned limitations. The range of layers was established with an upper limit of 10 and a lower limit of 2. The researchers have the option to augment these values to enhance the likelihood of achieving a superior number of layers. However, this increment would increase the duration of the search process, as the algorithms would be required to investigate a substantial number of regions. With regard to the upper and lower limits of the range of neurons, they have been established as 80 and 500, correspondingly. Also, it is possible to increase the upper limit of neurons to potentially discover several other solutions, however, this action may require an augmented exploration process from the metaheuristics to cover the regions that might involve the optimal value. Thus, the aforementioned upper limit of 500 was deemed preferable in order to mitigate computational expenses. After determining the upper and lower bound of each dimension, the algorithm will start its optimization process with randomly distributing d-dimensions of N solutions within the upper bound and lower bound of each dimension. The obtained solutions will be repaired to convert the decimal values for the number of neurons and layers into integers.

3.3.2 Constructing DNN

Afterward, the DNN will be created under the parameters found in each solution, as shown in Algorithm 3.3. This algorithm

---

Algorithm 3.3 DNN

Input: Number of classes (n), $\vec{X_i}$
Output: model
/* Building model */
1: **inp:** Create an **input layer** to receive the input dataset
2: **x = inp;**
3: **while** $i < X_1$ %% Loops to create the layers with the corresponding number of neurons
4:   **x = Dense(X_{i+2}, activation = 'Relu')(x)**
5:   $i = i + 1;$
6: **end while**
7: **x = Dense(n, activation = 'softmax')(x)**
8: **model** = Model(inputs = **inp**,outputs = **x**)
9: **model.compile(loss = 'categorical_crossentropy', optimizer = Adam(X_2))**

---

takes the number of classes (n) and the current solution ($\vec{X_i}$) as inputs. Then, it creates the input layer to receive the dataset. The number of layers estimated in the current solution will be created in Lines 3−6, in which the corresponding number of neurons is set as estimated in the same solution. After constructing the DNN model, in Line 9, it is configured with the loss function and the Adam optimizer using the learning rate from the given solution. In this chapter, CCE is used as a loss function due to its wide use for multiclass classification problems. This function is mathematically formulated as follows:

$$\text{Minimize: loss}(CCE) = -\sum_{i=1}^{M} y_i \cdot \log \breve{y}_i, \qquad (3.27)$$

where $\breve{y}$ represents the predicted outputs of the samples in the training dataset, y is a vector including the true classes for the training samples, and M stands for the total number of samples. It is worth mentioning that during compiling the model, the weight parameters will be randomly initialized to set the initial weights that are then optimized using the Adam optimizer.

3.3.3 Evaluation

After constructing the DNN model, it will be trained under the training dataset for two epochs. Then, the loss value is returned to determine the quality of the current solution. This process is applied for each initialized solution in the current population. Afterward, the metaheuristics start to update those solutions in an attempt to search for better solutions that might achieve a better DNN architecture. Those updated solutions will be first repaired to convert the number of layers and neurons into integers. Then, the new DNN architectures are designed using those solutions. Those architectures are training and the loss value for each solution is returned. Those loss values are compared and the solutions with the lowest fitness value are set as the best-so-far solution. Finally, the pseudocode of the classical GTO as an illustrative example used to estimate the hyperparameters of DNN is listed in Algorithm 3.4. Fig. 3.1 presents the different steps for adapting the metaheuristic algorithms for estimating the hyperparameters of the DNN.

Algorithm 3.4 The pseudocode of GTO for tuning hyperparameters

Input: (X_train, Y_train), (X_vad, Y_val), Epochs (T)

Output: X^*

1. Initializes randomly N individuals, $\vec{X_i}(i \in N)$.
2. Set β_1 , W, and p.
3. *for* each i solution
4.   model = DNN$(\vec{X_i})$
5.   model.fit(X_train, Y_train, epochs = 2, batch_size = batch_size);
6.   Store the loss value for the *ith* solutions
7. *end*
8. Identify the solution with the lowest loss value as the near-optimal solution achieved yet, X^*
9. t = 0;
10. **while** (t < T_{max})
11.   **Update** C and L according to (3.5) and (3.7), respectively.
12.   // **Exploration**
13. r: a numerical value selected at random in the interval (0, 1)
14.   *for* each i solution
15.   Update X_i using Eq. (3.4)
16.   model = DNN$(\vec{X_i})$
17.   model.fit(X_train, Y_train, epochs = 2, batch_size = batch_size);
18.   Replace X_i with G_i if the loss value of the new solution is better
19.   Update X^* if there is better
20. $t++;$
21.   *End*
22.   // **Exploitation**
23.   *for* each i solution
24.   update X_i using (3.16)
25.   model = DNN$(\vec{X_i})$
26.   model.fit(X_train, Y_train, epochs = 2, batch_size = batch_size);
27.   Replace X_i with G_i if the loss value of the new solution is better
28.   Update X^* if there is better
29. $t++;$
30.   *End*
31. *End while*

3.3.3.1 Performance metrics

In this chapter, three different performance metrics are used to evaluate the performance of the constructed deep-learning neural networks. Those metrics include F1-score, precision, and accuracy. Precision is used to compute the percentage of the correctly-classified instances with a class A among all the instances classified

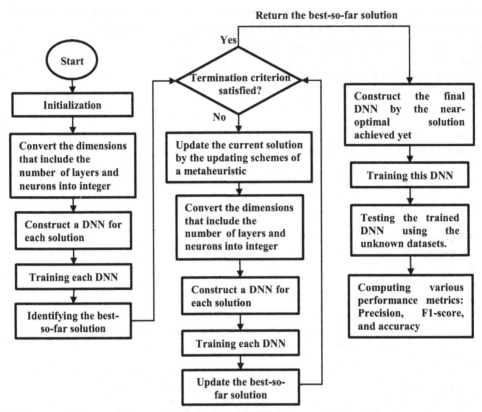

Figure 3.1 A general framework for metaheuristics-based DNN's hyperparameters tuning.

with the same class. The mathematical formula that could be used to compute this percentage is as follows:

$$\text{Precision} = \frac{TP}{TP + FP} \qquad (3.28)$$

where *TP* refers to true positive, and *FP* refers to false positive. A model's accuracy indicates how often it accurately categorizes a data point. Accuracy can be thought of as the proportion of the correctly-classified instances from all the instances in the dataset. To compute the accuracy, the following mathematical formula can be used:

$$\text{Accuracy} = \frac{TP + TN}{TP + FP + TN + FN} \qquad (3.29)$$

where *TN* represents true negative, and *FN* is false negative. The F1-score is a mathematical synthesis of the recall and precision indicators. The F1 score can have a value of one in the best scenario and zero in the worst case. The F1 score can be computed using the following formula:

$$F1 - score = 2 \times \frac{Precision \cdot Recall}{Precision + Recal} \qquad (3.30)$$

3.3.3.2 Dataset preprocessing

Before developing a DL-based model, it is necessary to complete the step of "data preprocessing", which involves cleaning raw data and putting it in a format that is appropriate for the model in question. In order to make the dataset more precise for a DL-based model, the first stage of the preprocessing step is called "data cleaning". This stage involves the removal of any invalid or unnecessary data from the dataset. As a result of the enormous size of the datasets that were utilized for this research, any and all tuples within the datasets that had missing data were eliminated, and the remaining data were sent to the following stage of the preprocessing procedure. Following the cleaning of the dataset, the standardization method was applied to it in order to standardize all of the columns and give them all the same scale. This was done to ensure that during the optimization phase, no column would be dominant over the others. The mathematical model of this method is as follows:

$$\vec{X'} = \frac{\vec{X} - \overline{X}}{a}, \qquad (3.31)$$

where $\vec{X'}$ represents the normalized vector, $\vec{X}$ is the input vector to be normalized, $\overline{X}$ refers to the mean vector, and a is the standard deviation. Following the process of scaling each column in the dataset, the dataset was analyzed to determine whether or not it was balanced. If the dataset was balanced, the process of splitting the data would be carried out to split the data into 80% training dataset and 20% testing dataset. But, if the dataset was not balanced, stratified sampling would be required to be performed before the process of dividing the data.

3.4 Dataset description and experiment settings

In this chapter, four different metaheuristic algorithms, namely TLBO, GTO, DE, and GWO are employed to search for the hyperparameters of the DNN in an attempt to reveal the best algorithm, which is able to reach the near-optimal architecture that is able to accurately tackle the HAR in the healthcare system. Two widely used datasets, namely UCI-HAR and USC-HAD are employed in this study. The UCI-HAR dataset is considered to be one of the most important datasets that were made available in 2012 for the purpose of evaluating the effectiveness of newly published models [9]. SITTING (HA4), WALKING (HA1), STANDING (HA5), WALKING_DOWNSTAIRS (HA3), WALKING_UPSTAIRS (HA2), and LAYING (HA6) are the six human actions that are included in this dataset. This dataset's data samples were separated into two distinct datasets: the training dataset contained 7352 samples, while the test dataset contained 2947 samples. These samples had 128 time-series data spread across nine channels, each of which was a part of the sample's overall composition. In Table 3.1, the characteristics of the UCI-HAR dataset are presented. These characteristics include the overall number of data points as well as the number of data points for each human activity that is included in this dataset. The USC-HAD dataset consists of 195,374 data points. These data points can be broken down into a total of twelve human activities, as listed in Table 3.2. Those activities include Walking Frontward (HA1), Walking Left (HA2), Walking Right (HA3), Walking Upstairs (HA4), Walking Downstairs (HA5), Running Frontward (HA6), Jumping Up (HA7), Sitting (HA8), Standing (HA9), Sleeping (HA10), Elevator Up (HA11), and Elevator Down (HA12) [10].

To construct and train the recommended deep neural network, the programming language Python, the Keras package, and a TensorFlow backend were utilized. Because the Keras package contains a neural network library that was built on top of Theano or TensorFlow, it makes it possible for researchers to easily design a neural network [11]. The Keras package provides

Table 3.1 Characteristics of the UCI-HAR dataset.

Activity	Data points per activity	Proportion percentage
WALKING (HA1)	1722	16.7%
WALKING_UPSTAIRS (HA2)	1544	14.9%
WALKING_DOWNSTAIRS (HA3)	1406	13.6%
SITTING (HA4)	1777	17.2%
STANDING (HA5)	1906	18.5%
LAYING (HA6)	1944	18.8%
Total data points	10299	100%

Table 3.2 Statistics of the USC-HAD dataset.

Activity	Data points per activity	Proportion percentage
Walking forward (HA1)	12,300	6.30%
Walking left (HA2)	16,400	8.39%
Walking right (HA3)	18,700	9.57%
Walking upstairs (HA4)	30,700	15.71%
Walking downstairs (HA5)	28,700	14.69%
Running forward (HA6)	8200	4.20%
Jumping up (HA7)	7000	3.58%
Sitting (HA8)	20,000	10.24%
Standing (HA9)	9500	4.86%
Sleeping (HA10)	25,000	12.80%
Elevator up (HA11)	9687	4.96%
Elevator down (HA12)	9187	4.70%
Total data points	195,374	100%

the vast majority of the building pieces that are required to develop somewhat sophisticated deep-learning models. All experiments are conducted on a PC with the following capabilities: 32 gigabytes of random access memory (RAM), a 2.40 GHz Intel Core i7−4700MQ CPU, and Windows 10 as the operating system. The maximum number of iterations and population size for all studied metaheuristics are limited to 5 and 10, respectively, to ensure a fair comparison among algorithms. After estimating the architecture of the deep learning network by each metaheuristic, this architecture is extensively trained on each training dataset under a number of epochs up to 40 to observe the quality of each architecture for reaching better classification accuracy. The batch size values heuristically selected for two validated used were 128, and 50. The number of epochs in the experiments was 200, and 0.001, respectively.

3.5 Results and discussion

This chapter includes conducting some experiments to reveal the performance of metaheuristics for tuning the hyperparameters of the DNN. In those experiments, all metaheuristics are executed 10 independent times. In each run of those, the DNN is constructed and trained using the training dataset for only two epochs, and the loss values within the optimization process are compared to identify the best-so-far solution that is returned after satisfying the termination conditions. The average loss value, referred to F-value, of those runs is computed for each algorithm and reported in Figs. 3.2 and 3.3 for both UCI-HAR and USC-HAD, respectively. Those figures reveal that GTO could achieve the lowest loss values for the former dataset, while DE could be better for the latter dataset. This do not mean that those algorithms could achieve the near-optimal architecture because the algorithm might perform well on the training dataset while its performance is degraded on the unknown dataset, also referred to as the testing dataset. This problem is known as the overfitting problem.

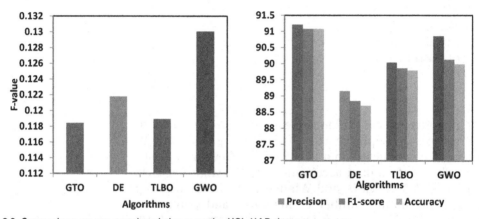

Figure 3.2 Comparison among metaheuristics over the UCI_HAR dataset.

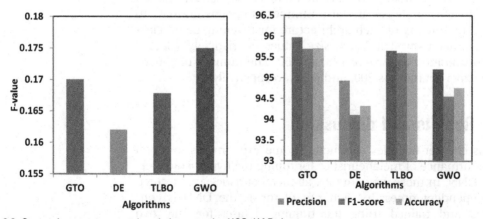

Figure 3.3 Comparison among metaheuristics over the USC_HAD dataset.

Therefore, the best solution from those runs is extracted to construct the final DNN architecture employed to tackle the HAR in the healthcare system. This architecture is trained for 40 epochs on the training samples of two employed datasets. Then, the values of the various performance metrics described before are computed on the testing dataset and reported in Figs. 3.2 and 3.3, respectively. Fig. 3.2 reports the precision, F1-score, and accuracy values obtained under various metaheuristics on the UCI-HAR dataset. From this figure, we can conclude that the architecture obtained by GTO is better than all the other algorithms because it can be better in terms of all the performance metrics on the testing dataset. Following GTO, GWO could achieve better values for those metrics, while DE is the worst-performing algorithm. To further confirm our hypothesis, the outcomes over the other dataset, called USC_HAD, are reported in Fig. 3.3, which shows the superiority of GTO compared to the others, where it could achieve better values for all performance metrics, followed by TLBO as the second-best one, while DE is the worst. As a result, GTO is a strong alternative for finding the near-optimal hyperparameter values of the DNN to improve its classification accuracy for the HAR in medical applications. Ultimately, we can conclude that metaheuristic techniques are indispensable in several fields, especially in the medical field, due to their ability to tackle several optimization problems with high accuracy and at a less computational cost. For example, they could be applied to search for the near-optimal parameters of the DNN to find the DNN architecture that could maximize the classification accuracy for HAR in the medical field.

3.6 Chapter summary

The deep learning techniques include several hyperparameters that need to be accurately estimated to maximize their performance for analyzing the data returned from the wearable sensors related to the patients and connected through the IoT. This might improve the quality of service in the medical field. The traditional methods like exhaustive grid search and guestimating method could not precisely estimate the near-optimal values of those parameters due to the high difficulty level of this optimization problem. Therefore, the scientists pay attention to applying the metaheuristic algorithms, which could achieve outstanding outcomes for several applications in a reasonable amount of time, to estimate the hyperparameters of the deep learning and machine learning models. In this chapter, we investigated the performance of four metaheuristic algorithms, namely DE, TLBO, GTO, and GWO, for estimating the optimal values of those hyperparameters for improving the performance of the DNN to accurately estimate the human activities for improving the medical care services. The experimental findings show that GTO is the most effective for tackling this optimization problem.

References

[1] M.A. Khan, Challenges facing the application of IoT in medicine and healthcare, International Journal of Computations, Information, and Manufacturing 1 (1) (2021).

[2] B. Pradhan, S. Bhattacharyya, K. Pal, IoT-based applications in healthcare devices, Journal of Healthcare Engineering 2021 (2021) 1–18.

[3] A. Subasi, M. Radhwan, R. Kurdi, and K. Khateeb, IoT based mobile healthcare system for human activity recognition, in *Proceedings of the Fifteenth Learning and Technology Conference (L&T)*, 2018, pp. 29–34: IEEE.

[4] D. Mukherjee, R. Mondal, P.K. Singh, R. Sarkar, D. Bhattacharjee, EnsemConvNet: a deep learning approach for human activity recognition using smartphone sensors for healthcare applications, Multimedia Tools and Applications 79 (2020) 31663–31690.

[5] A. Jalal, S. Kamal, and D. Kim, A depth video-based human detection and activity recognition using multi-features and embedded hidden Markov models for health care monitoring systems, 2017.

[6] E. Tuba, N. Bačanin, I. Strumberger, M. Tuba, Convolutional neural networks hyperparameters tuning, Artificial Intelligence: Theory and Applications, Springer, 2021, pp. 65–84.

[7] B. Abdollahzadeh, F. Soleimanian Gharehchopogh, S. Mirjalili, Artificial gorilla troops optimizer: a new nature-inspired metaheuristic algorithm for global optimization problems, International Journal of Intelligent Systems 36 (10) (2021) 5887–5958.

[8] S. Mirjalili, S.M. Mirjalili, A. Lewis, Grey wolf optimizer, Advances in Engineering Software 69 (2014) 46–61.

[9] H. Yu, et al., Fedhar: semi-supervised online learning for personalized federated human activity recognition, IEEE Transactions on Mobile Computing (2021).

[10] S. Xu, L. Zhang, W. Huang, H. Wu, A. Song, Deformable convolutional networks for multimodal human activity recognition using wearable sensors, IEEE Transactions on Instrumentation and Measurement 71 (2022) 1–14.

[11] A. Gulli, S. Pal, Deep Learning with Keras, Packt Publishing Ltd, 2017.

4

Improved gradient-based optimizer for medical image enhancement

4.1 Introduction

Essentially, image enhancement (IE) aims to make images more easily understood by humans and give more accurate and clearer images for the fields that are sensitive to their quality [1]. In other words, IE aims at adjusting images so that they are better suited for usage in automated image processing techniques, like analysis, recognition, detection, and segmentation [2]. IE takes the image as input and tries to change some or all its attributes to be clearer [1]. There are several enhancement techniques with strong performance to improve a digital image without distorting it. These techniques could be categorized into two primary classes:

- **Spatial domain methods**: These methods manipulate the image pixels for reaching the desired enhanced image. The main advantages of these techniques are that they are easy to be understood and need low computational costs for reaching desired enhancement.
- **Frequency domain methods**: In these methods, the images are first converted into the frequency domain. To be clearer, the Fourier transform of these images is first computed and then manipulated by various enhancement operations to get the enhanced Fourier transform signals. The enhancement operations are conducted to improve the distribution, contrast, or brightness of the images. In the end, these signals are transformed into enhanced images by the inverse Fourier transform.

Enhancing medical images is a necessary step to aid in diagnosing several superior diseases in addition to accurately discovering pathological lesions [3]. The medical imaging technique known as computed tomography is widely regarded as an essential tool for diagnosing a wide variety of illnesses, including vascular lesions and tumors [3]. However, unfortunately, speckle noise ruins the images generated using this tool and makes them unsuitable to

Metaheuristics Algorithms for Medical Applications. DOI: https://doi.org/10.1016/B978-0-443-13314-5.00009-6

interpret clinical data. In light of this, medical IE is required to remove noise and produce images that are clearer for accurate diagnosis.

This chapter first discusses different methods proposed for IE problems. Then, it overviews the classical gradient-based optimizer (GBO). Furthermore, the main steps required to adapt metaheuristics for solving the IE are discussed. Some experiments and comparisons are presented in this chapter to reveal the performance of some metaheuristics for this problem. Finally, the chapter summary is discussed.

4.2   Methods

The majority of IE techniques typically employ a reliable transformation function to map the pixels of an input image that needs to be improved [4]. However, unfortunately, such a function has some unknown parameters that need to be accurately optimized to significantly enhance the quality of the medical images. Therefore, the researchers have paid attention to estimating the near-optimal value for these parameters by the metaheuristic algorithms as the most effective techniques for optimization problems over the last few decades; these techniques are also known as approximation techniques. These techniques are not problem-specific and hence could be applied to several optimization problems by making some modifications to the updated solutions to become applicable to the tackled problems. Then, these solutions are employed to minimize or maximize the desired objective function according to the needs of the tackled optimization problems. The objective function used herein with the studied metaheuristics is discussed within this section, following the description of the specific transformation function employed in this chapter to map the image's pixels. In addition, we overview the classical GBO as one of the recently published, high-performing algorithms.

4.2.1   Transformation function

In general, a two-dimensional matrix with N rows and M columns could be used to represent any image, where each coordinate (x, y) in this matrix includes a value known as intensity or gray level. Traditional techniques for enhancing images seek to eliminate noise in addition to enhancing the sharpness and contrast of the image's edges. In the beginning, Jourlin [3] developed a model called the logarithmic image processing (LIP) algorithm so that it could address this issue. For the purpose of signal and image processing, the LIP is considered a mathematical model that offers a collection of generalized adaptations of mathematical operations such as subtraction, multiplication, addition, and convolution. According to the LIP model, the image's brightness is represented by the amount of light that is allowed to travel through a light filter that has an absorption function. The percentage of incident light that is absorbed by the light filter is the definition of the absorption function. There are several other IE techniques belonging to the spatial domain category, such as piecewise linear transformation functions, intensity transformation, thresholding transformation, power-law transformations, and gray-level slicing [1]. In this chapter, one of the widely used transformation functions proposed is used to perform the enhancement process, driven by the metaheuristics [5]. The enhancement of the pixel (x, y) in image A using this transformation could be formulated as follows:

$$P(x,y) = T[A(x,y)] \tag{4.1}$$

where $A(x,y)$ denotes the gray value of the pixel (x,y) in the original image, $P(x,y)$ represents the enhanced gray value for the same pixel, and T is the transformation function. A window with a size of $n*n$ is utilized for the process of extracting the local information. According to that, the transformation function T could be defined as follows to enhance the image pixel (x,y):

$$P(x,y) = B(x,y)[R(x,y) - c*z(x,y)] + z(x,y)^a \tag{4.2}$$

Given that a and c are both parameters that have to be accurately estimated. The local mean of each pixel (x, y) in the input picture, calculated over a $n*n$ window, is as follows:

$$z(x,y) = \frac{1}{n*n}\sum_{i=0}^{n-1}\sum_{j=0}^{n-1} R(i,j) \tag{4.3}$$

$B(x,y)$ is considered the enhancement function that keeps both global and local data and could be mathematically defined as follows:

$$B(x,y) = \frac{k*A}{\sigma(x,y) + b} \tag{4.4}$$

where k and b are two unknown parameters, which have to be estimated more precisely for reaching the required enhanced image. $\sigma(x,y)$ refers to the local standard deviation of the pixel (x,y) of the given image over the $n*n$ window. The global mean could be computed using the following formula:

$$z(x,y) = \frac{1}{M*N}\sum_{i=0}^{M-1}\sum_{j=0}^{N-1} R(i,j) \tag{4.5}$$

The local standard deviation of the pixel (x, y) in the given image, calculated over the $n * n$ window, could be computed as follows:

$$z(x,y) = \sqrt{\frac{1}{n*n}\sum_{i=0}^{n-1}\sum_{j=0}^{n-1}\left(R(i,j)-z(x,y)\right)^2} \qquad (4.6)$$

The new transformation function, which stretches the image's contrast, can be obtained by replacing Eq. (4.4) with Eq. (4.2) as follows:

$$P(x,y) = \frac{k*A}{B(x,y)}\left[R(x,y) - c*z(x,y)\right] + z(x,y)^a \qquad (4.7)$$

The previous equation involves four known parameters, b, a, k, and c, which have to be accurately estimated to maximize the performance of the transformation function. The purposes of these parameters are as follows: The output image's brightening bias is represented by parameter a, which enables precise control over the required level of smoothing for the enhanced image. When parameter b is used, it helps to ensure that a zero-standard deviation value in the pixels of the immediate neighborhood does not have a major impact on the degree to which the final image is whitened. The parameter c, which allows for a proportion of the mean to be removed from the original pixels in the given image, controls the degree of darkening effects that are formed in the output image. The parameter k strikes a fair equilibrium between pixels located in the middle of the gray scale. This safeguards against the enhancement process, making the pixels too black or too bright [4].

The metaheuristic algorithms have played a significant role in estimating the near-optimal value for the unknown parameters of various transformation functions. For example, the chimp optimization algorithm was employed for estimating the near-optimal values of the incomplete beta function [6]. Furthermore, in this algorithm, the image contrast was further improved using bilateral gamma correction. Moreover, the elitism genetic algorithm was applied to enhance the biomedical images for improving the image quality for achieving better analysis [7]. In a new attempt to accurately choose the unknown coefficients of the incomplete beta function, the whale optimization algorithm was integrated with the chameleon swarm algorithm to propose a new variant, namely HWOA, with a better exploration and exploitation operator [8]. There are several other metaheuristic-based algorithms were proposed for tackling the IE problem [9]. Due to the importance of the metaheuristic algorithms for this problem, in this chapter, we will present a new

IE method based on the GBO and a novel updating strategy to search for the near-optimal parameters of the transformation function for significantly enhancing the quality of the medical images and reaching better analysis. In the next subsection, the used objective function employed is described in detail.

4.2.2 Objective function

It is required to have an objective function that is made of three performance metrics to evaluate and measure the quality of the enhanced medical image. These three performance metrics are the sum of the edge intensities, the number of edges, and the entropy value. This objective function is what is employed with the investigated metaheuristic algorithms to determine the best values for the four unknown coefficients of the transformation function T. This is done to get to the desired enhanced image. The more this objective function is maximized, the more the original images are enhanced. Under the previously stated measures, the objective function could be defined as follows:

$$F(I_e) = \log\left(\log(E(I_s))\right) * \frac{n_{\text{edges}}(I_s)}{M * N} * H(I_e) \qquad (4.8)$$

where I_e represents the improved image that was produced by applying the transformation function in Eq. (4.7). On the other hand, Sobel edge detection generates the edge image, I_s, from the enhanced image. $E(I_s)$ stands for the sum of all the pixel intensities in the Sobel edge image. The number of pixels whose intensity is higher than a predetermined threshold is denoted by n_{edges}. Using the enhanced image I_e as a starting point, the following is how you would generate an edge image:

$$I_s(i,j) = \sqrt{\delta m I_e(i,j)^2 + \delta n I_e(i,j)^2} \qquad (4.9)$$

$$\delta m I_e(i,j) = PI_e(i+1,j-1) + 2PI_e(i+1,j) + PI_e(i+1,j+1)$$
$$- PI_e(i-1,j-1) - 2PI_e(i-1,j) - PI_e(i-1,j+1) \qquad (4.10)$$

$$\delta n I_e(i,j) = PI_e(i-1,j+1) + 2PI_e(i,j+1) + PI_e(i+1,j+1)$$
$$- PI_e(i-1,j-1) - 2PI_e(i,j-1) - PI_e(i+1,j-1) \qquad (4.11)$$

The entropy value represented by $H(I_e)$ could be computed using the following formula according to the histogram of the enhanced image:

$$H(I_e) = \sum_{i=0}^{255} h_i \log_2(h_i) \qquad (4.12)$$

where h_i represents the frequency with which the ith intensity value appears in the improved image.

4.2.3   Gradient-based optimizer

Ahmadianfar et al. [10] presented a new population-based optimization technique that he called the GBO. This algorithm was designed to solve problems involving engineering optimization and global optimization. This algorithm uses the Newton technique as a means of guiding the individuals involved in the optimization process to arrive at the near-optimal solution for a number of optimization issues. The GBO method, in its most basic form, is broken down into two distinct components described in more detail in the following two sections.

4.2.3.1   Gradient search rule phase

The GBO algorithm utilizes gradient-based directions to facilitate agent movements during searching for the solutions, thereby achieving rapid convergence and circumventing entrapment in local optima. At this phase, a crucial variable denoted as ρ_1 is employed to ensure a balance between exploitation and exploration to efficiently evade local minima and attain nearly optimal solutions at a faster pace. The formulation of the mathematical model for ρ_1 is presented below.

$$\rho_1 = 2 \times r \times \alpha - \alpha \qquad (4.13)$$

$$\alpha = \left| \beta \times \sin\left(\frac{3\pi}{2} + \sin\left(\beta \times \frac{3\pi}{2} \right) \right) \right| \qquad (4.14)$$

$$\beta = \beta_{\min} + (\beta_{\max} - \beta_{\min}) \times \left(1 - \left(\frac{t}{t_{\max}} \right)^3 \right)^2 \qquad (4.15)$$

where $\beta_{\min}$ and $\beta_{\max}$ include two fixed numerical values of 0.2 and 1.2, respectively. Afterward, the GSR with the factor ρ_1

could be mathematically defined as follows to equilibrium between exploitation and exploration:

$$\text{GSR} = rn \times \rho_1 \times \frac{2\Delta x \times X_n}{X_w^{(t-1)} - X_*^{(t-1)} + \varepsilon} \qquad (4.16)$$

where rn is a number generated randomly according to the normal distribution, ε is a very low value, specifically ranging in the interval (0, 0.1), to prevent division by zero in a case that both the best solution achieved yet $X_*^{(t-1)}$ and the worst solution $X_w^{(t-1)}$ have the same positions. Δx represents the disparity between two different solutions: $X_*^{(t-1)}$ and $X_a^{(t-1)}$ (selected randomly from the current population). Δx could be formulated as follows:

$$\Delta x = \vec{r} \times |S| \qquad (4.17)$$

$$S = \frac{\left(X_*^{(t-1)} - X_a^{(t-1)}\right) + \delta}{2} \qquad (4.18)$$

$$\delta = 2 \times r_2 \times \left(\left|\frac{X_a^{(t-1)} + X_b^{(t-1)} + X_c^{(t-1)} + X_d^{(t-1)}}{4}\right| - X_i^{(t-1)}\right) \qquad (4.19)$$

where r_2 is a numerical value selected at random in the interval (0, 1); a, b, c, and d represent the indices of four individuals chosen randomly from the current population such that $a \neq b \neq c \neq d$. Based on GSR, each solution in the current population could be updated as formulated in the following equation:

$$X1_i^{(t)} = X_i^{(t-1)} - \text{GSR} \qquad (4.20)$$

However, these updated solutions are not directed to the regions that might include the best solution achieved yet with the aim of reaching the near-optimal solution faster. Therefore a new mechanism known as the direction of movements is employed with the GSR mechanism to improve the search abilities of GBO. The new mathematical equation used to update the current positions of the solutions is formulated as follows:

$$X1_i^{(t)} = X_i^{(t-1)} - \text{GSR} + \text{DM} \qquad (4.21)$$

$$\text{DM} = r \times \rho_2 \times \left(X_*^{(t-1)} - X_i^{(t-1)}\right) \qquad (4.22)$$

$$\rho_2 = 2 \times r \times \alpha - \alpha \qquad (4.23)$$

According to Ref. [10], $X1_i^{(t)}$ could be extended as follows, under the Newton method, to further enhance the exploration and diversity of the population:

$$X1_i^{(t)} = x_i^{(t-1)} - rn \times \rho_1 \times \frac{2\Delta x * X_n}{yp_i^{(t-1)} - yq_i^{(t-1)} + \varepsilon} + r \times \rho_2 \times \left(x_*^{(t-1)} - x_i^{(t-1)}\right)$$

(4.24)

where $yp_i^{(t-1)}$ and $yq_i^{(t-1)}$ could be expressed as follows:

$$yp_i^{(t-1)} = r\left(\frac{\left[z_i^{(t-1)} + x_i^{(t-1)}\right]}{2} + r * \Delta x\right)$$

(4.25)

$$yq_i^{(t-1)} = r\left(\frac{\left[z_i^{(t-1)} + x_i^{(t-1)}\right]}{2} - r * \Delta x\right)$$

(4.26)

where the $z_i^{(t-1)}$ could be computed as follows:

$$z_i^{(t-1)} = x_i - \overrightarrow{rn} \times \frac{2\Delta x \times x_n}{X_w^{(t-1)} - X_*^{(t-1)} + \varepsilon}$$

(4.27)

where $\overrightarrow{rn}$ is a vector generated according to the normal distribution at random. The solution denoted as $X1_i^{(t)}$ is utilized to improve the exploration operator of the algorithm, with the aim of improving the search capability of the GBO method for achieving superior results. The possibility exists that the optimal solution is in close proximity to the best solution obtained yet. In such cases, a new vector, denoted as $X2_i^{(t)}$, is created by replacing $x_i^{(t-1)}$ in $X1_i^{(t)}$ with $x_*^{(t-1)}$. This approach enhances the local search capability in the vicinity of the best solution achieved yet, thereby expediting the convergence rate. In general, $X2_i^{(t)}$ could be generated according to the following formula:

$$X2_i^{(t)} = x_*^{(t-1)} - r \times \rho_1 \times \frac{2\Delta x \times X_n}{yp_i^{(t-1)} - yq_i^{(t-1)} + \varepsilon} + r \times \rho_2 \times \left(x_*^{(t-1)} - x_i^{(t-1)}\right)$$

(4.28)

According to Ref. [10], each individual in the current population could be updated based on the vectors $X1_i^{(t)}$ and $X2_i^{(t)}$, as well as another vector $X3_i^{(t)}$, as defined below:

$$X_i^{(t)} = r_a\left(r_b \times X1_i^{(t)} + (1 - r_b) \times X2_i^{(t)}\right) + \left(1 - r_a\right) \times X3_i^{(t)}$$

(4.29)

$$X3_i^{(t)} = x_i^{(t-1)} - \rho_1 \times \left(X2_i^{(t)} - X1_i^{(t)}\right)$$

(4.30)

4.2.3.2 Local escaping operator (LEO) phase

In order to further prevent becoming trapped in local minima and to speed up the convergence in the direction of the near-optimal solution, a novel operator known as LEO is utilized in conjunction with the GBO algorithm:

$$X_i^{(t)} = \begin{cases} x_i^{(t-1)} + f_1\left(u_1 x_*^{(t-1)} - u_2 x_k^{(t)}\right) + f_2\rho_1\left(u_3\left(X2_i^{(t)} - X1_i^{(t)}\right)\right) \\ \quad + \dfrac{u_2\left(x_a^{(t-1)} - x_b^{(t-1)}\right)}{2}, \quad r < 0.5 \text{ and } r_1 < pr \\[2ex] x_*^{(t-1)} + f_1\left(u_1 x_*^{(t-1)} - u_2 x_k^{(t-1)}\right) + f_2\rho_1\left(u_3\left(X2_i^{(t)} - X1_i^{(t)}\right)\right) \\ \quad + \dfrac{u_2\left(x_a^{(t-1)} - x_b^{(t-1)}\right)}{2}, \quad r \geq 0.5 \text{ and } r_1 < pr \end{cases} \tag{4.31}$$

where pr is a constant value that is predetermined between 0 and 1 (recommended 0.5), f_1, and f_2 are two numerical values chosen at random according to the uniform distribution between 1 and -1, and u_1, u_2, and u_3 are three numbers generated at random between 0 and 1:

$$u_1 = \begin{cases} 2r_1 & \text{if } \mu_1 < 0.5 \\ 1 & \text{otherwise} \end{cases} \tag{4.32}$$

$$u_2 = \begin{cases} r_1, & \text{if } \mu_1 < 0.5 \\ 1, & \text{otherwise} \end{cases} \tag{4.33}$$

$$u_3 = \begin{cases} r_1, & \text{if } \mu_1 < 0.5 \\ 1, & \text{otherwise} \end{cases} \tag{4.34}$$

where μ_1 is a numerical value ranging between 0 and 1 and selected randomly. r_1 is a numerical value generated randomly in the interval (0, 1) according to the uniform distribution. Regarding $x_k^{(t)}$, it is created according to the following formula:

$$x_k^{(t)} = \begin{cases} x_r, & \text{if } \mu_2 < 0.5 \\ x_a^{t-1}, & \text{otherwise} \end{cases} \tag{4.35}$$

where x_r is a solution created at random within the search boundary of the optimization problems, as defined below:

$$x_r = \vec{x}_l + \vec{r}(\vec{x}_u - \vec{x}_l) \tag{4.36}$$

where μ_2 is a numerical value chosen at random in the interval (0, 1). The GBO's pseudocode is shown in Algorithm 4.1.

Algorithm 4.1 GBO's pseudocode

1. Initialize N solutions, $X_i (i \in N)$.
2. Set pr and $\mathscr{E}$.
3. Evaluation
4. t = 1;
5. Extracting $X_w^{(t-1)}$ as the worst solution, and $X_*^{(t-1)}$ as the near-optimal solution obtained yet
6. **while** (t < T_{max})
7.   *for* each i solutions
8.   *for* each j dimensions
9.   Select randomly $a \neq b \neq c \neq d \neq i$.
10.   // GSR strategy.
11.   Update $X_{ij}^{(t)}$ according to Eq. (4.29)
12.   *End for*
13.   // LEO Strategy
14.   Generate the new solution $X_i^{(t)}$ according to Eq. (4.31)
15. *End*
16. $t++$
17.   Update $X_w^{(t-1)}$ and $X_*^{(t-1)}$
18. *End*
19. *Return* $X_*^{(t-1)}$.

4.3 Metaheuristics-based image enhancement technique

4.3.1   Step 1: initialization

All the metaheuristic algorithms start with initializing a number of the candidate solutions within the search space of the optimization problems, where each candidate solution consists of k dimensions that represent four unknown parameters (k, c, b, and a) in the IE. The mathematical formula employed to initialize the candidate solutions within the search space of these parameters is as follows:

$$\vec{X}_i = \vec{L} + \left(\vec{U} - \vec{L} \right) * \vec{r} \tag{4.37}$$

where $\vec{L}$ is the lower bound vector, $\vec{U}$ represents the upper bound, and $\vec{r}$ is a vector generated at random in the range (0, 1). The lower bound values for those unknown parameters are $a = 0$, $b = 0$, $c = 0$, and $k = 0.5$, which is formulated in the lower vector $\vec{L}$ as follows: $\vec{L} = [0, 0, 0, 0.5]$, while the upper vector is $\vec{L} = [1.5, 0.5, 1, 1.5]$, as defined in Ref. [11]. The solutions are distributed between both lower and upper vectors according to the uniform distribution to generate the initial solutions that could be updated within the optimization process for reaching better solutions. After the distribution process, the evaluation step starts to evaluate each initial solution based on the fitness function defined in Eq. (4.8). This objective function needs to be maximized for reaching the near-optimal values of the unknown parameters that could present a highly enhanced image. Therefore, the solution with the highest objective value is considered the best solution achieved yet $X_*^{(t-1)}$, which is employed later within the optimization process for improving the quality of the other solutions in the population.

4.3.2 Step 2: novel self-adaptive strategy (SAS)

Unfortunately, the GBO algorithm might fall into local minima that prevent it from reaching a better solution within the whole optimization process. Also, it suffers from a slow convergence speed that makes it unable to reach the fittest solution in a small number of function evaluations. Therefore, in this chapter, we try to improve its performance using a recently proposed strategy known as the novel SAS for accurately solving the IE [12]. The proposed strategy aims to identify solutions that closely approximate the best-known solution, which may be confined to a local minimum. Then, it tries to conduct a strong exploration process around those solutions to mitigate the impact of such local minima. In addition, this approach involves evaluating whether the current solution significantly deviates from the optimal solution obtained thus far. If so, the current solution is steered toward the near-optimal solution achieved yet to effectively explore the surrounding solution in an attempt to achieve improved outcomes in fewer iterations, thereby expediting the convergence rate. Better results with the classic optimization approach may be achieved by applying this strategy with a proportion, denoted $\mathfrak{T}$; $\mathfrak{T}$ is set to 1 in the trials presented here.

This approach is built on a mathematical model with two folds, each of which consists of two steps. The first fold is employed if the difference in fitness between the optimal solution obtained yet and the current solution, as calculated by Eq. (4.38), is smaller than a predetermined value J, and the second fold is used otherwise. In the first iteration, we assume that the best solution found so far is a local optimum or very close to the optimal one. If the current solution is a local minimum, the first fold will initially zero in on the near-optimal solution achieved yet in an effort to find better solutions with fewer iterations. However, as the current function evaluation progresses, the fold will instead direct exploration of a different region in an effort to break out of local optima. Using Eq. (4.39), we can represent the first fold mathematically. In the same vein, it was proposed that the second fold begins the optimization process by zeroing in on the best solution found thus far. This fold uses a percentage of the updating process to update these solutions with a randomly generated step size within the search bounds, in an effort to prevent becoming caught in local minima. In Eq. (4.40), we have the mathematical model of this fold.

$$\mathcal{Q} = \left| \frac{f\left(X_i^{(t-1)}\right) - f\left(X_*^{(t-1)}\right)}{f\left(X_*^{(t-1)}\right)} \right| \tag{4.38}$$

$$X_i^{(t)} = \begin{cases} X_*^{(t-1)} + r_4\left(-X_i^{(t-1)} + X_d^{(t-1)}\right) \\ \quad + (1-r_4)\left(-X_e^{(t-1)} + X_g^{(t-1)}\right), \ r_1 < \dfrac{t}{t_{\max}} \ \text{and} \ r_2 < r_3 \\ X_i^{(t-1)} + r_6\left(-X_e^{(t-1)} + X_g^{(t-1)}\right) \\ \quad + (1-r_6)\left(X_*^{(t-1)} - X_g^{(t-1)}\right), \qquad\qquad \text{otherwise} \end{cases} \tag{4.39}$$

$$X_i^{(t)} = \begin{cases} X_*^{(t-1)} + r_4\left(-X_i^{(t-1)} + X_*^{(t-1)}\right) \\ \quad + (1-r_4)\left(-X_e^{(t-1)} + X_f^{(t-1)}\right), \qquad r_1 < \dfrac{t}{t_{\max}} \\ X_*^{(t-1)} + (r_5 + r(1-r_5)).2g.\left(-X_e^{(t-1)} + X_f^{(t-1)}\right) \\ \quad + \mathcal{F}\left(\vec{U} - \vec{L}\right)\mathbb{U}, \qquad\qquad \text{otherwise} \end{cases} \tag{4.40}$$

$$g = 1 - \frac{t}{t_{\max}} \tag{4.41}$$

where r_2, r_3, r_4, r_5, and r_6 are numerical values chosen at random at the interval of 0 and 1, d, e, and g are the indices of three randomly chosen solutions from the current population. $\mathbb{U}$ is a binary vector generated according to the following formula:

$$\mathbb{U} = \begin{cases} 0, & \vec{r} < \rho \\ 1, & \text{otherwise} \end{cases} \tag{4.42}$$

where $\vec{r}$ is a predefined threshold value. The pseudocode of the SAS strategy is clearly described in Algorithm 4.2. This strategy is integrated with the classical GBO to present a new strong variant with better exploration and exploitation operators. This variant is named improved GBO (IGBO).

Algorithm 4.2 SAS strategy's pseudocode

Input: J, $\mathfrak{T}$

1. R: A numerical value chosen at random in the interval of 0 and 1.
2. *If* $R < \mathfrak{T}$
3.   *for* each i solutions
4.   Create $\mathcal{Q}$ according to Eq. (4.38)
5.   *if* $\mathcal{Q} < J$
6.   Compute X_i^t according to Eq. (4.39)
7.   *else*
8.   Compute X_i^t according to Eq. (4.40)
9.   *end for*
10.   *if* $F(X_i^t) < F(X_i^{(t-1)})$
11. $X_i^{(t-1)} = X_i^t$
12.   *end*
13.   *end*
14. *end*

4.3.3   Step 3: evaluation stage

In this stage, each algorithm is assessed based on a fitness function that needs to be maximized or minimized according to the need of the tackled optimization problem. The IE could be solved using the fitness function defined in Eq. (4.8). During the optimization process of each metaheuristic algorithm, the updated solutions are evaluated using this objective function to determine their quality. Afterward, the objective values of all solutions are compared with each other to update the local best and the best solutions obtained yet in an attempt to improve the solutions' quality and promising region during the optimization process.

4.3.4   Step 5: pseudocode of the proposed IGNDO

After initializing N solutions as discussed in the first step, their objective values are computed and compared to identify the near-optimal solution achieved yet X^* that is later employed during the optimization process to search for better solutions. Following that, the optimization process of each algorithm is started to update these solutions within the search space. The updated solutions are evaluated to determine their objective values and the solution with the highest objective value is compared with the current near-optimal solution achieved yet to use the best one in the next generation. In the proposed IGBO, the SAS strategy is integrated with the classical GBO to improve its exploration and exploitation operators within the whole optimization process, as depicted in Fig. 4.1 and listed in Algorithm 4.3. In brief, the

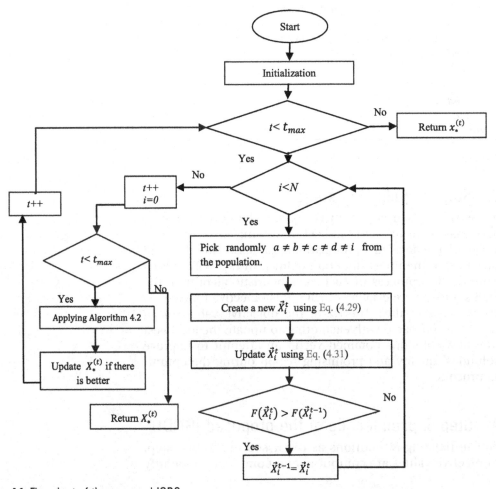

Figure 4.1 Flowchart of the proposed IGBO.

Algorithm 4.3 Pseudocode of GBO

1. Initialization process for randomly generating the initial population, $X_i(i \in N)$.
2. Set the parameters pr and $\mathcal{E}$.
3. Evaluation
4. $t = 1$;
5. Extracting $X_w^{(t-1)}$ as the poorest solution, and $X_*^{(t-1)}$ as the near-optimal solution obtained yet
6. **while** $(t < T_{\max})$
7.   *for* each i solutions
8.   *for* each j dimensions
9.   Pick randomly $a \neq b \neq c \neq d \neq i$.
10.   // GSR strategy.
11.   Generate the new dimension $X_{ij}^{(t)}$ by Eq. (4.29)
12.   **End**
13.   // LEO Strategy
14.   Generate the new solution $X_i^{(t)}$ by Eq. (4.31)
15.   **End**
16. $t++$
17.   Update $X_w^{(t-1)}$ and $X_*^{(t-1)}$
18.   %% Applying the SAS strategy %%
19.   Update the current solutions using Algorithm 4.2.
20. $t++$
21.   Update $X_w^{(t-1)}$ and $X_*^{(t-1)}$
22. **End**
23. **Return** $X_*^{(t-1)}$.

---

classical GBO will generate its updated solutions that are evaluated and submitted to the SAS strategy to perform further updating for accurately exploring and exploiting the search space in an attempt to solve the medical IE problem carefully.

4.4 Practical analysis

In this section, the proposed IGBO is evaluated using six brain tumor images and compared to four metaheuristics, including classical GBO, NOA, TLBO, and DE, to show its effectiveness and efficiency. The comparison in this section is in terms of the fitness value (F-value) to show efficacy and the computational cost to show efficiency. Regarding the controlling parameters of the employed optimizers, they are set as suggested in the original papers. The SAS strategy integrated with the proposed IGBO includes two main effective parameters, namely, J and ρ, which are set as described in Ref. [12]. All algorithms are implemented using MATLAB R2019a on a device with the following properties: 32 gigabytes of random access memory (RAM), a Core i7 processor, and a Windows 10 operating system. The maximum iteration and population size of 100 and 30 are set for all algorithms to ensure a fair comparison.

All algorithms were executed 30 independent times on 6 medical images. Then, the average fitness value and computational cost were computed and reported in Fig. 4.2, which illustrated that IGBO could reach the highest fitness value, and hence the enhanced images produced by it are better than all the other compared algorithms. It was also observed that DE is the second best with a fitness value of 126.99, followed by the classical GBO as the third best, while NOA is the worst performing one. From that, we could affirm that IGBO is more effective than all the others. Regarding the computational cost presented in the same figure, IGBO could come in the second rank with a value of 2.5, following the DE as the best one with a value of 2.39, while NOA is the most time-consuming one. Despite that, IGBO is preferred for enhancing the medical images and displaying the details more clearly to help in diagnosing several diseases because it can achieve a better fitness value in a reasonable amount of time when compared to the others. Fig. 4.3 shows the difference between the original images and the images enhanced by IGNBO. From this figure, it is clear that IGBO could show the details inside the medical images more clearly.

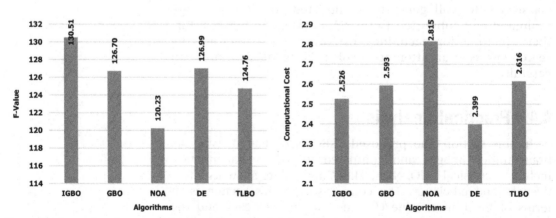

Figure 4.2 Comparison in terms of *F*-value and computational cost.

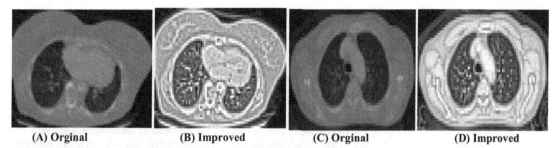

(A) Orginal   (B) Improved   (C) Orginal   (D) Improved

Figure 4.3 Comparison between (A and C) original and (B and D) enhanced images for two different images.

4.5 Chapter summary

This chapter looks at how well some recently published and well-known metaheuristic algorithms, such as GBO, NOA, TLBO, and DE, work to solve the problem of enhancing medical images. In addition, GBO is integrated with a recently published strategy known as the self-adaptive method to propose a new variant with better exploration and exploitation operators. This new variant was called IGBO. IGBO was evaluated using six brain tumor images and compared to four previously mentioned algorithms to show its effectiveness and efficacy. The experimental findings show that IGBO can show the details inside the medical images more clearly than all the others. As a result, IGBO is considered a powerful alternative metaheuristic algorithm for addressing IE in the medical field.

References

[1] R. Maini, H. Aggarwal, A comprehensive review of image enhancement techniques, arXiv, 2010.
[2] G. Singh, A. Mittal, Various image enhancement techniques-a critical review, International Journal of Innovation and Scientific Research 10 (2) (2014) 267−274.
[3] A.S. Ashour, et al., Computed tomography image enhancement using cuckoo search: a log transform based approach, Journal of Signal and Information Processing 6 (03) (2015) 244.
[4] M.O. Oloyede, et al., Exploratory analysis of different metaheuristic optimization methods for medical image enhancement, IEEE Access 10 (2022) 28014−28036.
[5] C. Munteanu, A. Rosa, Gray-scale image enhancement as an automatic process driven by evolution, IEEE Transactions on Systems, Man, Cybernetics, Part B 34 (2) (2004) 1292−1298.
[6] N. Du, et al., Color image enhancement: a metaheuristic chimp optimization algorithm, Neural Processing Letters 54 (6) (2022) 4769−4808.

[7] S. Chakraborty, et al. Contrast optimization using elitist metaheuristic optimization and gradient approximation for biomedical image enhancement, in: 2019 Amity International Conference on Artificial Intelligence (AICAI). 2019. IEEE.

[8] M. Braik, Hybrid enhanced whale optimization algorithm for contrast and detail enhancement of color images, Cluster Computing (2022) 1−37.

[9] J. Jiang, et al., Group theoretic particle swarm optimization for gray-level medical image enhancement, Mathematical Biosciences and Engineering 20 (6) (2023) 10479−10494.

[10] I. Ahmadianfar, O. Bozorg-Haddad, X. Chu, Gradient-based optimizer: a new metaheuristic optimization algorithm, Information Sciences 540 (2020) 131−159.

[11] S. Suresh, S. Lal, Modified differential evolution algorithm for contrast and brightness enhancement of satellite images, Applied Soft Computing 61 (2017) 622−641.

[12] M. Abdel-Basset, et al., Improved meta-metaheuristic algorithms for optimal parameters selection of proton exchange membrane fuel cells: a comparative study, 11, IEEE Access, 2023, pp. 7369−7397.

5

Metaheuristic-based multilevel thresholding segmentation technique for brain magnetic resonance images

5.1 Introduction

Today's medical professionals use e-healthcare and automated tools to make more accurate diagnoses for their patients. Examining internal organs for anomalies is a time-consuming process that can be approached either by invasive surgery or by noninvasive imaging. Magnetic resonance (MR) imaging is used to take detailed images of these irregularities, and then the images are analyzed to determine where the disease is and how severe it is. Examining medical images entails a number of steps, including preprocessing, investigation, categorization, and postprocessing, and is an essential procedure in the healthcare arena. Medical image segmentation has become the commonly utilized technique in many real-time applications to separate foreground and background from an image. This can be used for medical image synthesis and analysis by extracting different homogenous zones. Many segmentation strategies have been proposed to deal with the medical image segmentation problem (MISP), including region-based, feature selection-based clustering, edge-based, and threshold-based approaches. When compared to the other methods, threshold-based segmentation is the most straightforward, quick, and precise method. This is why threshold-based segmentation is widely used to deal with ISP. There are two types of threshold-based segmentation: multilevel and bilevel. The image in the bilevel consists of a foreground and a background (object). When there are more than two homogenous regions in an image, a multilevel threshold is used instead. While a multilevel threshold's potential benefits in overcoming MISP for images with multiple regions are substantial, the time required to implement such a

Metaheuristics Algorithms for Medical Applications. DOI: https://doi.org/10.1016/B978-0-443-13314-5.00003-5

threshold grows exponentially with increasing the threshold level [1]. Therefore the researchers have widely applied metaheuristic algorithms to solve this problem in a reasonable amount of time with better accuracy. The metaheuristic algorithms could fulfill strong outcomes for several optimization problems in medical image processing, like image registration [2], image enhancement [3], and image denoising [4].

This chapter discusses the performance of some metaheuristic algorithms with the Otsu method and Kapur's entropy as fitness functions for segmenting brain MR images at different threshold levels ranging between 3 and 30. Also, a recently proposed strategy for improving the performance of metaheuristic algorithms will be added to the investigated algorithms to show how well it works for dealing with the MISP. Lastly, a summary of the chapter is given to show which of the investigated algorithms is best for segmenting the brain MR images.

5.2 Techniques for image segmentation

Image segmentation methods are divided into two primary categories: layer-based segmentation and block-based segmentation [5]. In this chapter, we will tackle the second technique in detail to review the different methods found under this category and the difference between them. The block-based segmentation technique is based on various features in the image, which might be the color information, or information for edges, boundaries, and texture. This technique includes three categories divided according to two properties: discontinuity and similarity [5]:

- Region-based segmentation
- Edge- or boundary-based segmentation
- Clustering-based segmentation
- Thresholding-based segmentation
- Partial differential equation (PDE).

Region-based segmentation approaches separate the image into regions with related characteristics. The region-based algorithms detect these regions, which consist of a collection of pixels, by first selecting a seed point, which may be a little or a major fraction of the input image. Following the detection of the seed points, these algorithms would either enhance them with more pixels or reduce them so that they could be combined with other seed points. On this basis, there are two subcategories of region-based segmentation: region growth and region splitting and merging. The clustering-based segmentation is another technique that divides an image into clusters, having pixels with similar characteristics. If the pixels are more similar to pixels existing in a cluster, they will be set to this cluster according to this technique. There are several clustering methods, like k-means, fuzzy c-means (FCM), and improved k-means algorithms. The goal of edge-based segmentation is to identify the boundaries of diverse image objects. This is a crucial step since it enables you to determine the properties of the numerous objects in the image, as the image's edges contain useful information. A typical rationale for the extensive use of edge detection is that it facilitates the removal of unnecessary or irrelevant information from an image. It drastically reduces the image's size, making analysis of the image easier. Using edge-based segmentation techniques, the edges of the image are recognized based on changes in texture, contrast, gray level, color, and other properties. There are a number of edge-based segmentation approaches that fall into two categories: zero-crossing-based edge detection and search-based edge detection.

The approaches that are based on PDE are the most efficient ways of segmentation [6]. These are suitable for applications that are sensitive to time. Both the convex nonquadratic variation restoration and the nonlinear isotropic diffusion filter are fundamental PDE methods. The former is used to improve the edges, and the latter is used to eliminate the noise in the images. The PDE technique produces fuzzy edges and bounds that can be adjusted using nearby operators. The image noise is reduced using the fourth-order PDE method, while the edges and boundaries are better detected using the second-order PDE method.

Thresholding-based segmentation can be broken down into two distinct classes: *bilevel* and *multilevel*. The former separates an image into two groups: *background* and *foreground*. Nevertheless, the bilevel threshold runs into trouble when an image has more than two homogenous objects. The *multilevel threshold* incorporates the subdivision of a given image into several homogenous objects, which allows it to deal with the limitation of the bilevel threshold. The thresholding-based segmentation can be expressed as an optimization problem using either nonparametric or parametric methods [7]. In the parametric method, the probability density function is used to compute certain parameters for each region in order to estimate the optimal threshold values. The nonparametric approach, however, aims to maximize one of the functions, such as fuzzy entropy [8], Kapur's entropy (maximizing class entropy) [7], or Otsu function (maximizing between-variance) [9]. Unfortunately, with these methods, determining the ideal threshold values for multilevel thresholding is computationally intensive and time-consuming, particularly as threshold levels increase. Therefore, due to their ability to overcome the time complexity problem of several optimization problems, metaheuristic algorithms have been employed as a robust alternative to traditional techniques to avoid time-consuming problems. Several metaheuristics-based image segmentation techniques for medical images have been proposed over the last few years. For example, a multilevel thresholding algorithm based on an exchange market optimization algorithm was proposed to estimate the near-optimal threshold values that could precisely segment the medical images to aid the healthcare centers in accurately detecting and diagnosing diseases [10]. In addition, Dorgham et al. [11] used the monarch butterfly optimization to search for the near-optimal threshold values on a collection of computed tomography (CT) images under a number of threshold levels ranging between 1 and 4. This algorithm could be better than several other rival algorithms for accuracy and convergence rate. The FCM clustering technique was combined with the crow search algorithm (CSA) for solving the multilevel thresholding medical image segmentation. This approach was validated using a collection of abdomen CT images and compared to several optimization algorithms to show its effectiveness [12]. The experimental findings show that CSA is a promising approach. Table 5.1 presents some of the recently proposed multilevel thresholding medical image segmentation techniques based on the metaheuristics algorithms.

5.3 Problem formulation

5.3.1 Kapur's entropy

This section will concentrate on describing the mathematical model of Kapur's entropy, which is used to acquire the ideal threshold values. This method aims to maximize the entropy of segmented regions for reaching these threshold values [19]. Assuming that the threshold values that segment an image into

Table 5.1 Some recent metaheuristics proposed for MISP.

Algorithms	Contributions and disadvantages

Whale optimization algorithm integrated with slime mould algorithm (HSMA_WOA) [13]	• Contributions:
	  • To segment the COVID-19 X-ray images, this research proposed a new technique.
	  • In this technique, the whale optimization algorithm is integrated with the slime mould algorithm to capitalize on their complementary strengths and mitigate their individual drawbacks.
	  • Subsequently, 12 medical images were used to validate HSMA_WOA, and its results were contrasted to those of a variety of metaheuristic-based algorithms to gauge their effectiveness.
	  • In conclusion, the experimental results demonstrate that the HSMA_WOA is the best option.
	• Disadvantages:
	  • Its performance has been further investigated for several other images.

Improved marine predators algorithm [14]	• Contributions:
	  • Recently, a new metaheuristic technique was presented for the image segmentation problem of the COVID-19 X-ray images with the purpose of reaching similar regions that assist the machine learning and deep learning techniques to accurately predict and classify the persons infected with COVID-19.
	  • This technique improved the performance of a recently proposed metaheuristic algorithm called the marine predators algorithm based on the ranking-based strategy to improve its convergence speed for reaching better outcomes in smaller function evaluations.
	  • The experimental findings revealed the strong performance of this improved technique, which could lead to strong outcomes for several metrics like SSIM, PSNR, UQI, standard deviation, and fitness values.
	• Disadvantages:
	  • Needs a higher computational cost than the compared algorithms.

Improved whale optimization algorithm (LCWOA) [15]	• The classical WOA was improved using both the chaotic random mutation strategy and the Levy operator to avoid stagnation into local minima in addition to accelerating its ability to achieve better outcomes. This variant was named LCWOA. This algorithm was applied to find the near-optimal threshold values for the skin cancer images. • The experimental findings show that LCWOA has robust performance in obtaining optimal segmentation results.
Modified reptile search algorithm (mRSA) [16]	• In this study, the reptile search algorithm (RSA) was combined with a strong metaheuristic algorithm called RUNge Kutta optimizer to present a strong variant, namely mRSA. This variant has a strong convergence speed, could avoid falling into local minima, and can balance between the exploitation and exploration capabilities.

(*Continued*)

Table 5.1 (Continued)

Algorithms	Contributions and disadvantages
	• This algorithm was verified by a collection of magnetic resonance imaging (MRI) brain images to reveal its ability to search for the near-optimal threshold values that could accurately separate the homogenous regions within those images.
	• Overall experimental findings show that the mRSA has a robust optimization process.
Improved jellyfish search algorithm (IJSA) [17]	• Jellyfish search algorithm (JSA)-based multilevel thresholding image segmentation was developed. The JSA was enhanced using two mechanisms: Ranking-based updating and adaptive method to present a new variant called IJSA able to avoid local minima and accelerate convergence to optimal solutions.
	• Seven MRI images were used to validate the performance of IJSA for solving the image segmentation at threshold levels ranging between 3 and 30.
	• IJSA was compared to several metaheuristic-based algorithms in terms of PSNR, fitness, SD, SSIM, and FSIM.
	• The experimental results show that IJSA is a strong alternative for medical image segmentation.
Improved equilibrium optimizer (IEO) [18]	• The equilibrium optimizer was combined with the dimension learning hunting to present a new robust variant named IEO.
	• To maximize fuzzy entropy, this variant was used to segment several CT images of COVID-19.
	• The experimental results show that IEO has the potential as a useful tool for image segmentation, as shown by the segmentation results.

Note: FSIM, feature similarity index metric; *PSNR*, peak signal-to-noise ratio; *SSIM*, structured similarity index metric.

k homogenous regions are represented as $t_0, t_1, t_2, \ldots,$ and t_k and Kapur's entropy needs to be applied to get these values that maximize the entropy between them, the Kapur's entropy could be mathematically expressed as follows:

$$F(t_0, t_1, t_2, \ldots, t_k) = T_0 + T_1 + T_2 + \ldots + T_k \qquad (5.1)$$

where:

$$T_0 = -\sum_{i=t_0}^{t_1-1} \frac{X_i}{W_0} * \ln \frac{X_i}{W_0}, \quad X_i = \frac{Z_i}{W}, W_0 = \sum_{i=t_0}^{t_1-1} X_i \qquad (5.2)$$

$$T_1 = -\sum_{i=t_1}^{t_2-1} \frac{X_i}{W_1} * \ln \frac{X_i}{W_1}, \quad X_i = \frac{Z_i}{W}, W_1 = \sum_{i=t_1}^{t_2-1} X_i \qquad (5.3)$$

$$T_2 = -\sum_{i=t_2}^{t_3-1} \frac{X_i}{W_2} * \ln \frac{X_i}{W_2}, \quad X_i = \frac{Z_i}{W}, W_2 = \sum_{i=t_2}^{t_3-1} X_i \qquad (5.4)$$

$$T_k = -\sum_{i=t_k}^{L-1} \frac{X_i}{W_k} * \ln \frac{X_i}{W_k}, \quad X_i = \frac{Z_i}{W}, W_k = \sum_{i=t_k}^{L-1} X_i \qquad (5.5)$$

where $T_0, T_1, T_2, \ldots,$ and T_k represent the entropies of the various objects, and Z_i represents the number of pixels with intensity i. $W_0, W_1, W_2, \ldots,$ and W_k represent the percentage of each region to the whole image W.

5.3.2 Otsu method

This method was suggested as a variance-based methodology for finding threshold values that maximize the between-class variance, or equivalently, minimize the intraclass intensity variance, in order to extract the heterogeneity from an image [9]. This method could be applied using the following mathematical model to find the optimal k threshold levels $[t_0, t_1, t_2, \ldots, t_m]$ that could extract various objects from an image:

$$F(t_0, t_1, t_2, \ldots, t_m) = \sigma_0^2 + \sigma_1^2 + \sigma_2^2 + \ldots + \sigma_m^2 \qquad (5.6)$$

where

$$\sigma_0^2 = \omega_0 (\mu_0 - \mu_T)^2, \omega_0 = \sum_{i=t_0}^{t_1-1} p_i, \mu_0 = \sum_{i=t_0}^{t_1-1} \frac{ip_i}{\omega_0} \qquad (5.7)$$

$$\sigma_1^2 = \omega_1 (\mu_1 - \mu_T)^2, \omega_1 = \sum_{i=t_1}^{t_2-1} p_i, \mu_1 = \sum_{i=t_1}^{t_2-1} \frac{ip_i}{\omega_1} \qquad (5.8)$$

$$\sigma_2^2 = \omega_2 (\mu_2 - \mu_T)^2, \omega_2 = \sum_{i=t_2}^{t_3-1} p_i, \mu_2 = \sum_{i=t_2}^{t_3-1} \frac{ip_i}{\omega_2} \qquad (5.9)$$

$$\sigma_m^2 = \omega_m (\mu_m - \mu_T)^2, \omega_m = \sum_{i=t_m}^{L-1} p_i, \mu_m = \sum_{i=t_m}^{L-1} \frac{ip_i}{\omega_m} \qquad (5.10)$$

where $\sigma_0^2, \sigma_1^2, \sigma_2^2, \ldots,$ and σ_m^2 represent various similar classes' variances; $\omega_0, \omega_1, \omega_2, \ldots, \omega_m$ are the class probabilities;

$\mu_0, \mu_1, \mu_2, \ldots, \mu_m$ are the class mean; L represents the maximum gray level; and μ_T is computed as follows:

$$\mu_T = \sum_{i=0}^{L-1} i p_i \qquad (5.11)$$

5.4 How to implement a metaheuristic for the MISP

Step 1: Initialization

All the metaheuristic algorithms start with initializing a number of the candidate solutions within the search space of the optimization problems, where each candidate solution consists of k dimensions that represent the threshold levels in the MISP. The mathematical formula employed to initialize the candidate solutions within the search space of the MISP is as follows:

$$\vec{X}_i = \vec{X}_L + \left(\vec{X}_U - \vec{X}_L\right) * \vec{r} \qquad (5.12)$$

where $\vec{X}_L$ is a vector containing the smallest possible values for the dimensions of the optimization problem. This vector is initialized with 0 since the lowest possible gray intensity for each pixel is 0. $\vec{X}_U$ represents the upper bound and includes 255 as the upper gray level, $\vec{r}$ is a vector initialized at random according to the uniform distribution, and $\vec{X}_i$ is the ith candidate solution. However, the obtained solutions are continuous and MISP is discrete, so these solutions have to be converted into discrete to apply to this problem. Let us give an example to determine how to convert the obtained continuous solutions into discrete ones. A candidate solution initialized according to the aforementioned equation is depicted in Fig. 5.1. However, this solution could not be directly used to solve the MISP because its values are continuous. Therefore, these values should be changed to integers because each pixel in the gray image is represented by an integer value, ranging between the lower gray level and upper gray level. To make these solutions applicable, they are rounded to get rid of the decimal values, as shown in Fig. 5.2. Afterward, these integers are sorted in ascending order, as shown in Fig. 5.3. Following that, the Kapur's entropy or Otsu method as an objective function is used to evaluate the fitness values of those solutions.

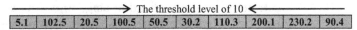
Figure 5.1 Solution representation to MISP.

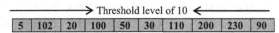
Figure 5.2 Unsorted integer threshold values.

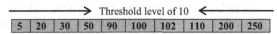
Figure 5.3 Sorted integer threshold values.

Step 2: premature convergence strategy (PCS)

A unique strategy referred to as the premature convergence method was presented to aid the metaheuristic algorithms to accelerate its convergence speed while avoiding local minima [20]. This approach additionally contains a control factor r assigned numerical values chosen randomly in the interval (0, 1). By this control factor, the exploitation capability is greatly boosted when $r > 0.5$, the exploration operator is employed to update the current position when $r < 0.5$, and both exploitation and exploration operators are balanced when $r = 0.5$. Mathematically, the PCM is formulated based on the following equation:

$$\vec{X}_i^t = \vec{X}^* + (1 - r)^* \left(\vec{X}_a^t - \vec{X}_b^t \right) + (r)^* \left(\vec{X}^* - \vec{X}_i^t \right) \qquad (5.13)$$

where a and b are two solutions chosen randomly from the current population. $\vec{X}^*$ is the best-so-far solution. This strategy is integrated with the investigated metaheuristic algorithms to observe its ability for helping those algorithms to achieve better performance when tackling the image segmentation problem.

Step 3: evaluation stage

In this stage, the performance of each algorithm is evaluated based on an objective function that needs to be maximized or minimized according to the nature of the tackled optimization problem. The image segmentation problem as mentioned above could be solved using several objective functions; two of them, Kapur's entropy and Otsu method, are considered in this chapter to investigate their performance with different metaheuristic algorithms. Both of them need to be maximized for achieving better solutions. During the optimization process of each metaheuristic algorithm, the updated solutions will be first fixed as illustrated in the initialization stage and evaluated using one of those two objective functions. After computing the objective value for each solution, all solutions' objective values are compared with each other. The local best solution for each solution is updated if the newly generated solution is better. In addition, the best solution obtained yet in an attempt to improve the promising region during the optimization process is also updated if there is a better solution.

Step 4: constructing the segmented image

In the end, once the process of optimization has been finished, the best possible threshold values will be returned to be used in the construction of the segmented image. However, how exactly will the segmented image be constructed utilizing these thresholds? Let us say the initial image is called A and it has N rows and M columns. The segmented image for image A under the best-so-far threshold values can be created, as illustrated in Algorithm 5.1.

Algorithm 5.1 Segmented image generation steps (GSI)

1. B: is a matrix of N*M to include the pixels of the segmented image.
2. $W^* = [0\vec{X}^* \ 255]$.
3. **for** i = 0: N
4.   **for** j = 0: M
5.   **for** m = 0: t-1
6.   **if** $A(i,j) \geq W^*_{(m)}$ 38 &$A(i,j) \leq W^*_{(m+1)}$
7. $B(i, j) = W_m^*$;
8.   **end**
9.   **end**
10.   **end**
11. **end**
12. **return** B;

Step 5: pseudocode of the adapted metaheuristics

After initializing N solutions as discussed in the first step, their objective values are computed and compared to identify the best-so-far solution X^* that will be later employed during the optimization process to search for better solutions. Following that, the optimization process of each algorithm is started to update these solutions within the search space of the optimization problem. The updated solutions are first fixed as described in the first step and evaluated to determine their objective values, and the solution with the highest objective value is compared with the current best-so-far solution to use the best one in the next generation. In brief, the pseudocode of adapting a metaheuristic algorithm for an image segmentation problem is listed below:

- **Step 1**: Initialize N solutions in addition to setting the controlling parameters for each algorithm; input the images to be segmented.
- **Step 2**: Rounding toward 0 and sorting each solution to become applicable to the tackled problems.
- **Step 3**: Evaluate each solution and identify the best solution obtained even now.
- **Step 4**: Run the optimization process of each algorithm to update the initialized solutions for fulfilling better solutions.
- **Step 5**: Repeating **steps 2–4** until the termination criterion is satisfied.
- **Step 6**: Finally, create the segmented images based on the best threshold values obtained by each algorithm, as described above.

Step 6: time complexity of a metaheuristic for MISP

In this subsection, the big-O time complexity is extensively discussed to demonstrate the speedup of the metaheuristic algorithms for solving the MISP. The initial factors that significantly affect these algorithm's speedup are the following:

- The population size: N
- The number of dimensions (d)
- The maximum iteration: T_{max}
- The time complexity of PCS.

The time complexity of the majority of metaheuristic algorithms is mainly based on the number of dimensions and the population size. Based on these factors, the time complexity in big-O for a metaheuristic at one iteration is as follows:

$$T = O(Nd) \tag{5.14}$$

In each iteration, the additional method, PCM, will affect the computational cost of the algorithms, so the time complexity for this method has to be analyzed to show its growth rate compared to the classical algorithms. This method also relies on the number of dimensions and the population, so its time complexity in big-O is the same as the classical algorithms. For the whole optimization process, the time complexity of the metaheuristics-based medical image segmentation techniques is of $O(T_{max}dN)$.

5.5 Practical analysis

In this section, the performance of classical investigated metaheuristic algorithms in addition to their improved variants will be investigated to show their efficiency and efficacy for segmenting six brain MR images under various threshold levels (T), ranging between 3 and 30. To assess the efficacy of each algorithm, three performance metrics, namely, structured similarity index metric (SSIM), peak signal-to-noise ratio (PSNR), and feature similarity index metric (FSIM), are used to observe the quality of the segmented images relative to the original images in addition to the objective values (F-value) and standard deviation (SD) to show effectiveness and stability. The description of all these metrics except the SD has been discussed in detail in Chapter 2. Regarding SD, it is used to measure how close the objective values achieved by each optimizer within 30 independent times are. The SD metric could be computed using the following mathematical formula:

$$SD = \sqrt{\frac{1}{n-1} \sum_{i=1}^{n} \left(f_i - \overline{f} \right)^2} \qquad (5.15)$$

where n indicates the number of independent runs, f_i stands for the ith fitness value, and $\overline{f}$ represents the average of all obtained fitness values for the independent runs. All conducted experiments were run using a computer with 32 gigabytes of random access memory (RAM), a Core i7 processor, and a Windows 10 operating system. The algorithms were implemented using MATLAB R2019a.

5.5.1 Evaluation using SD metric

The average SD of fitness values obtained using both the Otsu method and Kapur's entropy was calculated over all medical brain test images and reported in Fig. 5.4 to assess the similarity between the outputs provided by each metaheuristic algorithm. It is clear from this figure that the PCM strategy could enhance the stability of the investigated algorithms under considering objective function. For example, under Kapur's entropy, the SD values of both classical NOA and the improved variant are 0.0917 and 0.0563, respectively, which are significantly minimized by INOA in comparison to the classical variant. This illustrates the effectiveness of PCM when hybridizing to the metaheuristic algorithms, where it could preserve stability as much as possible for all independent runs. This figure also shows that both TLBO with Kapur's entropy and DE with the Otsu method are capable of producing more convergent results than the other algorithms.

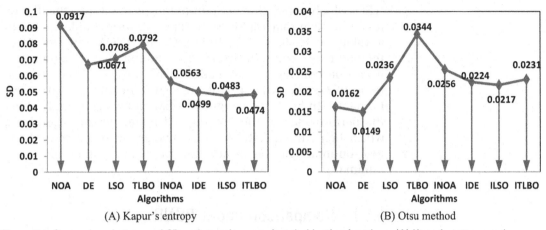

Figure 5.4 Comparison in terms of SD under various employed objective functions: (A) Kapur's entropy and (B) Otsu method.

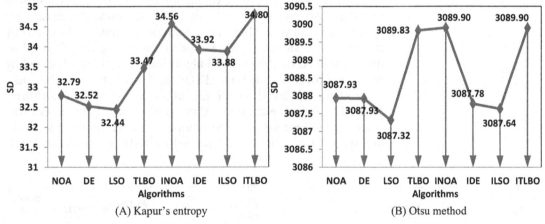

Figure 5.5 Comparison in terms of *F*-value under various employed objective functions: (A) Kapur's entropy and (B) Otsu method.

5.5.2 Comparison under fitness values

The average fitness values of each algorithm after running 30 independent times under each threshold level on all test images are shown in Fig. 5.5. According to this figure, the performance of various algorithms has been influenced by the integrated PCM, where the performance of all algorithms with Kapur's entropy is significantly improved, while the performance of both IDE and ILSO under the Otsu method is a little poor compared to the classical algorithms, in contrast to both INOA and

ILSO, which could show strong performance. From this figure, it can be seen that ITLBO with Kapur's entropy ranks first with a value of 34.80, and both ITLBO and INOA with the Otsu method could come in first with a value of 3089.90. From this, it can be concluded that TLBO is the top performing one in terms of *F*-value, while LSO is the algorithm with the worst performance. In brief, the integrated PCM could significantly affect the performance of the investigated metaheuristic algorithms, which helps them fulfill better convergence speed toward the near-optimal solution in addition to avoiding stuck into local minima.

5.5.3 Comparison under PSNR values

In this section, the PSNR metric is used to evaluate and compare the quality of the segmented images estimated by the investigated metaheuristics and their improved versions. Fig. 5.6 displays the average PSNR values for all threshold levels overall medical test images throughout 30 independent times. This figure demonstrates that the segmented images obtained by the improved variants with Kapur's entropy are not as good as those obtained by the classical algorithms, and those obtained by some improved algorithms (INOA and ITLBO) with the Otsu method are better than all the other investigated algorithms. Also, this figure elaborates that TLBO with Kapur's entropy achieves the best value when compared to the others and ranks first with a value of 28.30, followed by NOA as the second best

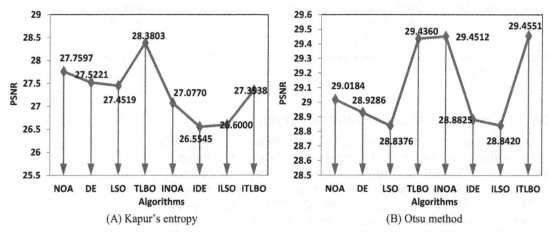

(A) Kapur's entropy   (B) Otsu method

Figure 5.6 Comparison in terms of PSNR under various employed objective functions: (A) Kapur's entropy and (B) Otsu method.

one. Regarding the performance of the investigated algorithms with the Otsu method, ITLBO could segment the images better than all the other algorithms, where it could reach an average PSNR value of 29.4551, followed by INOA as the second best one with a value of 29.4512. In brief, the empirical findings in this section illustrate that the PCM strategy could have a positive influence on some of the algorithms under the Otsu method and a negative influence on the other algorithms under the same method. Therefore, this method is considered an effective method for improving the performance of metaheuristic algorithms when tackling various optimization problems. Finally, it is concluded that TLBO with Kapur's entropy shows better performance than all the other algorithms, and it is considered a strong alternative to all the investigated algorithms under the same objective function. On the other hand, both INOA and ITLBO with the Otsu method could excel at all the other algorithms.

5.5.4 Comparison under SSIM values

Here, the quality of the segmented images estimated by the researched metaheuristics and their refined variants is evaluated and compared using the SSIM metric. In Fig. 5.7, we see the average SSIM values for all threshold settings across all 30 medical test images. This figure shows that the segmented images produced by the enhanced variations using Kapur's entropy are inferior to those produced by the classical algorithms, while the segmented images produced by the enhanced algorithms using the Otsu approach are superior. In addition, this figure explains

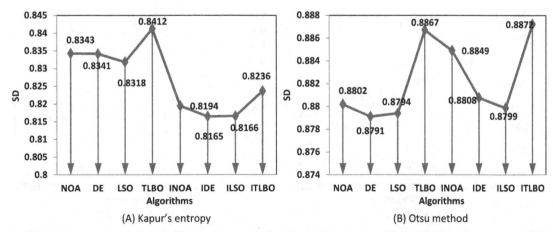

Figure 5.7 Comparison in terms of SSIM under various employed objective functions: (A) Kapur's entropy and (B) Otsu method.

how TLBO with Kapur's entropy outperforms the rival optimizers and came in first, with a value of 0.8412; NOA comes in second. Among the studied algorithms, ITLBO performed the best when using the Otsu method to segment images, with an average SSIM of 0.8872. This was followed by TLBO, which achieved an SSIM of 0.8867. In essence, this section's empirical findings show that the PCM strategy may have a favorable influence on some algorithms under the Otsu method and a detrimental effect on other algorithms. As a result, this strategy is often regarded as an efficient way for enhancing the efficiency of metaheuristic algorithms for dealing with a wide range of optimization problems. In the end, it is determined that TLBO with Kapur's entropy outperforms every other algorithm studied for the same objective function and is thus a formidable contender among the alternatives. However, by using the Otsu approach, both INOA, and ITLBO can outperform the others.

5.5.5 Comparison under FSIM values

In this section, we will examine the performance of various studied metaheuristics in terms of the FSIM metric. This test is intended to further demonstrate any technique is capable of reaching better-segmented images than the others. As shown in Fig. 5.8, TLBO with both the Otsu method and Kapur's entropy occupies the first rank with outstanding FSIM values of 0.9114 and 0.9361, respectively, followed by the ITLBO as the second best one. As stated previously, SSIM and FSIM are more important than the other metric because they examine the similarity,

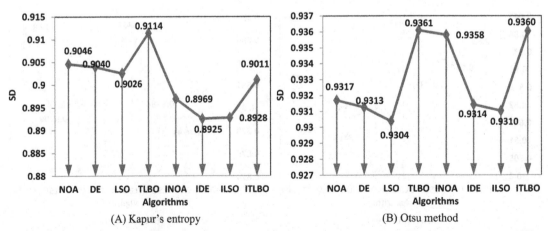

Figure 5.8 Comparison in terms of FSIM under various employed objective functions: (A) Kapur's entropy and (B) Otsu method.

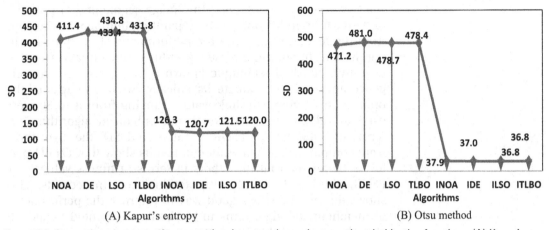

(A) Kapur's entropy   (B) Otsu method

Figure 5.9 Comparison in terms of computational cost under various employed objective functions: (A) Kapur's entropy and (B) Otsu method.

contrast distortion, and luminance of the segmented images. Since both ITLBO and TLBO could produce robust outcomes for SSIM, PSNR, and FSIM, they are considered the most efficient methods for segmenting medical images to enhance patient care quality.

5.5.6 Computational cost analysis

Finally, this section observes the efficiency of the variously studied metaheuristics in terms of computing the computational cost required by each algorithm till reaching the segmented images. Fig. 5.9 presents the average computational cost incurred by each employed metaheuristic algorithm within 30 times for all threshold levels over all test images. This figure indicates that the improved variants need much less time than the classical variants. For example, the classical NOA needs around 411 seconds to segment the medical images, whereas the improved variant only needs about 126 seconds. Hence, the improved variants are more efficient than all the classical algorithms. Based on that, it can be seen that ITLBO has the highest efficiency and efficacy.

5.6 Chapter summary

This chapter discusses the performance of some recently published and well-established metaheuristic algorithms with two distinct objective functions, namely, Kapur's entropy and the Otsu method, for solving the image segmentation problem of medical brain MR images by separating homogenous regions from the images to improve the performance of machine learning models. In addition, these algorithms were enhanced with a recently published technique known as the premature convergence approach to evaluate its efficacy. Six MR images of the brain with varying threshold values ranging from 3 to 30 were used to validate the traditional and enhanced algorithms. In terms of SSIM, FSIM, PSNR, F-value, and SD, the algorithms were compared. The experimental results show that ITLBO performs better than all the others in terms of fitness values, SD, PSNR, SSIM, FSIM, and computational cost in seconds. This shows that the PCM is a good way to improve the performance of metaheuristic algorithms to get better-segmented images. It also shows that ITLBO is a strong alternative way to segment medical images to improve patient care.

References

[1] M. Abdel-Basset, et al., HWOA: a hybrid whale optimization algorithm with a novel local minima avoidance method for multi-level thresholding color image segmentation, Expert Systems with Applications 190 (2022) 116145.

[2] J. Santamaría, et al., An overview on the latest nature-inspired and metaheuristics-based image registration algorithms, Applied Sciences 10 (6) (2020) 1928.

[3] S. Chakraborty, et al., Bio-medical image enhancement using hybrid metaheuristic coupled soft computing tools, in: Proceedings of the 2017 IEEE 8th Annual Ubiquitous Computing, Electronics and Mobile Communication Conference (UEMCON), 2017.

[4] S. Kockanat, N. Karaboga, Medical image denoising using metaheuristics, in: A. Nakib, E.-G. Talbi (Eds.), Metaheuristics for Medicine and Biology, Springer, Berlin, Heidelberg, 2017, pp. 155–169.

[5] Y. Yang, et al., Layered object models for image segmentation, IEEE Transactions on Pattern Analysis and Machine Intelligence 34 (9) (2011) 1731–1743.

[6] D. Kaur, Y. Kaur, Various image segmentation techniques: a review, International Journal of Computer Science and Mobile Computing 3 (5) (2014) 809–814.

[7] J.N. Kapur, et al., A new method for gray-level picture thresholding using the entropy of the histogram 29 (3) (1985) 273–285.

[8] D. Oliva, M.A. Elaziz, S. Hinojosa, Fuzzy entropy approaches for image segmentation, in: D. Oliva, M. Abd Elaziz, S. Hinojosa (Eds.), Metaheuristic Algorithms for Image Segmentation: Theory and Applications, Springer International Publishing, 2019, pp. 141–147.

[9] N. Otsu, A threshold selection method from gray-level histograms, IEEE Transactions on Systems, Man, and Cybernetics 9 (1) (1979) 62–66.

[10] R. Kalyani, P. Sathya, V. Sakthivel, Medical image segmentation using exchange market algorithm, Alexandria Engineering Journal 60 (6) (2021) 5039–5063.

[11] O.M. Dorgham, et al., Monarch butterfly optimization algorithm for computed tomography image segmentation, Multimedia Tools and Applications 80 (2021) 30057–30090.

[12] A. Lenin Fred, et al., Fuzzy-crow search optimization for medical image segmentation, Applications of Hybrid Metaheuristic Algorithms for Image Processing (2020) 413–439.

[13] M. Abdel-Basset, V. Chang, R. Mohamed, HSMA_WOA: a hybrid novel slime mould algorithm with whale optimization algorithm for tackling the image segmentation problem of chest X-ray images, Applied Soft Computing 95 (2020) 106642.

[14] M. Abdel-Basset, et al., A hybrid COVID-19 detection model using an improved marine predators algorithm and a ranking-based diversity reduction strategy, IEEE Access 8 (2020) 79521–79540.

[15] L. Liu, et al., An efficient multi-threshold image segmentation for skin cancer using boosting whale optimizer, Computers in Biology and Medicine 151 (2022) 106227.

[16] M.M. Emam, E.H. Houssein, R.M. Ghoniem, A modified reptile search algorithm for global optimization and image segmentation: case study brain MRI images, Computers in Biology and Medicine 152 (2023) 106404.

[17] M. Abdel-Basset, et al., An improved jellyfish algorithm for multilevel thresholding of magnetic resonance brain image segmentations, Computers, Materials & Continua 68 (3) (2021) 2961–2977.

[18] E.H. Houssein, et al., An efficient multi-thresholding based COVID-19 CT images segmentation approach using an improved equilibrium optimizer, Biomedical Signal Processing and Control 73 (2022) 103401.

[19] J.N. Kapur, P.K. Sahoo, A.K. Wong, A new method for gray-level picture thresholding using the entropy of the histogram, Computer Vision, Graphics, and Image Processing 29 (3) (1985) 273–285.

[20] M. Abdel-Basset, et al., Recent meta-heuristic algorithms with a novel premature covergence Method for Determining the parameters of PV cells and modules, Electronics 10 (15) (2021) 1846.

6

Metaheuristic algorithm's role for machine learning techniques in medical applications

6.1 Introduction

Machine learning (ML) is a branch of artificial intelligence that focuses on the development of algorithms to enable the computers learn independently based on the given data and their past experiences. ML techniques have been designed based on mathematical models able to learn from the training data to aid in making predictions without being explicitly programmed. Over the last few decades, ML has evolved a new branch known as deep learning, which uses several layers to automatically extract the relevant features for achieving better classification/clustering accuracy. In brief, each ML technique belongs to one of the following categories:

- **Supervised learning**: The techniques in this category are trained on labeled data to learn their characteristics. Afterward, they are used to estimate the class of unseen data. There are several techniques that belong to this category, including random forest (RF), k-nearest neighbors (KNN), decision tree (DT), and neural networks. Some of those supervised learning techniques will be tackled in detail in this chapter.
- **Unsupervised learning:** In this particular category, the computer is allowed to learn on its own without receiving any kind of oversight. Unsupervised learning is a type of ML in which the learning algorithm is given training data that has not been labeled, categorized, or classed. This algorithm then attempts to reorganize the input data into new features or a set of objects with patterns that are similar to one another. The K-mean clustering algorithm is one of the more well-known unsupervised learning algorithms [1].
- **Reinforcement learning (RL):**
  - RL is a learning method based on a feedback to identify if the taken actions are rewarded or penalized based on the desired target.

Metaheuristics Algorithms for Medical Applications. DOI: https://doi.org/10.1016/B978-0-443-13314-5.00007-2

- Automatic learning from this feedback improves the agent's performance.
- The agent explores its environment to learn the optimal behaviors to fulfill the maximum reward.

In recent years, ML methods have been extensively employed to address a variety of complex problems in a variety of application domains, including financial, industrial, marketing, security, environmental, and medical applications. ML approaches are distinguished by their capacity to evaluate a large amount of data for discovering exciting links and present interpretation, in addition to recognizing different patterns. ML can improve the reliability, predictability, performance, and precision of diagnostic systems for a variety of diseases [1]. In brief, ML can aid in the resolution of diagnostic issues in various medical fields, including cancer diagnostics, medical imaging, and wearable sensors. Also, ML is employed to investigate crucial clinical parameters, such as medical information extraction and diseases prediction. Consequently, it aids in planning and supporting the patient's status. In addition, it ensures efficient healthcare monitoring by assisting with data analysis and providing intelligent alerts as needed [1]. Metaheuristics play a vital role in the ML techniques, where they could be applied to estimate their hyperparameters to maximize their performance for achieving better accuracy, in addition to applying them as feature selection techniques to extract the most relevant features that will maximize the performance of these techniques. Furthermore, the metaheuristics techniques could be applied as an optimizer to estimate the near-optimal weights and the coefficient values for the neural network and linear regression. The most common application of the metaheuristics to maximize the performance of ML is feature selection. Before starting the training process, the feature selection technique has to be applied to extract the most relevant features for maximizing the performance of the ML technique.

This chapter will overview some ML techniques and clarify their roles in the medical field. In addition, the role of metaheuristic algorithms for each technique from those will also be clarified to show the readers the importance of the metaheuristics for the ML techniques.

6.2 Support vector machine

One of the most popular supervised learning approaches is support vector machines (SVMs). It is based on using a

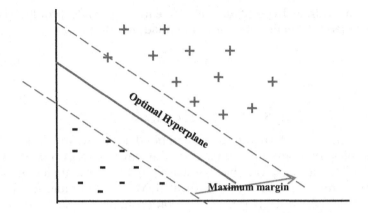

Figure 6.1 Two-dimensional hyperplane SVM.

hyperplane to distinguish between the various classes (Fig. 6.1). However, nonlinearly separable data has a major effect on SVM performance and can be solved by employing kernel functions. Those functions linearly divide data by mapping the current features onto a higher-dimensional space. Selecting the appropriate kernel function is one challenge of using SVMs, and adjusting the parameters of that function is another. Finding the optimal decision plane is a computational optimization problem that aids kernel functions in determining the best space for linearly separating the classes using a nonlinear transformation [2].

Let us assume that we have a training dataset with M samples $(S = S_1, S_2, S_3, \ldots, S_M)$ such that each sample contains d attributes and belongs to one of those two classes $(y_i \in \{-1, 1\})$. The training set is denoted as $((S_1, y_1), (S_2, y_2), (S_3, y_3), \ldots, (S_M, y_M))$, where $\{y_1, y_2, \ldots, y_M\}$ stand for the class labels related to S_1, S_2, ..., and S_M. In linearly separable data, the decision border between the two classes, $\{-1, 1\}$, is given as $w^T S + b = 0$, where w represents a weight vector, b denotes the bias, and S denotes the training sample. Then, the SVM classifier aims to find the near-optimal values of both w and b in order to orient the hyperplane as far away from the closest samples as possible and to create the two planes:

$$H_1 \rightarrow w^T S + b \geq +1 \text{ for } y_i = +1 \qquad (6.1)$$

$$H_2 \rightarrow w^T S + b \leq -1 \text{ for } y_i = -1 \qquad (6.2)$$

The intersection of these two planes is stated as follows:

$$y_i(w^T S_i + b) - 1 \geq 0 \forall i = 1, 2, 3, \ldots \ldots, M \qquad (6.3)$$

An optimal hyperplane for a linearly separable problem is obtained by tackling the following quadratic problem:

$$\min\frac{1}{2}\|w\|^2 \qquad (6.4)$$

Subject to

$$y_i(w^T S_i + b) - 1 \geq 0 \forall i = 1, 2, 3, \ldots\ldots, M$$

In the case of linearly nonseparable data, there are classified samples that are not subject to the constraint of Eq. (6.4). Therefore a slack variable known as ε_i has been included to loosen the constraints of the linear SVM. It is desirable for this variable, which measures the separation between the ith training sample and the corresponding margin hyperplane, to be as small as possible. After ε_i is plugged into the SVM's objective function represented in Eq. (6.4), we get the following:

$$\min\frac{1}{2}\|w\|^2 + C\sum_{i=1}^{M}\varepsilon_i \qquad (6.5)$$

Subject to

$$y_i(w^T S_i + b) - 1 + \varepsilon_i \geq 0 \forall i = 1, 2, 3, \ldots\ldots, M \qquad (6.6)$$

where C is responsible for determining the relative importance of the slack variable penalty in relation to the overall size of the SVM margin.

Another technique to deal with data that cannot be separated linearly is to use kernel functions to transform the data into a higher-dimensional space by applying a nonlinear kernel function (φ). In this scenario, the data can be separated linearly. Under the kernel function, the following will be the objective function of the SVM:

$$\min\frac{1}{2}\|w\|^2 + C\sum_{i=1}^{M}\varepsilon_i \qquad (6.7)$$

Subject to

$$y_i(w^T \varphi(S_i) + b) - 1 + \varepsilon_i \geq 0 \forall i = 1, 2, 3, \ldots\ldots, M$$

There are several kernel functions [3]:
- Linear kernel is represented as follows:
  - $K(S_i, S_j) = S_i, S_j,$
- Polynomial kernel of degree is represented based on the following formula:
  - $K(S_i, S_j) = (S_i, S_j + c)^2,$

- The radial basis function is formulated as follows:
  - $K(S_i, S_j) = \exp\left(\frac{\|S_i - S_j\|^2}{2\sigma^2}\right).$

SVM has been applied to several problems in the medical field to assist doctors in diagnosing several diseases. For example, in Ref. [4], the least square SVM was proposed to diagnose breast cancer disease. This clarifies the importance of SVM for predicting various diseases. However, SVM has some hyperparameters that have to be accurately optimized before the training process for maximizing its performance. Estimating the optimal values for these parameters is considered an optimization problem; hence, the metaheuristic algorithms as strong optimization techniques could be employed with the SVM for optimizing their parameters to maximize its classification accuracy when diagnosing various diseases, as done in several studies in the literature [5].

6.3 K-nearest neighbor algorithm

This algorithm is one of the simplest ML techniques, which is classified as a supervised learning algorithm due to the need for a labeled dataset. It could be used to solve both regression and classification problems. This algorithm's ease of use and broad applicability makes it a promising tool for a variety of research challenges in fields like data compression, data mining, market forecasting, and medical applications, where it has been shown to outperform numerous sophisticated supervised algorithms [6]. The KNN technique is also known as a nonparametric algorithm or an instance-based algorithm. Instead of learning a discriminative function from the provided training dataset, this algorithm merely memorizes the samples. This is why it is known as an instance-based algorithm. In addition, it is classified as a nonparametric method because it makes no assumptions about the distribution of the underlying data. The KNN classifier is based on the principle that the data points that are the most similar and that correspond to the same label have a greater probability. This means that this algorithm's learning is predicated on the concept of how similar a data point is to others. When applied to a given problem, the algorithm typically begins by calculating the KNNs in the training data and then set the label with the highest probability from those neighbors to the new unknown data point. According to the idea of similarity metrics, these nearest neighbors are calculated. As a method of determining the point from the given dataset that is most likely to be close to the input sample, the nearest neighbor determination based on a distance metric is used in this case. The KNN algorithm's classification also takes into account which points have the highest probabilities. The KNN classifier's steps are outlined in Algorithm 6.1. There are

---

Algorithm 6.1 Steps of KNN

Input: D, Unlabeled data points
1. Set any odd integer to k
2. s: an array to include the distance between the unknown data point and the others
3. For each d in D:
4.   s: Compute the distance from d to all classified data points
5.   Sort s in descending order
6.   Select the top k classified data points from the sorted s
7.   Assigning the unknown data point to the class with the highest frequency among the classes in the selected points
8. End for

---

several distance metrics used in the literature to compute the distance between the unseen data point and the classified data points; some of these metrics are Manhattan, Euclidean, and Minkowski. Euclidean is the most popular distance metric in the KNN techniques. These metrics are not limited to the KNN, but also can be used to calculate the distance between any two vectors with real values. The mathematical model of the Euclidean distance to calculate the distance between two real-valued vectors, x and y, which has size of n, is as follows:

$$d_1 = \sqrt{\sum_{i=1}^{n} (x_i - y_i)^2} \tag{6.8}$$

The mathematical model of the Manhattan metric for the same two vectors is as follows:

$$d_2 = \sum_{i=1}^{n} |x_i - y_i| \tag{6.9}$$

where $|\cdot|$ returns the absolute value. Minkowski metric is expressed as below for the same two vectors:

$$d_3 = \left(\sum_{i=1}^{n} |x - y| \right)^{1/p} \tag{6.10}$$

Minkowski metric is considered the generalization of both Manhattan and Euclidean metrics, where if $p = 1$, then Eq. (6.10) is reduced to Eq. (6.9). In the same context, if $p = 2$, then Eq. (6.10) is reduced to Eq. (6.8).

In literature, KNN has been applied to several medical problems, like medical fraud detection, heart disease diagnosis, and breast cancer diagnosis [7]. Nevertheless, the method is subject to the challenge of determining the optimal initialization of the K value. Therefore, the metaheuristics have been widely applied in the literature for the optimal selection of this parameter before starting the training process to improve the classification and prediction accuracy [5].

6.3.1 Weighted KNN (wKNN) algorithm

Properly determining the value of k is crucial to the efficacy of the algorithm. Outliers can influence the algorithm if k is very tiny. The neighborhood may include more points with unrelated labels if k is made larger. Although this is a concern, the classical KNN algorithm also has issues due to its reliance on the majority vote. This can be problematic when the distances to the nearest neighbors vary widely; it can also be problematic when the closest neighbors so faithfully represent the class of the object [6]. Therefore the wKNN algorithm was proposed to overcome these flaws. wKNN uses a kernel function to assign weights to the k closest points. This entails giving greater weight to near points and less weight to distant points. In wKNN, the kernel function is utilized to weigh the neighbors according to their distance. Some works employ two weighting techniques: uniformity and distance. If all the points in any neighborhood have the same weight, it is uniform. In the alternative method, point weighting is determined by the inverse of their distance. The steps of this algorithm are listed as follows:

Step 1: Input the dataset.
Step 2: Calculate the distance between the unseen record and each record in the input dataset
Step 3: Choose the nearest K neighbors to the unseen record whose class needs to be estimated.
Step 4: Utilize distance-weighted voting to determine the class label of the unseen record, as defined in Ref. [6].

This algorithm has been also applied for several medical problems like breast cancer classification [6]. However, it has several hyperparameters that need to be accurately predicted to maximize its performance when tackling the classification problems. The metaheuristics techniques could be employed to optimize these parameters to maximize their performance [6].

6.4 Naive Bayes algorithm

Naive Bayes (NB) classifiers are straightforward probabilistic classifiers that employ Bayes' theorem under the strong assumption of independence. It is more accurate to refer to the underlying probability model as the self-determining feature model. NB classifiers, at their most fundamental level, work under the assumption that the presence of one feature of a class is independent of the presence of any other feature. Even if the assumption is false, the NB classifier still shows decent performance. The NB classifier's strength is in its ability to estimate the means and variances of the variables needed for classification using a minimal quantity of training data. Due to the lack of information on the independent variables, we just need to calculate the variances of the variables for each label.

6.4.1 Why is this algorithm known as naive Bayes?

The NB method consists of the two words naive and Bayes, which can be stated as follows: It is dubbed naive because it implies that the existence of one feature is independent of the occurrence of other features. The NB model is simple to build and very successful for extremely big datasets. Compared to complex classification approaches, NB offers simplicity. Bayes' theorem provides a method for determining posterior probability:

$P(c|x)$ from $P(c)$, $P(x)$, and $P(x|c)$. This method is represented as follows [8]:

$$P(c|x) = \frac{P(x|c).P(c)}{P(x)} \qquad (6.11)$$

where $P(c|x)$ represents the posterior probability of target c given the attribute x, $P(c)$ is the former probability of the target c, $P(x)$ represents the former probability of the attribute x, and $P(x|c)$ is the probability of attribute x given the class c. The classification procedure using the NB algorithm can be explained in three straightforward steps:

1. Generate a frequency table using the input dataset,
2. Create a Likelihood table by describing the probabilities
3. Utilize the Bayesian equation to calculate the postclass probability.

The class with the largest posterior proportion is considered the class resulting from the prediction. It is practically impossible to obtain a set of entirely independent predictors in practice. The classification accuracy of the NB algorithm could be improved by accurately estimating the used probability terms. This problem is considered as an optimization problem and could be tackled by the metaheuristic algorithms as discussed extensively in Ref. [9].

6.5 Random forest

The RF is a popular ensemble learning framework for problems involving classification and regression [10,11]. This framework consists of numerous independent DTs that are sampled at random. In the framework, the bootstrap sampling approach is used to construct a new bootstrap training set by drawing a random sample of the data from the first training set. Additionally, the DTs that correspond to each new bootstrap training set are constructed using the bootstrap sampling approach as well. It is feasible to utilize the out-of-bag (OOB) in order to evaluate the efficiency of a DT. The OOB is constructed on the basis of new bootstrap training sets. The ratio of bootstrap training sets to OOB data is about equivalent to two to one in the majority of instances. After that, the features that are used for each resampling procedure will be picked at random. By taking the average of the predictions made by the DTs, one can make predictions about the new data [10,11]. The output of RF's prediction, denoted by the letter R, is expressed as follows:

$$R = \frac{1}{n}\sum_{i=1}^{n} R_i(x) \qquad (6.12)$$

where R_i represents the outcome of the ith prediction model and n indicates the total number of DTs used in the model. The number of trees, denoted by n, and the minimum size of the random feature set at each tree, denoted by MF, are the two hyperparameters in the RF model. It is interesting to note that it has been proved that increasing n might result in the overfitting problem. In addition to this, the value of the Gini index can be utilized in the RF approach in order to automatically complete the selection of the features [10,11]. To maximize the performance of the RF model, its previously mentioned hyperparameters need to be accurately estimated. This problem is considered an optimization process because the values of these parameters might differ for each classification problem. Therefore, to adapt the RF model for each classification problem, it could be integrated with the metaheuristics that could estimate its parameters effectively to maximize the classification accuracy. Several researches considered this problem as an optimization problem and solved it using the metaheuristic techniques [12].

6.6 K-means clustering algorithm

K-means clustering is a form of unsupervised learning that splits the dataset, which is unlabeled, into a number of distinct groups. If K is equal to 2, then there will be two clusters; if K is equal to 3, then there will be three clusters; and so on. It is listed as one of the most used ML algorithms for data mining due to its simplicity, strong performance, low computational cost, and flexibility [13]. The main process of this algorithm includes two stages. The first one includes selecting randomly K data points known as centroids to represent the centers of the clusters. The second stage is based on employing the Euclidean distance metric to determine the distance between the remaining data objects and the cluster centers, and these objects are assigned to the closest clusters [13]. As soon as all of the data objects have been assigned, the new centroid for each cluster can be updated by recalculating the average of all data objects assigned. After that, the iterative method is carried out until the criterion function has reached its minimum value. Supposing that there are a dataset X including n data points such that $X_i = (x_1, x_2, \ldots, x_n)$ and K clusters, where $K < n$ is a predefined number to represent the number of clusters, the K-means algorithm is applied to partition those data points into K clusters with a criterion function based on minimizing the squared error between the points within the cluster. Following that, K data points are randomly selected from the dataset X to represent the centroids of the clusters. Then, the distance between those centroids and each remaining data point is computed and this point is assigned to the cluster with the smallest distance. The centroid for each cluster is updated based on computing the average of all the data points assigned to this cluster, as defined in the following formula:

$$\mu_i = \frac{1}{S_i} \sum_{x \in C_i} x \tag{6.13}$$

where S_i represents the number of data points assigned to the cluster C_i. μ_i is the centroid of the ith cluster. The assignment and updating process is repeated until the criterion function is minimized. This function is based on minimizing the sum of the squared error between the points within the cluster. The mathematical model of this criterion function is as follows:

$$J_{\text{SSE}} = \sum_{i=0}^{K} \sum_{x \in C_i} (x - \mu_i)^2 \tag{6.14}$$

Fig. 6.2 shows the flowchart of the K-means clustering algorithm. This algorithm plays a vital role in exploring the structure of the medical dataset. The vast majority of clustering algorithms generate exclusive clusters, which means that a given sample can only belong to a single cluster [14]. On the other hand, the vast majority of real-world medical datasets contain information that is fundamentally redundant. This phenomenon is best described by overlapping clustering approaches, which let a single sample

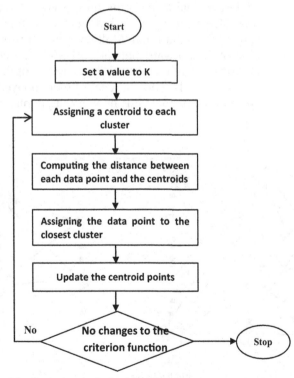

Figure 6.2 The flowchart of the K-means clustering algorithm.

to belong to more than one cluster. The term "overlapping K-means" refers to a method that is an extension of the conventional K-means algorithm and is considered to be one of the easiest and most effective ways for overlapping clustering. One of the most essential requirements for a fruitful clustering operation is the identification of the centroids that are most suited for use with the clustering algorithm. The challenge of clustering and the problem of locating the optimal centroids are both nondeterministic polynomial time-hard problems; hence, the application of metaheuristic algorithms may be an acceptable method for addressing both concerns. This problem has been handled by several authors using metaheuristic algorithms [13].

6.7 Multilayer perceptron

Feedforward neural networks are supervised ML techniques that consist of neurons dispersed over completely interconnected layers. The initial (input) layer maps network input variables, while the final layer is the output layer. Between the initial and final layers are a set of hidden layers, that might involve one, two, or more than that. Multilayer perceptron (MLP) is a frequent type of feedforward network. In MLP, the connections between neurons are unidirectional. The weights of the links lie within the interval $[1, -1]$. There is a set of hidden layers between the input and output in the MLP network, as depicted in Fig. 6.3. Before

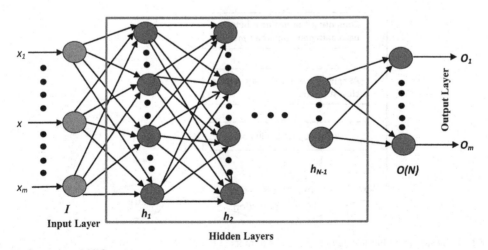

Figure 6.3 Structure of MLP.

calculating the node output value, the weighted total for the jth node in the ith is computed as follows:

$$S_j = \sum_{j=1}^{m} w_{i-1j}I_{i-1j} + \beta_j \qquad (6.15)$$

where I_{i-1j} represents the input from the $(i-1)$th layer to the jth neuron, w_{i-1j} represents the connection weight between the input the $(i-1)$th layer to the jth neuron, m represents the number of inputs to the jth neuron, and β_j represents the bias value for this layer. After computing the linear summation of multiplying the weights vector by the input vector to the jth neuron in the ith layer, the activation function is applied to compute the final output of this neuron based on this summation S_j. There are several activation functions proposed in the literature that have been proposed in an attempt to reach better performance for MLP. Some of these activation functions are as follows:

- **Step function:** The step function (SF) is a form of activation function that is considered to be one of the simplest. In this case, a threshold value is used, and if the value of S_j is higher than the threshold, then the neuron will become active; otherwise, the neuron becomes inactive. The mathematical formulation of this function is as follows:

$$SF(S_j) = \begin{cases} 1 & if \quad S_j > 0 \\ 0 & else \end{cases} \qquad (6.16)$$

- **Rectified linear units (ReLU):** This function provides a solution to the problem of vanishing gradients, allowing models to learn more quickly and perform their operations more efficiently. This function's mathematical model is as follows:

$$ReLU(S_j) = \max(0, S_j) \qquad (6.17)$$

This means that when the input is negative, ReLU will produce an output of 0, and when the input is positive, the output will be x.

- **Scaled exponential linear unit (SELU):** This function is mathematically expressed as follows:

$$SELU(S_j) = \begin{cases} \lambda S_j & if \ S_j > 0 \\ \lambda\alpha(e^{S_j} - 1) & Otherwise \end{cases} \qquad (6.18)$$

where λ and α have approximations of 1.0507 and 1.6732, respectively.

- **Exponential linear unit (ELU):** This activation function tackles some of the concerns that have arisen with ReLUs, while keeping some of their advantageous characteristics.

If the input x-value is greater than zero, then it is equivalent to the ReLU; in this case, the output will be a y-value equal to the input x-value. However, if the inputted value x is less than 0, we will obtain a relatively negative result. Following is the mathematical model for this function:

$$\text{ELU}(S_j) = \begin{cases} S_j & \text{if } S_j > 0 \\ \alpha(e^{S_j} - 1) & \text{Otherwise} \end{cases} \qquad (6.19)$$

where α is a fixed value.

- **Tanh activation function:** This activation function returns a value between 1 and -1 where if the input value is large, then the output value is close to 1.0 and vice. Following is the mathematical formulation of this activation function:

$$\tanh(S_j) = \frac{\sinh(S_j)}{\cosh(S_j)} = \frac{e^{S_j} - e^{-S_j}}{e^{S_j} + e^{-S_j}} \qquad (6.20)$$

- **Sigmoid activation function:** This activation function returns a value between 0 and 1. Following is the mathematical formulation of this activation function:

$$sj = \frac{1}{1 + e^{-S_j}} \qquad (6.21)$$

Finally, the output layer takes the output from the previously hidden layer to give the final prediction or classification based on employing one of the following activation functions according to the tackled problem: Step, sigmoid, tanh, and softmax activation functions. Note that, the last three previously mentioned functions could be used for binary classification problems taking into consideration the fact that their output needs to be compared with a threshold value to determine the final output. The most common activation function for multiclass classification problems is the softmax activation function. The softmax layer is responsible for estimating the final output according to the following formula:

$$\text{Softmax}(S_j) = \frac{e^{S_j}}{\sum_{j=1}^{C} e^{S_j}} \qquad (6.22)$$

The MLP has been extensively applied to tackle medical problems. For example, in Ref. [15], it was applied to diagnose the low back pain [15]. Also, it was applied to tackle several other problems in the medical field, like heart disease diagnosis, long-term forecasting of survival in liver transplantation, chronic kidney disease prediction, and so on [16]. MLP has some hyperparameters that have to be accurately estimated to get the optimal architecture that could achieve better classification accuracy according to the employed dataset. Those parameters are represented in the number of layers, activation function, batch size, learning rate, and number of neurons for each layer. Also, the optimizer employed to update the MLP's weights has a controlling parameter known as learning rate (LR), which needs to be also estimated precisely. The estimation of these parameters are considered an optimization problem that could be solved using the metaheuristic technique as performed in several researches in the literature [16].

6.8   Decision tree induction

The DTs are a form of supervised learning that may be utilized for both regression and classification problems, but in most cases, it is most useful for solving classification problems [11]. It is a classifier that is constructed like a tree, with internal nodes representing the features of a dataset, branches representing the decision rules, and each leaf node representing the conclusion of the classification. In general, there are two nodes in a DT: the leaf node and the decision node. Leaf nodes are the results of the decisions that have been made and do not contain any more branches, whereas decision nodes are used to make any decision and can contain many branches. The judgments or the examinations are carried out on the basis of the characteristics of the dataset that is provided. DT is a graphical depiction that allows one to obtain all of the possible answers to a problem or choice depending on the conditions that have been presented. It is referred to as a DT due to the fact that, just like a tree, it begins with the root node and then develops on subsequent branches to form a structure that resembles a tree.

DTs are a powerful ML technique due to their interpretability and simplicity. Since the DT induction (DTI) technique establishes the attribute's relevance when constructing test conditions, it gives a built-in mechanism for selecting certain features [11]. The performance of the DTI mechanism influences not only the performance but also the expressiveness of the induced DTs. In brief, this mechanism includes four characteristics:
- The splitting criterion for determining the quality of the test conditions,
- The mechanism to deal with the missing data,
- The strategy to handle both categorical and numerical attributes, and
- The tree pruning techniques to avoid overfitting.

There are two forms of DTs that can be induced, multivariate and univariate, depending on the number of attributes being examined in each test condition:

- In the univariate DT, the training set is typically divided into subsets using a single attribute. The univariate DTs have two benefits: they are easy to understand, and their induction techniques are straightforward. However, numerous internal nodes are included in induced DTs when the training instance distribution is complicated.
- In contrast, each multivariate DT test condition employs a unique set of features. These classifiers typically show greater performance than univariate DTs while being more compact. Although a greater computational effort is needed to induce them, they are less expressive.

The vast majority of DTI approaches make use of a recursive-partitioning strategy that implements some sort of splitting criterion in order to divide the training records. In most cases, this strategy is supplemented with a *pruning method*, which works toward enhancing the performance of the classifier. The two DTI algorithms that are most frequently used to accomplish this *induction method* are known as C4.5 and CART (Classification and Regression Trees). Nevertheless, a number of studies show that recursive partitioning includes three main flaws:

- Selection bias toward multivalued traits
- Overfitting
- Instability to modest changes in the training set

Overfitting occurs in a DT when the classification performance of the DT is worse than its learning performance and when it is more complicated. According to Ref. [17], this problem arises when the data contain noise or irrelevant features or when there is only a limited training set available. In addition, a number of studies have demonstrated that certain splitting criteria are biased in the selection of one attribute type over others, although this selection influences the performance of DT. Both the information gain criterion and the Gini index, for instance, have a tendency to favor characteristics with multiple values [17]. Last but not least, according to [17], the most significant issue with DTI approaches is their sensitivity to relatively few alterations in the training set. It was also noted that in recursive partitioning, the selection of the splitting attribute and the precise positioning of the cutpoints significantly rely on the particular training instances distribution. The incremental induction of trees under classifier ensembles like RF, boosting, and bagging and the application of contemporary mixed-integer optimization techniques are fruitful alternative approaches for avoiding these flaws [17]. Developing the DTs could be dealt as an optimization problem, which could be tackled using the optimization techniques. However, this optimization problem is considered NP-hard. Therefore the traditional techniques could not produce solutions with high quality. Therefore the metaheuristics were applied as a strong alternative for generating DTs that are more precise than those created using conventional methods [17].

6.9 Logistic regression

Logistic regression considers a statistic-based technique that is analogous to the linear regression, where both of them require finding the values of the coefficients. However, the output of linear regression is continuous values, while logistic regression generates the probability that determines if the input instance belongs to the given class or not [18]. It could be applied for the binary classification problem where any quantity will be converted to a value of around 0 or 1. The classical logistic function σ, which normalizes any continuous value t into a value between 0 and 1, is formulated as follows:

$$\sigma(t) = \frac{1}{1 + e^t} \tag{6.23}$$

After computing the values of coefficients for separating the various classes, the logistic regression could predict the class probability for the sample x according to the following formula:

$$\sigma(x) = \frac{1}{1 + e^{-(w_0 + w_1 x)}} \tag{6.24}$$

where w_0 represents the bias or intercept term and w_1 is the coefficient for the input x.

6.10 Chapter summary

In this chapter, we elaborated on the role of the metaheuristics for the ML techniques as well as the importance of the ML techniques in medical applications. In a broad sense, this chapter showed that the majority of the ML techniques have some hyperparameters that need to be accurately estimated for each tackled classification problem. The optimal estimation of this parameter is considered hard to be tackled by the traditional technique because some ML techniques, like MLP, might have a huge number of hyperparameters that could not be estimated by these techniques. In addition, these techniques might be unable to find the most precise values for these parameters that could maximize the performance of ML techniques. Therefore the metaheuristic, as a strong and highly performing technique, could be used to tackle this problem in a reasonable amount of time and with higher accuracy.

References

[1] M. Shehab, et al., Machine learning in medical applications: a review of state-of-the-art methods, Computers in Biology and Medicine 145 (2022) 105458.

[2] O. Chapelle, et al., Choosing multiple parameters for support vector machines, Machine Learning 46 (1) (2002) 131−159.

[3] A. Tharwat, A.E.J.A.I. Hassanien, Chaotic antlion algorithm for parameter optimization of support vector machine, Applied Intelligence 48 (3) (2018) 670−686.

[4] K. Polat, S. Güneş, Breast cancer diagnosis using least square support vector machine, Digital Signal Processing 17 (4) (2007) 694−701.

[5] K. Korovkinas, P. Danėnas, G. Garšva, Support vector machine parameter tuning based on particle swarm optimization metaheuristic, Nonlinear analysis: Modelling and Control 25 (2) (2020) 266−281.

[6] S.S. Chakravarthy, N. Bharanidharan, H. Rajaguru, Deep learning-based metaheuristic weighted K-nearest neighbor algorithm for the severity classification of breast cancer, IRBM 44 (3) (2023) 100749.

[7] M. Shouman, T. Turner, R. Stocker, Applying k-nearest neighbour in diagnosing heart disease patients, International Journal of Information and Education Technology 2 (3) (2012) 220−223.

[8] M. Alwateer, et al., Ambient healthcare approach with hybrid whale optimization algorithm and naïve Bayes classifier, Sensors 21 (13) (2021) 4579.

[9] D.M. Diab, K.M. El Hindi, Using differential evolution for fine tuning naïve Bayesian classifiers and its application for text classification, Applied Soft Computing 54 (2017) 183−199.

[10] Y. Dai, et al., A hybrid metaheuristic approach using random forest and particle swarm optimization to study and evaluate backbreak in open-pit blasting, Neural Computing and Applications (2022) 1−16.

[11] J. Li, C. Li, S. Zhang, Application of six metaheuristic optimization algorithms and random forest in the uniaxial compressive strength of rock prediction, Applied Soft Computing 131 (2022) 109729.

[12] H. Khajavi, A. Rastgoo, Predicting the carbon dioxide emission caused by road transport using a Random Forest (RF) model combined by Meta-Heuristic algorithms, Sustainable Cities and Society (2023) 104503.

[13] G. Komarasamy, A. Wahi, An optimized K-means clustering technique using bat algorithm, European Journal of Scientific Research 84 (2) (2012) 263−273.

[14] S. Khanmohammadi, N. Adibeig, S. Shanehbandy, An improved overlapping k-means clustering method for medical applications, Expert Systems with Applications 67 (2017) 12−18.

[15] D.G. Bounds, et al. A multilayer perceptron network for the diagnosis of low back pain, in *ICNN*, 1988.

[16] W. Penny, D. Frost, Neural networks in clinical medicine, Medical Decision Making 16 (4) (1996) 386–398.

[17] R. Rivera-Lopez, et al., Induction of decision trees as classification models through metaheuristics, Swarm and Evolutionary Computation 69 (2022) 101006.

[18] T.M. Le, et al., A novel wrapper–based feature selection for early diabetes prediction enhanced with a metaheuristic, IEEE Access 9 (2020) 7869–7884.

Metaheuristic algorithms collaborated with various machine learning models for feature selection in medical data: Comparison and analysis

7.1 Introduction

A variety of datasets mainly of biomedical nature are highly dimensional. This indicates that there are numerous features per sample. The majority of these features are redundant or useless, and they produce noise that degrades the efficiency of a classifier used for medical diagnosis. It is consequently vital to employ dimensionality reduction approaches that select the most informative subset of characteristics [1]. Dimensionality reduction (Dr) can be used to clean up datasets by removing superfluous details without sacrificing accuracy. There are two main types of Dr strategies. The primary method is called feature extraction, which involves the extraction of new feature spaces from the overall features of the dataset. Feature selection (FS), as the second type of Dr technique, aims at selecting a minimal subset of the overall features utilized to describe the data [2]. Hence, FS aids in reducing redundancy and irrelevance and also improves the performance of the machine learning (ML) and deep learning models in several cases. FS approaches are classified into three categories: filter-based, wrapper-based, and embedded. Filter methods were proposed to select the optimal subset of the overall features without the need for a classifier to measure its accuracy; on the contrary, the wrapper-based methods employ a classifier to observe the quality of the obtained subset of features. Embedded methods can be considered as a special class of wrapper-based methods, where the FS technique is only applicable to a specific classifier [2]. Conventional FS techniques are centered on exploring all the subsets to find suitable subsets.

Metaheuristics Algorithms for Medical Applications. DOI: https://doi.org/10.1016/B978-0-443-13314-5.00004-7

The search may be exhaustive, in which all 2^d subsets are generated and evaluated for d features. This is essentially impossible due to the exponentially increased computing time, even when dealing with small datasets. Moreover, random search, greedy search, and heuristic search have been employed. Nonetheless, many of these search algorithms may become stuck in local optimums and are computationally expensive [2].

This chapter first discusses different techniques proposed for FS. Then, it explains the main steps required to adapt any continuous metaheuristics algorithm for solving this problem. Afterward, some experiments analyzed using various performance metrics are conducted and reported to clarify the effectiveness of some metaheuristics. Finally, the chapter summary is presented to show the conclusions.

7.2 Feature selection techniques

There are three categories for the FS techniques: the first one is filter methods that aim to extract the near-optimal subset of features using a filter function to extract the more effective features out of the overall feature without the need for a machine learning classifier; the second is dependent on a classifier to determine if the extracted subset of feature is useful or not; the last class includes embedded methods. These classes are extensively discussed in the rest of this section to illustrate the different techniques found in each class in addition to their advantages and disadvantages.

7.2.1 Filter methods

The standard filter algorithm has two stages [3]. First, it assigns a score to each feature according to a set of criteria. Features could be evaluated using a univariate or multivariate approach. The univariate approach ranks features in isolation from the feature space, while the multivariate scheme assesses features in batches. The multivariate approach can, thus, easily account for duplicate features. The second stage is to select the highest-ranked features to use as inputs to the machine learning classification models. The merits of the filter-based technique are that it is computationally efficient, prevents overfitting, and has been shown to perform well with specific datasets as discussed in Ref. [4]. The selected subset of features may not be optimal due to the possibility of obtaining a redundant subset, which is one of the downsides of filter-based algorithms. Another

Figure 7.1 Feature selection using filter-based approaches.

disadvantage of the filter-based techniques is that while performing a feature ranking, it is possible to disregard significant characteristics that are not particularly helpful on their own but are relevant when combined with other characteristics [4]. Because the machine learning classifiers are neglected, it can become difficult to find a classifier that is adequate for the task at hand. In addition, there is no one best way to decide which dimension the feature space should have [4]. Fisher score, mutual information (MI)-based approaches, and ReliefF and its variants are just some of the performance criteria that have been developed in the past decade for filter-based FS. Some of those methods will be discussed in the rest of this section. The main framework used to select the optimal subset of features using filter-based techniques is depicted in Fig. 7.1.

7.2.2 Chi-square feature selection

The chi-squared metric is a well-known FS technique that is based on measuring the independence level between the feature x_i and the class label y_i. The chi-square metric is formulated as follows [5]:

$$X^2(\mathbf{x_i}, y_i) = \sum \frac{(\mathbf{O_i} - \mathbf{E_i})}{\mathbf{E_i}} \tag{7.1}$$

where O_i represents the observed frequency, and E_i is the expected frequency. The observed frequency is a phrase about the number of rows in the given dataset that have the attribute x_i and the target or class y_i. The expected frequency is based on computing the occurrence percentage of the feature x_i in the total dataset multiplied by the total number of appearing in the class y_i with this feature.

7.2.3 Classical Fisher score

High-quality features should consistently give the same values to instances of the same class and different values to instances of different classes. By using this logic, we can derive the Fisher score for the ith feature $S(i)$ as [6]:

$$S(i) = \frac{\sum_{k=1}^{K} n_j \left(\mu_{ij} - \mu_i \right)}{\sum_{k=1}^{K} n_j \rho_{ij}^2} \tag{7.2}$$

where μ_{ij} is the mean of the ith feature for the jth class, ρ_{ij}^2 represents the variance of the same feature for the same class, n_j is the number of instances labeled with the jth class, and μ_i represents the mean of the ith feature. The higher the Fisher score is, the better will be the chosen feature.

7.2.4 Generalized Fisher score

Feature redundancy is a problem for the Fisher score because each feature is evaluated independently. To overcome the abovementioned issue, Gu et al. [6] recently presented a generalized Fisher score to jointly choose features, which seeks to identify a subset of features that maximizes the lower bound of the classic Fisher score:

$$\left\| W^T \mathbf{diag}(p)X - G \right\|_F^2 + \gamma \|w\|_F^2 \tag{7.3}$$

subject to:

$$p \in \{0, 1\}^m$$

where p is the vector of selecting the features, d represents the feature number to select, m is the overall number of features, and G represents a matrix to be as an indicator to a special label, and computed as follows:

$$G(i,j) = \begin{cases} \sqrt{\dfrac{n}{n_j}} - \sqrt{\dfrac{n_j}{n}} & \textit{if} \quad x_i \in c_j \\[3mm] -\sqrt{\dfrac{n_j}{n}} & \textit{else} \end{cases} \tag{7.4}$$

where c_j represents the jth class label, and x_i is the ith instance in the given dataset.

7.2.5 Correlation criteria

Pearson's correlation coefficient is a measure of how strongly and in what direction two variables are related to one another.

In other words, it determines the linear relationship between X and Y. Positive linear correlation is ranged between 0 and 1, whereas no linear correlation is represented by the value 0, and negative linear correlation is ranged between 0 and -1. A positive correlation means that if feature X increases, then feature Y likewise increases, and vice versa, if feature Y decreases, then feature X also decreases. Both features have a linear relationship and move together. A negative correlation means that if a feature X grows, then a feature Y decreases, and vice versa, if the Pearson's correlation coefficient is 0, then there is no correlation between the two variables. The formula for calculating the Pearson's correlation coefficient is as follows [7]:

$$S(i) = \frac{\delta(X_i, Y)}{\sqrt{\omega(X_i)^* \omega(Y)}} \tag{7.5}$$

$$\delta(X_i, Y) = \frac{\sum_{k=1}^{m} (x_{k,i} - \overline{x_i})(y_k - \overline{y})}{\sqrt{\sum_{k=1}^{m} (x_{k,i} - \overline{x_i})^2 \sum_{k=1}^{m} (y_k - \overline{y})^2}} \tag{7.6}$$

where δ represents the covariance, ω stands for the variance, m is the number of instances in the dataset, X_i is a vector including the values of the ith feature, and Y is a vector including all the target values.

7.2.6 Mutual information

MI considers one of the most popular FS techniques due to its simplicity and low computational cost. Before describing how the MI measures the relevance of each feature, we must first describe the Shannon entropy as [4]:

$$H(X) = -\sum_x p(x)\log(p(x)) \tag{7.7}$$

This equation was proposed to represent the uncertainty for various class labels. The conditional entropy between two variables X and Y is computed as follows:

$$H(X|Y) = -\sum_x \sum_y p(x,y)\log(p(x|y)) \tag{7.8}$$

where x represents the feature, and y represents the target or class. According to the abovementioned equation, if we observe a variable X, we can lower the degree of uncertainty in the output Y. The reduced degree of uncertainty can be computed as follows:

$$I(X, Y) = H(X) - H(X|Y) \tag{7.9}$$

This equation calculates MI between two variables Y and X, where 0 indicates complete independence and greater than 0 indicates closer dependence between the feature and the target. In the last case, there is a dependent relationship between the two variables because one variable can reveal details about the other. All of the previous definitions are applied to discrete variables, but the same holds true for continuous variables; all you have to do is swap out the summations for integrations. The MI can be thought of as a distance metric, defined as follows [4]:

$$k(f,g) = \int f(y) \log\left(\frac{f(y)}{g(y)}\right) \tag{7.10}$$

where k represents the Kullback–Leibler divergence between two densities, which can be also employed as a measure of MI. If we use the abovementioned equations to determine MI, we need to know the probability density function (PDF) of the variables. We are unable to accurately calculate the PDF due to the limited sample size of the data collected [4]. A variety of techniques for calculating the MI have been discussed in the literature [4]. Finding the MI between each feature and the output class labels and ranking them based on this value is one of the simplest approaches for FS.

7.3 Wrapper-based methods

These methods are based on employing a machine learning classifier as a black box to return the classification accuracy under the obtained subset of features to assess its quality. However, finding the optimal subset of features among 2^d considers the NP-hard problem due to the exponential growth computational cost when increasing the number of features (d represents the number of features). Therefore, several techniques have been recently proposed to aid in finding this optimal subset that will maximize the performance of the machine learning model. For example, the Branch and Bound approach made use of a tree structure to evaluate a variety of subsets for a specified number of FSs. However, the search would become increasingly difficult as the number of features increased. When used for bigger datasets, exhaustive search techniques have high computational costs. Therefore, simplified algorithms such

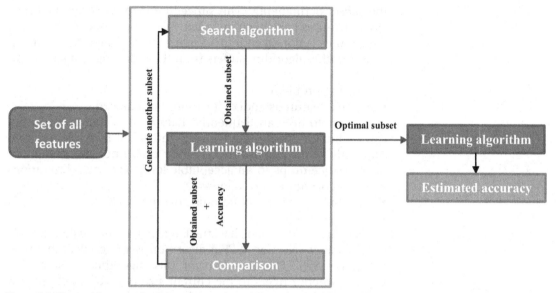

Figure 7.2 General framework of the wrapper-based feature selection techniques.

as sequential search or metaheuristic algorithms such as genetic algorithm or nutcrackers optimization algorithm (NOA) are used because they are capable of producing good results and are computationally efficient. However, these algorithms still suffer from several shortcomings, like slow convergence speed, lack of population diversity, and stagnation into local minima, that prevent them from reaching the near-optimal solution. Because of this, there is always a challenge for the researchers to solve. In this section, we will thoroughly explain the sequential search algorithm in addition to presenting the main steps required to adopt a metaheuristic algorithm for extracting the optimal subset of features. The main framework used to select the optimal subset of features using wrapper-based techniques is depicted in Fig. 7.2.

7.3.1 Sequential selection algorithms

Due to their iterative nature, those algorithms are categorized as sequential. When given an empty set, the sequential feature selection (SFS) algorithm adds a single feature that maximizes the objective function [4]. In the next phase, the remaining features are added one at a time to the existing subset, and the resulting subset is then assessed. If a single feature provides the highest possible level of classification accuracy, it is added to the subset permanently. This procedure is repeated until all necessary features have been included. Since the interdependence of the features is not taken into account, this SFS algorithm is naive. However, this algorithm suffers from the following two shortcomings [4]:

- Nesting problem.
- Once a feature is added, it cannot be removed.

Similar to SFS, an Sequential Backward Selection algorithm can be built by beginning with the full set of features and subsequently removing features, one by one, until the predictor's performance drops to an acceptable level. The main limitations of this algorithm are as follows:

- Requires more computational cost than SFS
- Nesting problem

Due to its additional backtracking phase, the sequential forward floating selection (SFFS) algorithm is more adaptable than the naive SFS. The flowchart of this algorithm is shown in Fig. 7.3, where i refers to the current size of a subset of features and d is the needed dimension. The initial phase of the algorithm is identical to the SFS algorithm, in that it gradually increases the number of features dependent on the fitness function. With the SFFS method, another step is added to analyze subsets generated by removing a single feature at a time from the initial subset. If

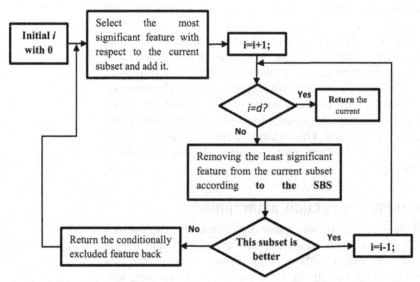

Figure 7.3 Flowchart of the SFFS technique.

the value of the objective function is improved by removing a feature, that feature is eliminated and the algorithm returns to the first step with the new, smaller subset; otherwise, the algorithm is back to the initial stage to insert a new feature. The algorithm will repeat this process until the desired number of features is reached or the desired level of performance is achieved. Nested subsets are a problem for SFFS methods since forward inclusion was always unconditional, so strongly correlated variables might be included if they improve the performance in the SFS evaluation. Therefore, another variant known as adaptive SFFS has been proposed to avoid the nesting problem [4].

7.3.2 Metaheuristic-based feature selection

The metaheuristic techniques could fulfill significant success for several optimization problems in a reasonable amount of time due to their outstanding characteristics:

- Strong performance to explore several solutions during the optimization process.
- Their ability to exploit the promising regions obtained by the exploration stage to search for better solutions faster.
- Less computational cost because it has a simple mathematical model.

This success motivates the author over the last few years to adapt them to solve the FS that is considered NP-hard and cannot be easily solved by the traditional methods. Some of the proposed wrapper-based techniques for medical data are listed in Table 7.1.

To make the metaheuristic algorithms applicable for solving the FS, they must be adapted using the following steps:

Step 1: initialization

These algorithms initialize randomly a number of solutions within the search space of the tackled problems. Since the FS problem needs a binary solution to determine those features that are selected and those that are removed, the initial solutions will be randomly distributed with a value of 0 to determine the unselected features and 1 to determine the selected features, as depicted in Fig. 7.4. Following that, these initial solutions will be evaluated using the objective function discussed later to determine the quality of each solution and extract the best one that could achieve the lowest fitness value (F-value). The optimization process of the metaheuristic algorithms will be fired after finishing the evaluation step to

Table 7.1 Some metaheuristics proposed for feature selection in the medical dataset.

Algorithms	Contributions
Improved generalized normal distribution optimization (IGNDO) [8]	• To select features from medical data, the GNDO algorithm was introduced. • This algorithm is based on the utilization of the transfer function called arctangent to transform the continuous values produced by GNDO into binary values. In addition, the classical GNDO was improved using a unique restarting strategy to retain the diversity among its solutions during the optimization process. • This strategy is based on reinitialization of the individuals that exceed a predefined threshold distance from the best solution obtained yet. The reinitialization process is performed based on an efficient updating system. • This method is merged with GNDO to suggest another binary variation called improved IGNDO. • This variant has a strong ability to retain the diversity of the solutions, which helps prevent becoming stagnation into local optima and speeds up convergence. • IGNDO was validated on 13 medical examples obtained from the UCI repository, and thoroughly contrasted with 7 metaheuristic techniques to disclose its effectiveness. • The experimental outcomes have demonstrated that IGNDO is superior to all the compared algorithms under various employed performance metrics.
Chaotic Harris Hawks optimization (CHHO) [9]	• This study improved the classical HHO using two mechanisms to propose a new strong variant called CHHO. • The first mechanism is based on initializing the individuals based on the chaotic maps to distribute them as accurately as possible to cover the majority of the possible permutations for the optimization problems. • The second strategy involves applying the simulated annealing to the best solution obtained even now to improve the exploitation capability of HHO. • CHHO was tested using a set of medical datasets taken from the UCI repository. The experimental outcomes show that this algorithm is a strong alternative for tackling the FS problem
Binary moth-flame optimization (B-MFO) [10]	• This study presented a new binary variant of the moth-flame algorithm, namely B-MFO, for identifying efficacious features from medical datasets of varying sizes. • Three different transformation functions called shaped, V-shaped, and U-shaped were used to convert the continuous solutions generated by the classical MFO to binary solutions to become applicable for tackling the FS problem. • This paper assessed various categories of B-MFO across seven medical datasets and conducted a comparative analysis with four established binary algorithms.
Enhanced whale optimization algorithm (E-WOA) [11]	• This study aimed to enhance the performance of the WOA by incorporating a pooling mechanism and three search strategies, namely, preferential selecting, migrating, and enriched encircling prey. • The resulting variant, E-WOA, demonstrated significant improvements in its efficacy. • A binary variant of E-WOA, called BE-WOA, was employed to propose a FS technique for medical datasets.

(Continued)

Table 7.1 (Continued)

Algorithms	Contributions
Hybrid brain storm optimization (HBSO) algorithm [12]	• The validation of the BE-WOA involves the use of datasets about medical diseases, and a comparison is made with other optimization algorithms. • The comparison is based on different performance measures such as fitness, accuracy, sensitivity, precision, and a number of features. • This study presented a hybridization approach based on combining the firefly algorithm integrated with the brainstorm algorithm. This variant was called HBSO. • HBSO was utilized as a wrapper method to address FS problems on classification datasets. • This algorithm was subjected to evaluation using a total of 21 datasets and subsequently compared against 11 other metaheuristic algorithms. • Furthermore, it has been implemented on the dataset pertaining to the coronavirus disease. • The experimental results obtained provide evidence for the resilience of this algorithm.

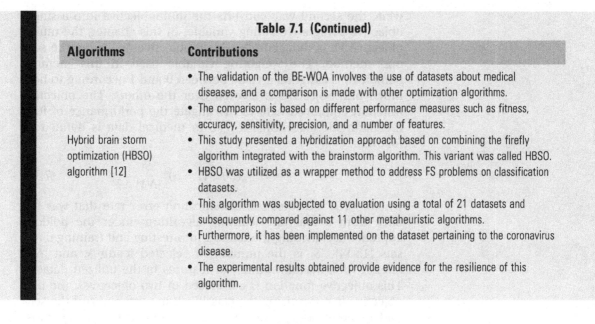

Figure 7.4 A binary solution.

generate new solutions in an attempt to search for better solutions. However, these solutions are represented in continuous values that cannot be applied to tackling the FS. For this reason, we will employ two widely used families of transfer functions to discretize these continuous values before applying them to the FS. The next part will provide a detailed explanation of these transfer functions.

Step 2: evaluation phase

Since the FS aims to increase accuracy while concurrently reducing feature length, it is regarded as a multiobjective problem. However, the vast majority of metaheuristic algorithms have only been presented to deal with optimization problems with a single objective; hence they are not applicable to multiobjective problems. Numerous studies have addressed this issue in two different ways: the first made use of Pareto optimality, while the second way converts the multiobjective into a single objective using a weighting variable. In this chapter, the multi-objective FS is reduced to a single-objective one using the second method. The weighting variable used in this method, namely α, is assigned a value between 0 and 1 according to how much one objective is favored over the others. The objective function employed here to investigate the performance of four metaheuristic algorithms for FS in medical data is defined as follows:

$$f = \alpha^{*}\gamma_{R}(D) + (1 - \alpha)^{*}\frac{|S|}{|N1|} \qquad (7.11)$$

where $\gamma_{R}(D)$ indicates the classification error rate that was fed back from a machine learning algorithm under the holdout approach for dividing the dataset into testing and training datasets [13,14], $|S|$ is the number of selected features, and $|N1|$ refers to the overall number of features in the utilized dataset. This objective function is composed of two objectives: the first objective is maximizing the classification accuracy and the second objective is minimizing the selected features. The most important objective is maximizing the classification accuracy, so this objective is favored by increasing the value of the weighting variable.

Step 3: S-shaped and V-shaped transformation functions

The vast majority of presented metaheuristic algorithms are intended to deal with continuous problems; nevertheless, most algorithms are inapplicable when it comes to tackling binary problems [8]. As a result, two well-known families of transfer functions, the S-shaped and the V-shaped families, which are mathematically provided in Table 7.2, have been

Table 7.2 Mathematical model of S-shaped and V-shaped.

S-shaped	V-shaped
S1 $F(\vec{x}) = \frac{1}{1+e^{-a}}$	V1 $F(\vec{x}) = \left|\frac{2}{\pi}\arctan\left(\frac{\pi}{2}a\right)\right|$
S2 $F(\vec{x}) = \frac{1}{1+e^{-2^{*}a}}$	V2 $F(\vec{x}) = \left|\tanh(a)\right|$
S3 $F(\vec{x}) = \frac{1}{1+e^{-\frac{a}{2}}}$	V3 $F(\vec{x}) = \left|\frac{a}{\sqrt{1+a^{2}}}\right|$
S4 $F(\vec{x}) = \frac{1}{1+e^{-\frac{a}{3}}}$	V4 $F(\vec{x}) = \left|\text{erf}\left(\frac{\sqrt{\pi}}{2}a\right)\right|$

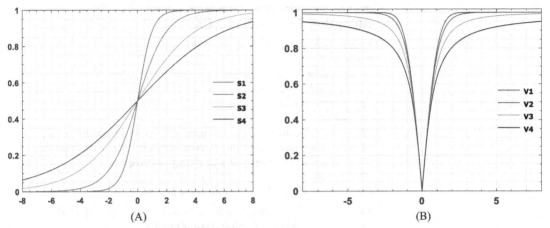

Figure 7.5 (A) S-shaped and (B) V-shaped transformation functions.

developed in order to normalize the continuous solutions between 0 and 1. Afterward, these normalized solutions will be converted, in accordance with Eq. (7.12), to the values 0 and 1 to be suitable for binary problems. The difference between transfer functions with an S-shaped and a V-shaped profile is depicted in Fig. 7.5. These transfer functions, in conjunction with the classical investigated algorithms, are utilized to present binary variants called BNOA, BTLBO, BLSO, and BDE, which can be utilized for the purpose of addressing binary optimization problems. As an illustrative example, Algorithm 7.1 presents the steps of adapting NOA to binary optimization problems. Fig. 7.6 presents the flowchart of adapting metaheuristics for the FS problem.

$$\vec{x}_{\text{bin}}(\vec{x}) = \begin{cases} 1 & \text{if } F(\vec{x}) \geq r \text{ and} \\ 0 & \text{otherwise} \end{cases} \qquad (7.12)$$

7.4   Experiment settings

In this section, we will practically investigate the performance of four studied metaheuristic algorithms for selecting the most relevant features in medical data. These data include five medical datasets, namely, heart-statlog, diabetes, spect, spectIF, and sonar, taken from the UCI repository. All the studied algorithms are executed 25 independent times, and their performance is analyzed using three different metrics, precision, recall, and

Algorithm 7.1 Steps of NOA

Input: population size N, $\vec{L}$, $\vec{U}$, and T_{max};
Output: $\vec{X}_{best}^{t}$
1. Initialize N solutions using Eq. (1.2);
2. Evaluation and estimation of the best-so-far solution.
3. $t = 1$; //the current evaluation//
4. **while** ($t < T_{max}$)
5. σ and σ_1: two numbers chosen at random between 0 and 1.
6. φ is a numerical value selected randomly between 0 and 1.
7.   **If** $\sigma < \sigma_1$ //* ***Foraging and storage strategy****//
8.   **for** $i = 1:N$
9.   **if** $\varphi < P_{a_1}$ /* **Exploration phase1***/
10.   Updating $\vec{X}_i^{t+1}$ using Eq. (**1.3**) and Eq. (**1.19**)
11.   **else** /*Exploitation phase1*/
12.   Updating $\vec{X}_i^{t+1}$ using Eq. (**1.5**) and Eq. (**1.19**)
13.   **end if**
14.   Apply Eq. (7.11) to transform $\vec{X}_i^{t+1}$ into $\vec{X}_i^{cb}$
15.   Compute the objective value: $f(\vec{X}_i^{cb})$
16.   Update the best-so-far $\overrightarrow{X_{best}^b}$, and best binary local solution $\overrightarrow{X_i^b}$
17. $t = t + 1$
18.   **end for**
19.   **else** //* ***Cache-search and recovery strategy*** *//
20.   Compute RP matrix by Eqs. (**1.8**), (**1.9**) and (**1.10**).
21.   **for** $i = 1:N$
22.   **if** $\phi < P_{a_2}$ /*Exploitation phase2*/
23.   Updating $\vec{X}_i^{t+1}$ using Eq. (**1.17**) and Eq. (**1.19**)
24.   **else** /*Exploration phase2*/
25.   Updating $\vec{X}_i^{t+1}$ using Eq. (**1.18**) and Eq. (**1.19**)
26.   **end if**
27.   Apply Eq. (7.12) to transform $\vec{X}_i^{t+1}$ into $\vec{X}_i^{cb}$
28.   Compute the objective value: $f(\vec{X}_i^{cb})$
29.   Update the best-so-far $\overrightarrow{X_{best}^b}$, and best binary local solution $\overrightarrow{X_i^b}$
30.   **end for**
31. **end while**

F-value, to reveal the effectiveness of each algorithm. Three different ML techniques, namely, linear discriminant analysis (LDA), naive Bayes (NB), and K-nearest neighbor (KNN), are employed with the studied metaheuristics to investigate the effectiveness of various subsets of features on the performance of various ML classifiers. All the conducted experiments were run using a computer with 32 gigabytes of random access memory, a Core i7 processor, and a Windows 10 operating system. The

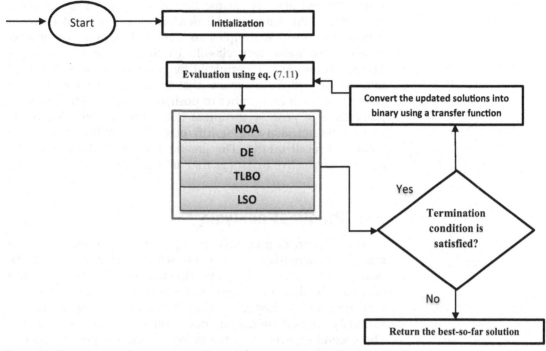

Figure 7.6 Flowchart of adapting metaheuristics for the feature selection problem.

algorithms were implemented using MATLAB R2019a under a maximum number of iterations and a population size of 40 and 30, respectively.

7.5 Performance metrics

In this chapter, three performance metrics are used to evaluate the quality of the features selected by each metaheuristic. These metrics are precision, recall, and F-value. The fitness metric has been described before in detail, but, in this section, both precision and recall are described to show their importance. Precision and recall are used to observe the quality of the ML models for predicting the correct classification, the mathematical model of these metrics is as follows:

$$\text{Precision} = \frac{\text{TP}}{\text{TP} + \text{FP}} \tag{7.13}$$

$$\text{Recall} = \frac{\text{TP}}{\text{TP} + \text{FN}} \tag{7.14}$$

where TP and FN refer to the true positive and false negative, respectively. Precision can be defined as the ratio of correctly categorized positive samples to the total number of positive samples that have been classified either correctly or wrongly. The recall metric is determined by computing the ratio of the number of positive instances that were correctly identified as positive to the total number of positive instances. This gives the percentage of positive instances that were correctly identified. The model's capacity to identify positive instances is evaluated using the recall metric. The greater the recall, the greater the number of positive instances that are classified.

7.6 Practical analysis

This section is presented to report the performance of the studied metaheuristics and show which one can achieve the near-optimal subset. Two experiments are performed in this chapter. The first one is used to investigate the performance of V-shaped and S-shaped transfer functions for converting the variously studied metaheuristics from continuous to discrete. The second experiment aims to investigate the performance of variously studied metaheuristics under different ML models to show whether the same subsets have similar results with different ML models or not.

In the first experiment, to observe the performance of various transfer functions, all algorithms with each transfer function have been executed 25 independent times, and the average F-values for each algorithm is computed and presented in Fig. 7.7. This figure illustrates that the performance of the metaheuristic algorithms significantly relies on the selected transfer function. For example, BLSO has strong performance with the transfer function S4, and both BDE and BTLBO have strong performance under S2, while the performance of BNOA is significantly improved when using V2. The studied metaheuristics with these highly effective transfer functions are employed in the next experiment to show their performance with various ML models.

In the second experiment, three different ML models are employed to observe the quality of the features selected by each algorithm. Starting with the first ML technique, known as LDA, all algorithms have been executed 25 independent times, and the accuracy of the subsets of features obtained within these runs is computed using this ML technique and reported in Fig. 7.8. This figure illustrates that the performance of BNOA was better in terms of the F-value, while the performance of DE

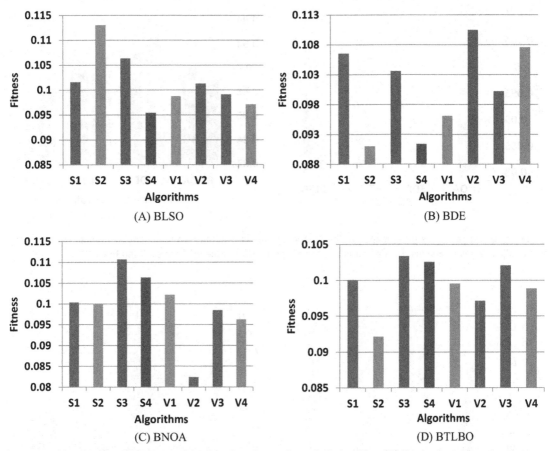

Figure 7.7 Observation of various transfer functions for each studied algorithm: (A) The performance of various transfer functions for BLSO; (B) The performance of various transfer functions for BDE; (C) The performance of various transfer functions for BNOA; (D) The performance of various transfer functions for BTLBO.

was maximized for both precision and recall. To display the performance under the NB technique, Fig. 7.9 is presented to compute the average of the performance metrics obtained by each algorithm on all used datasets within 25 independent times. From this figure, BNOA could come in the first rank for all used performance metrics, followed by DE as the second-best one, while BLSO is considered the worst-performing algorithm. To further investigate the performance of the metaheuristics, another ML model, known as the KNN, is used. Under this ML model, which is used to compute the classification accuracy of each subset of features, all algorithms are also executed 25 independent times, and the average values for various

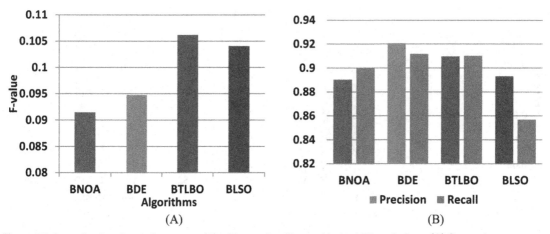

Figure 7.8 Investigating the performance of the binary algorithms with the LDA technique: (A) Comparison among algorithms in terms of F-value; (B) Comparison among algorithms in terms of Precision and Recall.

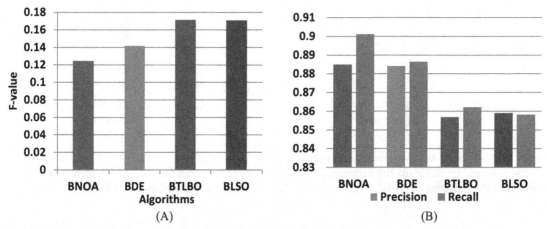

Figure 7.9 Investigating the performance of the binary algorithms with the NB technique: (A) Comparison among algorithms in terms of F-value; (B) Comparison among algorithms in terms of Precision and Recall.

performance metrics are reported in Fig. 7.10. According to this figure, BTLBO could show the best performance for the three used performance metrics, followed by BDE as the second-best one, while BNOA comes in at the last rank. Consequently, we can say that the performance of metaheuristic algorithms differs according to the ML technique used to compute the classification accuracy. For example, when using the LDA, BNOA could perform better for F-value, while BDE could perform

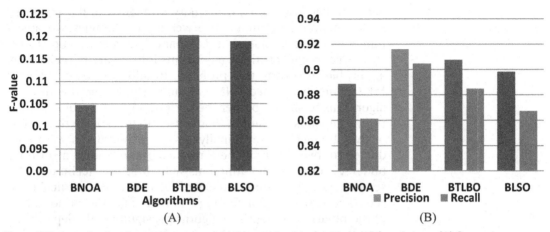

Figure 7.10 Investigating the performance of the binary algorithms with the LDA technique: (A) Comparison among algorithms in terms of F-value; (B) Comparison among algorithms in terms of Precision and Recall.

better for the other metrics. Meanwhile, when employing the NB technique, BNOA could be the best for all performance metrics. Under the last ML technique, BDE could be the best in terms of all performance metrics. This affirms that the performance of the proposed binary technique is significantly affected by the used ML model.

7.7   Chapter summary

The FS is considered a crucial preprocessing step for ML techniques when dealing with several applications, like those in the medical field. This step is used to preprocess the dataset to get rid of any noisy, redundant, or useless features that could make the ML models less accurate and useful. Several techniques were proposed for the FS, which falls into three categories, filter-based, wrapper-based, and embedded. The most widely used techniques due to their high accuracy are the wrapper-based techniques. These techniques employ an ML model to compute the accuracy of the obtained subset of features. The metaheuristic algorithms are considered wrapper-based techniques because they could be guided using the accuracy obtained by the ML technique. In this chapter, we review some of the filter-based techniques and wrapper-based techniques. Then, we employed four different metaheuristics, named BNOA, BLSO, BTLBO, and BDE, to investigate their performance in finding the near-optimal subset of features in the medical datasets. Because the FS is a binary problem and the employed algorithms are continuous, two well-known families of transfer functions called V-shaped and S-shaped transfer functions were employed to convert these algorithms into binary to make them applicable to solving this problem. In addition, three different ML techniques, named KNN, NB, and LDA, are used with these algorithms to show whether the performance of the binary algorithms depends on the ML model used to investigate the quality of the obtained subset. Finally, several experiments were conducted to investigate the performance of the studied algorithms under various transfer functions and three ML techniques for searching for the optimal subset of features in the medical datasets. The experimental findings showed that the performance of the binary metaheuristic algorithms significantly depends on the ML model and the used transfer function.

References

[1] E. Momanyi, D. Segera, A master-slave binary grey wolf optimizer for optimal feature selection in biomedical data classification, BioMed Research International 2021 (2021) 5556941.

[2] S. Nagpal, S. Arora, S. Dey, Feature selection using gravitational search algorithm for biomedical data, Procedia Computer Science 115 (2017) 258–265.

[3] J. Tang, et al., Feature selection for classification: a review, in: J. Tang, S. Alelyani, H. Liu (Eds.), Data Classification: Algorithms and Applications, CRC Press, 2014, p. 37.

[4] J. Miao, L. Niu, A survey on feature selection, Procedia Computer Science 91 (2016) 919–926.

[5] I.S. Thaseen, C.A. Kumar, Intrusion detection model using fusion of chi-square feature selection and multi class SVM, Journal of King Saud University-Computer and Information Sciences 29 (4) (2017) 462–472.

[6] Q. Gu, Z. Li, J. Han, Generalized Fisher score for feature selection, arXiv preprint, 2012.

[7] I. Guyon, A. Elisseeff, An introduction to variable and feature selection, Journal of Machine Learning Research 3 (2003) 1157–1182.

[8] M. Abdel-Basset, et al., Medical Feature Selection Approach Based on Generalized Normal Distribution Algorithm, 2021.

[9] Z.M. Elgamal, et al., An improved Harris Hawks optimization algorithm with simulated annealing for feature selection in the medical field, IEEE Access 8 (2020) 186638–186652.

[10] M.H. Nadimi-Shahraki, et al., B-MFO: a binary moth-flame optimization for feature selection from medical datasets, Computers 10 (11) (2021) 136.

[11] M.H. Nadimi-Shahraki, H. Zamani, S. Mirjalili, Enhanced whale optimization algorithm for medical feature selection: a COVID-19 case study, Computers in Biology and Medicine 148 (2022) 105858.

[12] T. Bezdan, et al., Feature selection by hybrid brain storm optimization algorithm for COVID-19 classification, Journal of Computational Biology 29 (6) (2022) 515−529.

[13] S. Yadav, S. Shukla, Analysis of k-fold cross-validation over hold-out validation on colossal datasets for quality classification, in: Proceedings of the 2016 IEEE Sixth International Conference on Advanced Computing (IACC), 2016.

[14] L.E. Peterson, K-nearest neighbor, Scholarpedia 4 (2) (2009) 1883.

Machine learning and improved multiobjective binary generalized normal distribution optimization in feature selection for cancer classification

8.1   Introduction

The development of the technology known as DNA microarrays has had a substantial effect on the research conducted in the field of biology. Researchers are able to conduct a simultaneous examination of thousands of genes, which allows them to investigate the biological behavior of these genes and determine their significance in the operation of cells. In addition, the use of microarray technology for the screening of multiple genomic profiles at the same time offers profound insights into a variety of genetic differences and alterations. It is helpful in the early diagnosis of a wide variety of serious illnesses including cancer. Over the course of the past two decades, a large number of researchers have helped advance oncological research by providing numerous benchmark microarray databases for a variety of tumor types [1]. The cancer databases include thousands of genes, each of which corresponds to a different sample. These datasets are used as benchmarks for a broad variety of different approaches that have been proposed for cancer classification. However, these datasets have a small number of samples, a large number of features, and imbalance distributions, which make them unsuitable in their current form for training the machine learning (ML) and deep learning models [2]. Therefore the scientists have sought to solve this challenge by applying the feature selection methods to search for the most associated features with the diseases in order to achieve two objectives:

Metaheuristics Algorithms for Medical Applications. DOI: https://doi.org/10.1016/B978-0-443-13314-5.00011-4

minimizing the number of genes to save the computational cost and maximizing the classification accuracy [2]. As mentioned in Chapter 7, the feature selection techniques are divided into three classes: *filter-based, wrapper-based,* and *embedded-based.* The *wrapper-based technique* is the most common method due to its simplicity and high accuracy [3]. However, it requires high-computational costs because it uses a ML model with optimization techniques to observe the quality of each subset of features.

The feature selection problem is generally classified into multiobjective because it has two objectives in conflicts that have to be simultaneously minimized. The first objective aims at minimizing the number of selected features as small as possible to avoid the curse of dimensionality for saving the computational cost, whereas the second objective is based on maximizing the classification accuracy. Therefore the applied optimization technique must search for the features that could achieve these two objectives together. However, the majority of the wrapper-based techniques deal with this problem as a single objective by improving some objectives on the account of others. In general, there are two approaches proposed in the literature to deal with multiobjective problems: prior-based and posterior-based [4]. The former has treated the multiobjective problem as a singular objective by utilizing weighted objective functions. In contrast, the latter aims to identify the most effective solutions, namely, nondominated solutions, which could simultaneously optimize at least one objective without deteriorating the others. Several works in the literature dealt with feature selection as a multiobjective optimization problem. For example, the spotted hyena optimizer is combined with the salp swarm algorithm to come up with a new variant with strong features that can pick the near-optimal features for classifying cancer [2]. The Pareto optimality theory was used with this hybrid algorithm to find a set of nondominated solutions that represent the solutions to this problem. This was done to improve both the number of features and the accuracy of classification.

This chapter starts with describing the concept and terminology of the multiobjective optimization problems. Then, it overviews the classical generalized distribution algorithm used to solve the multiobjective feature selection problem. Also, the main steps required to adapt the metaheuristics for this problem are listed and discussed. Afterward, some experiments are conducted to compare the performance of some metaheuristics with various ML techniques. Finally, the chapter summary is discussed.

8.2 Background

8.2.1 Multiobjective optimization

The multiobjective problems are those that have two or three objectives in conflict and need to be simultaneously optimized to determine the desired solutions for the decision makers. If these problems involve more than three objectives, they are called many-objective problems. The feature selection problem is considered a multiobjective problem because it involves only two objectives that have to be accurately optimized to reach the near subset of features, which could minimize the training time and maximize the classification accuracy in the field of ML and data mining. Generally, the following model mathematically formulates the multiobjective problems:

$$\text{Minimize } J\left(\vec{X_i}\right) = \left\{J_1\left(\vec{X_i}\right), J_2\left(\vec{X_i}\right), J_3\left(\vec{X_i}\right), J_4\left(\vec{X_i}\right), \ldots, J_m\left(\vec{X_i}\right)\right\}, m \geq 2 \tag{8.1}$$

$$\text{Subject to } nq_i\left(\vec{X_i}\right) \geq 0, i = 1, 2, \ldots, z \tag{8.2}$$

$$q_i\left(\vec{X_i}\right) = 0, i = 1, 2, \ldots, k \tag{8.3}$$

$$\vec{L} \leq \vec{X_i} \leq \vec{U}, i = 1, 2, \ldots, n \tag{8.4}$$

where L is the number of objectives to be simultaneously optimized. The multiobjective problems might involve some constraints that have to be satisfied during the optimization process. These constraints are divided into two categories: equality and inequality constraints. In the previous mathematical model, the inequality constraints are represented by nq, the number of inequality constraints is presented by the variable z, the equality constraints are presented by q, and the number of equality constraints is represented by the variable k. In addition, each solution $\vec{X_i}$ must be ranged within the lower bound $\vec{L}$ and the upper bound $\vec{U}$ for each decision variable in the optimization problem.

Selecting the most suitable solution for a single-objective problem is a straightforward process, as it involves the consideration of a solitary objective function. In the case of a minimization problem, solution A is deemed superior and selected as the optimal solution only if it attains a fitness value lower than that of solution B. However, problems with multiple objectives are hard to be easily tackled due to the presence of several objectives that have to be simultaneously optimized to find a solution. To solve these problems, the Pareto optimality theory is applied to extract the solutions that could minimize at least one objective without deteriorating the others, as shown in Fig. 8.1. These solutions are known as nondominated solutions. From Fig. 8.1, the dominant relationship between solution $\vec{X}_2$ and solution $\vec{X}_1$ can be inferred, as the former exhibits superior performance in two objectives and equivalent performance in the other objective. In academic discourse, it is commonly asserted that a solution is considered nondominated if it has superior performance in at least one of the objective functions while exhibiting equivalent values across the rest of the objectives. True Pareto-optimal solutions are defined as those that remain unaffected by the dominance of any other potential solution throughout the entire search space. The collection of Pareto-optimal solutions in the objective space is referred to as an efficient front [4].

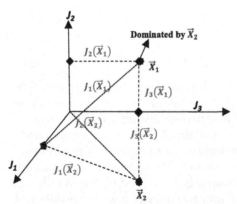

Figure 8.1 An illustrative example for the nondominated solutions.

8.2.2 Generalized normal distribution optimization

A new population-based optimization algorithm [5] known as generalized normal distribution optimization (GNDO) was recently suggested for the purpose of tackling the parameter estimation of photovoltaic models. This algorithm draws its motivation from the normal distribution theory, and its structure is predicated on two primary phases: exploitation and exploration. During the exploration phase, GNDO searches the entire search space to pinpoint the most promising regions, which may contain the best possible solution. The latter concentrates on this region to get to the best possible solution. These two phases of GNDO are broken down in great detail in the following paragraphs.

Phase 1: local exploitation

In this phase, GNDO is designed to exploit the promising region for searching for the near-optimal solution inside it. This region is estimated by computing the mean of three solutions, μ_i, using Eq. (8.6); these solutions are the following:

- The best solution achieved yet X^*.
- The ith solution X_i^t.
- The mean M of the whole population computed using Eq. (8.7).

Following that, GNDO during the optimization process exploits the solutions in these regions by generating a step size using Eq. (8.8) to be added to μ_i, as formulated in Eq. (8.5), for generating a new trial vector T_i^t, representing a new candidate solution to the optimization problems. This trial solution T_i^t will be compared to the present solution X_i^t to determine its efficacy, and if it is superior, it will be used in the next iteration instead of the current solution.

$$T_i^t = \mu_i + \delta_i \times \eta, \forall i = 1{:}N \tag{8.5}$$

$$\mu_i = (\vec{X}_i^{\,t} + \vec{X}^* + M)/3.0 \tag{8.6}$$

$$M = \frac{\sum_{i=1}^{N} X_i^{\,t}}{N} \tag{8.7}$$

$$\delta_i = \sqrt{\frac{1}{3}\left[(\vec{X}_i^{\,t} - \mu)^2 + (\vec{X}^{\,*} - \mu)^2 + (M - \mu)^2\right]} \tag{8.8}$$

η that is mathematically modeled in Eq. (8.9) stands for the penalty factor.

$$\eta = \begin{cases} \sqrt{-\log(\lambda_1)} \times \cos(2\pi\lambda_2), r_1 \leq r_2 \\ \sqrt{-\log(\lambda_1)} \times \cos(2\pi\lambda_2 + \pi), r_1 > r_2 \end{cases} \qquad (8.9)$$

r_1, r_2, λ_1, and λ_2 are numerical values chosen at random according to the normal distribution between 0 and 1.

Phase 2: global exploration

The optimization problem's search space will be thoroughly investigated in this phase to identify the most promising area that might contain the best answer. In this phase, GNDO generates the candidate solution according to the following formula:

$$T_i^t = X_i^t + \beta \times (|\lambda_3| \times v_1) + (1 - \beta) \times (|\lambda_4| \times v_2) \qquad (8.10)$$

λ_3 and λ_4 are numerical values chosen at random according to the normal distribution, and β is a numerical value chosen at random at the interval of 0 and 1. v_1 and v_2 are two step sizes computed according to the following formula:

$$v_1 = \begin{cases} X_i^t - X_{p1}^t, & \text{if } f(X_i^t) \leq f(X_{p1}^t) \\ X_{p1}^t - X_i^t, & \text{Otherwise} \end{cases} \qquad (8.11)$$

$$v_2 = \begin{cases} X_{p2}^t - X_{p3}^t, & \text{if } f(X_{p2}^t) \leq f(X_{p3}^t) \\ X_{p3}^t - X_{p2}^t, & \text{Otherwise} \end{cases} \qquad (8.12)$$

where $p1, p2,$ and $p3$ are the indices of three solutions selected at random from the current population, where those indices are different from each other and from the ith solution. The local and global search is randomly exchanged during the optimization process in an attempt to avoid local minima in addition to accelerating the convergence speed in the hope that the randomization process might probably achieve the equilibrium between these stages.

8.3 Multiobjective improved binary GNDO

In this chapter, we propose a new multiobjective improved binary GNDO for choosing the most important genes that have a high association with cancer diseases. This algorithm is called MIGNDO. Similar to the other metaheuristics-based feature selection techniques, the proposed MIGNDO starts with initializing randomly a number of the solutions with 0 to represent the unselected feature and 1 to indicate the selected feature. Then, two ML techniques are employed with the proposed algorithm to evaluate the quality of these solutions based on two objectives. The first one is based on minimizing the number of selected genes to significantly reduce the computational cost and is computed according to the following formula:

$$\text{Minimize } J_1 = \frac{|S|}{|N1|} \qquad (8.13)$$

where $|S|$ represents the selected number of genes/features and $|N1|$ is the overall number of genes in the input dataset. The second objective aims to maximize the accuracy of cancer classification. The mathematical model of this objective is as follows:

$$\text{Minimize } J_2 = 1 - \gamma \qquad (8.14)$$

where γ is the classification accuracy returned by the k-nearest neighbors (KNN) algorithm. After that, the Pareto optimality theory is applied to compare these solutions for determining the nondominated solutions and add them to an archive (Arc) to be preserved within the optimization process. Finally, the optimization process of GNDO is fired to update the initialized solutions in an attempt to search for better solutions. Generally, the obtained solutions by the standard metaheuristics involve continuous values that could not be applied to the feature selection problem. Therefore the transfer function, also referred to as the transformation function, is employed with these algorithms to normalize these continuous values within 0 and 1, which are then converted into 0 and 1 using the randomization process. There are several transfer functions proposed in the literature; the most common functions belong to the V-shaped and S-shaped families. All of them were studied in Chapter 7 to illustrate their effectiveness on the performance of the metaheuristic algorithms. In this chapter, we used the V2 transfer function to be integrated with the GNDO for proposing a multiobjective binary variant of GNDO, namely MGNDO. The V2 transfer function was selected due to its strong performance discussed before. In brief, the mathematical model of this transfer function is as follows:

$$F(\vec{X}) = \left| \tanh\left(\vec{X}\right) \right| \qquad (8.15)$$

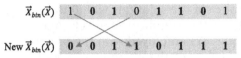

Figure 8.2 Simulation of the swap operator.

This function takes the continuous solution $\vec{X}$ as input and normalize it between 0 and 1. This normalized solution is converted into 0 and 1 using the following formula that employs a random vector $\overrightarrow{rand}$ of the same length of the normalized vector to be compared with each other for generating a binary vector $\vec{X}_{bin}$:

$$\vec{X}_{\text{bin}}(\vec{X}) = \begin{cases} 1 & \text{if } F\left(\vec{X}\right) \geq \overrightarrow{rand} \\ 0 & \text{Otherwise} \end{cases} \tag{8.16}$$

This binary vector is evaluated using the previously mentioned objective functions. The same steps are applied for all the continuous solutions generated by the classical GNDO. Afterward, the objective values of these solutions are compared under the Pareto optimality to extract the nondominated solutions from the current solutions. Each nondominated solution of these is compared to the solutions in the archive to determine whether it is dominated by any solution there. If so, it will be removed; otherwise, it will be added to the archive. Unfortunately, the MGNDO suffers from the low diversity inside the population which makes it unable to explore several regions within the search space that might involve the near-optimal solution. Therefore it is integrated with a swap operator that is applied to the obtained binary solution to select two distinct positions and swap them to generate a new different binary solution. Broadly speaking, this operator randomly selects a position with a value of 0 and another with a value of 1 and exchanges them to generate a new solution, which might be better than the current solution. Fig. 8.2 presents the concept of the swap operator. In this figure, we can see that two positions with distinct values in the current binary solution $\vec{X}_{\text{bin}}(\vec{X})$ are randomly selected. These two positions are exchanged in the new solution, while the other positions are set in the same order as found in $\vec{X}_{\text{bin}}(\vec{X})$. Finally, this operator is effectively integrated with MGNDO to generate an improved variant called MIGNDO. The pseudocode of this improved variant is listed in Algorithm 8.1.

Algorithm 8.1 MIGNDO

1. Input: N, t_{max}
2. t = 0 %% Current iteration
3. Initialize randomly N solutions with 0 (indicating the unselected genes) and 1 (distinguishing the selected genes)
4. Compute the objective value of each solution for each objective function
5. Compare each solution using the Pareto optimality and add the nondominated solutions to arc
6. **While** t < t_{max}
7.   **For** i = 1:N
8.   α: a numerical value chosen at random in the interval (0, 1)
9.   If α > 0.5
10.   Compute **M** using Eq. (8.7)
11.   Compute $\delta_i, \mu_i,$ and η
12.   Compute $T_i{}^t$ using Eq. (8.9).
13.   Normalize the trial solution using V2 (Eq. (8.15))
14.   Compute the binary vector $\vec{X}_{bin}$ using Eq. (8.16)
15.   Compute the objectives for $\vec{X}_{bin}$
16.   Adding $\vec{X}_{bin}$ to arc if it is not dominated
17.   Removing from Arc any solution dominated by $\vec{X}_{bin}$
18.   **If** $J\left(\vec{X}_{bin}\right)$ dominates $J(bX_i{}^t)$
19. $X_i{}^t = T_i{}^t$
20.   **End If**
21.   **Else**
22.   Compute $T_i{}^t$ according to Eq. (8.10).
23.   Normalize the trial solution using V2 [Eq. (8.15)]
24.   Compute the binary vector $\vec{X}_{bin}$ using [Eq. (8.16)]
25.   Compute the objectives for $\vec{X}_{bin}$
26.   Adding $\vec{X}_{bin}$ to arc if it is not dominated
27.   Removing from Arc any solution dominated by $\vec{X}_{bin}$
28.   **If** $J\left(\vec{X}_{bin}\right)$ dominates $J(bX_i{}^t)$
29. $X_i{}^t = T_i{}^t$
30.   **End If**
31.   Applying the swap operator to $\vec{X}_{bin}$ to generate $n\vec{X}_{bin}$
32.   Compute the objectives for $n\vec{X}_{bin}$
33.   Adding $n\vec{X}_{bin}$ to Arc if it is not dominated
34.   Removing from Arc any solution dominated by $n\vec{X}_{bin}$
35.   **End If**
36.   **End For**
37. **End while**

8.4 Practical analysis

In this chapter, the efficacy of the multiobjective improved GNDO (MIGNDO) is evaluated in comparison to three other metaheuristic algorithms, namely, multiobjective differential evolution (MDE), multiobjective teaching-learning-based optimization (MTLBO), and MGNDO. These algorithms are employed with two different ML techniques, namely, support vector machine (SVM) and KNN, to observe their stability when using different ML models. All these algorithms are assessed in terms of the number of selected genes or features (SF) and the classification accuracy for six distinct microarray datasets. These datasets are taken from http://csse.szu.edu.cn/staff/zhuzx/Datasets.html, and their characteristics are listed in Table 8.1. The definition of classifier accuracy pertains to the proportion of accurately classified samples relative to the overall number of samples:

$$\text{Accuracy}(\%) = \frac{C}{A}*100 \tag{8.17}$$

where the variable C denotes the number of correctly classified samples, while the variable A represents the overall number of samples in the used datasets. The evaluation of prediction accuracy for each subset was conducted through the utilization of two commonly employed classifiers, specifically SVM and KNN. The evaluation of each classifier is based on the training and testing samples. The population size (N) and the maximum number of iterations are limited to 20 and 30, respectively, for the proposed MIGNDO and the other compared algorithms to ensure a fair comparison. Due to the stochastic characteristic of these algorithms, they are executed 30 independent times to carefully investigate their performance under different seeds. All conducted experiments are run on a device with the following

Table 8.1 Characteristics of employed microarray datasets.

Id	Dataset	Features	Samples	Class	ID	Dataset	Features	Samples	Class
1	Colon tumor	2,000	60	2	4	Central nervous system	7,129	60	2
2	Small-blue-round-cell tumor	2,308	83	4	5	Breast cancer	24,481	97	2
3	Ovarian cancer	15,154	253	2	6	Lung cancer	12,533	181	2

characteristics: 32 gigabytes of random access memory, a Core i7 processor, and Windows 10 operating system. The algorithms are implemented using MATLAB R2019a.

To observe the effectiveness of the proposed MIGNDO with the KNN technique, it was executed 30 independent times on the considered datasets, and the average values for the number of selected genes and the classification accuracy were computed and reported in Fig. 8.3. This figure shows that MIGNDO could fulfill better classification accuracy with a value of 88.6, followed by MDE as the second best one with a value of 85.1, while the classical MGNDO is the worst performing one. Regarding the number of selected genes, which is considered to investigate the ability of the proposed MIGNDO to minimize the computational cost, it is computed and presented in the same figure. This figure shows that MIGNDO could reach the lowest number of selected genes relative to all the compared algorithms.

To investigate the performance of MIGNDO over another ML technique, specifically the SVM technique, it was run on the considered datasets 30 times independently, and the average values for the number of selected genes and the classification accuracy were calculated and reported in Fig. 8.4. From what can be seen in this figure, MIGNDO achieves the highest classification accuracy (83.24), followed by MDE (81.60), and the least effective method is the classical MGNDO (80.10). This figure also includes computation and presentation of the number of chosen genes that is used in the investigation of the proposed MIGNDO's capacity to reduce the computational time and effort needed by ML during the training process. This

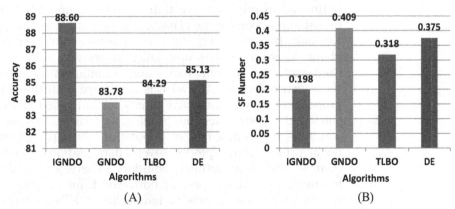

Figure 8.3 Comparison among multiobjective algorithms with KNN in terms of accuracy and SF number: (A) Comparison in terms of accuracy; (B) Comparison in terms of SF number.

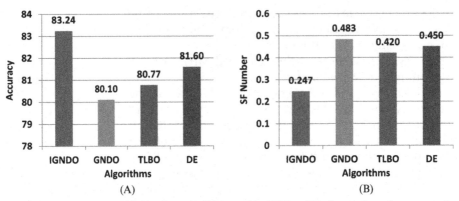

Figure 8.4 Comparison among multiobjective algorithms with SVM : (A) Comparison in terms of accuracy; (B) Comparison in terms of SF number.

figure demonstrates that of all the compared algorithms, MIGNDO achieved the fewest chosen genes. Since MIGNDO with both SVM and KNN could reach the smallest number of genes that are highly correlated with the cancer classification, it is considered a strong alternative algorithm to be employed with the ML for the cancer classification problem.

8.5 Chapter summary

Selecting the optimal genes from the microarray datasets to accurately classify cancer diseases is considered a crucial problem, referred to as gene selection or feature selection. However, this problem includes two objectives that have to be accurately optimized to minimize the training time required by each ML model and maximize the classification accuracy. In this chapter, we start by describing the multiobjective optimization problems. Then, the Pareto optimality theory was discussed to be used with the metaheuristics for simultaneously optimizing those two objectives. GNDO was combined with this theory to propose a new multiobjective binary variant called MGNDO for solving the gene selection problem. However, this algorithm was suffering from a lack of population diversity that prevents the algorithm from exploring several permutations, which might involve the near-optimal solution. Therefore MGNDO is improved by a swap operator borrowed from the genetic algorithms to propose a new variant called MIGNDO with better exploration capability. The efficacy of MIGNDO is observed by comparison to three other metaheuristic algorithms, namely,

MDE, MTLBO, and MGNDO. These algorithms are employed with two different ML techniques, namely, SVM and KNN, to observe their stability when using different ML models. All these algorithms are assessed in terms of the number of selected genes and the classification accuracy for six distinct microarray datasets. The experimental results elaborate on the efficacy of MIGNDO in comparison to the others.

References

[1] A. Sharma, R. Rani, C-HMOSHSSA: gene selection for cancer classification using multi-objective meta-heuristic and machine learning methods, Computer Methods and Programs in Biomedicine 178 (2019) 219−235.

[2] X. Deng, et al., Hybrid gene selection approach using XGBoost and multi-objective genetic algorithm for cancer classification, Medical & Biological Engineering & Computing 60 (3) (2022) 663−681.

[3] T.M. Le, et al., A novel wrapper−based feature selection for early diabetes prediction enhanced with a metaheuristic, IEEE Access 9 (2020) 7869−7884.

[4] M. Abdel-Basset, R. Mohamed, S. Mirjalili, A novel whale optimization algorithm integrated with Nelder−Mead simplex for multi-objective optimization problems, Knowledge-Based Systems 212 (2021) 106619.

[5] Y. Zhang, Z. Jin, S. Mirjalili, Generalized normal distribution optimization and its applications in parameter extraction of photovoltaic models, Energy Conversion and Management 224 (2020) 113301.

9

Metaheuristics for assisting the deep neural network in classifying the chest X-ray images infected with COVID-19

9.1   Introduction

There is a type of virus known as a coronavirus that attacks the respiratory system of humans. It is known as "corona" because of the "crown-like spikes" that cover its surface. This virus has been linked to a number of different respiratory illnesses [1]. In 1937, the coronavirus was found for the first time in birds. In 1960, researchers detected a form of coronavirus in the human nose. This discovery was made while they were studying the common cold. This particular type of corona is associated with a rather minor disease that manifests itself most frequently during the winter [1]. On December 1, 2019 [1], COVID-19 was found for the first time in Wuhan, China. The virus was originally found in an animal that had contracted a common infectious ailment. Many experts think that bats were the original hosts of COVID-19 and that the virus was transmitted from them to other animals and people. Although this has not been verified, researchers are still looking into its origin and dissemination [1]. Over the past two decades, the virus has changed names, first being called severe acute respiratory syndrome coronavirus in 2002 and then Middle East respiratory syndrome in 2012. The most recent strain of this virus, which was identified in Wuhan, is termed the 2019 coronavirus (2019-nCoV). This virus has the potential to cause life-threatening pneumonia [1].

The rapid spread of COVID-19 has led to the deaths of a significant number of people all across the world. This virus causes a variety of symptoms, including aches and pains in the muscles, a headache, difficulty breathing, a cough, and fever [2]. Other symptoms, such as fatigue, pains, and a loss of taste

Metaheuristics Algorithms for Medical Applications. DOI: https://doi.org/10.1016/B978-0-443-13314-5.00010-2

and smell, have also been reported by a few of the patients [3]. Despite that, several infected persons had not any symptoms [3]. This posed a challenge in identifying the COVID-19 infection. To stop the spread of the disease, numerous nations have declared a state of emergency. However, effective patient screening is still required before the disease may be treated. It is generally agreed that real-time–polymerase chain reaction (RT-PCR) is the best method for detecting COVID-19. The time it takes to get results can range from an hour to 2 days. However, because kits were not readily available, and because RT-PCR had a poor level of sensitivity, imaging approaches that utilized radiography arose as an additional choice for COVID-19 identification [3]. Computed tomography (CT) and chest X-rays scans are two of the most used techniques of radiography. However, X-rays are favored over CT because they are more widely available and have a smaller radiation impact on patients [4]. The manual examination of X-rays by radiological specialists takes a significant amount of time and can result in inaccurate reports [3]. Automatic X-ray analysis utilizing machine/deep learning (DL) models is the key to solving this problem. Recent years have seen an uptick in the use of DL methods in the field of medical imaging for illness diagnosis [3]. These methods are well-suited for the classification procedure of COVID-19 imaging patterns because they can automatically extract the image features [3].

This chapter first discusses the various DL techniques proposed for diagnosing COVID-19 disease. Second, it explains the metaheuristic roles in assisting the DL techniques for detecting this disease. In addition, the performance of various metaheuristics for producing segmented images that could assist the DL techniques in automatically and accurately classifying the COVID-19-infected persons is investigated. The next section reports some experimental findings that could elaborate on the performance of each studied metaheuristic. Finally, the chapter summary is presented.

9.2 Deep learning techniques for COVID-19 diagnosis

Over the last 4 years, several DL techniques were proposed to classify chest X-rays for detecting COVID-19. For example, the pretrained convolutional neural network (CNN) was evaluated for diagnosing COVID-19 infection [5]. In this technique, transfer learning was utilized to train the deep CNN due to the small samples of available COVID-19 datasets. Ozturk [6] provided a new approach for automatically detecting COVID-19 infection from X-ray images. The suggested model was built to deliver precise diagnoses for both multiclass classification and binary classification. A concatenated neural network that utilizes both ResNet50V2 and Xception networks was proposed to categorize X-ray images into three distinct classes: pneumonia, normal, and COVID-19 [7]. To categorize COVID-19 infection using chest X-ray images, a deep CNN model was suggested [8]. Based on the residual neural network, this model, known as CVDNet, was developed. To capture the local and global properties of the inputs, it is built utilizing two parallel levels with different kernel sizes. A novel deep CNN based on transfer learning was proposed for classifying the persons infected with the COVID-19 disease [9]. This model had 94.5% as overall classification accuracy, 98.4% as a sensitivity, and 98% as a specificity.

SqueezeNet is a well-designed CNN that was proposed for classifying images, especially those in the medical field [10]. In comparison to previous models, it uses a reduced number of parameters. The components of SqueezeNet were utilized to develop a new network architecture for classifying the COVID-19 infection [10]. This architecture was called COVIDiagnosis-Net. To tune the parameters of this architecture, the Bayesian optimization technique was used. In addition to that, multiscale offline image augmentation was done to compensate for imbalances in the data classes. This model could achieve an overall accuracy of 98.30% when it came to the three-group classification test. Ensemble learning (EL) is a powerful method for enhancing the accuracy of classifications [10]. EL takes the best features from multiple DL models and merges them into a single prediction. The multiple models are expected to show complementary performance when integrated. This will make the models based on the EL stronger against unseen data [10]. Rajaraman et al. [10] aggregate the prediction of nine distinct DL models for tackling the classification problem. They utilized various established ensemble techniques, such as max voting, averaging, weighted averaging, and stacking, to combine the outputs of these models. Additionally, they used an iterative pruning approach to search for the optimal number of layers for the network architecture. This resulted in a reduction in model complexity, while simultaneously maintaining model performance. This model was applied for classifying the COVID-19 infection. The experimental findings show the efficacy of the DL techniques based on the EL.

A hybrid DL model based on combining both HRNet and ResNet34 was proposed for performing the classification tasks to categorize chest X-ray images for detecting COVID-19 infection [11]. This model is called COVID-CheXNet. It could achieve outstanding outcomes when diagnosing COVID-19 diseases. Based on the previous review, DL techniques have a significant role in accurately detecting COVID-19 patients. However, these techniques still have some shortcomings that stand as a strict obstacle that prevents obtaining a better accuracy when applied to the classification tasks, especially those of the COVID-19 detection. Some of these demerits include tuning the hyperparameters and an image segmentation problem. The hyperparameter tuning is considered an indispensable step that has to be accurately performed to enhance the performance of the DL techniques when tackling classification tasks. Using inaccurate parameters might result in overfitting or underfitting problems. The overfitting problem occurs when the model performs well on the training dataset, while its performance on the unseen datasets is poor. On the contrary, the underfitting problem occurs when the model shows poor performance on both testing and training datasets. The image segmentation problem includes separating homogenous objects within the image to assist in improving the classification accuracy of the DL model.

Metaheuristic optimization algorithms have been widely employed in different aspects to improve the classification performance of both DL and machine learning models. For example, they could be applied for estimating the hyperparameters of those models, in addition to being used as an optimizer to optimize the weight parameters of the multilayer perceptron and various variants of deep neural networks (DNNs). Furthermore, they could be used as segmentation techniques with the assistance of a traditional image segmentation technique like Kapur's entropy and the Otsu function to segment the homogenous regions within the images. These segmented images might improve the classification accuracy of the DL models. In this chapter, we will investigate the influence of employing some metaheuristic algorithms for performing the segmentation process under different threshold levels (T) on the performance of the DL techniques.

9.3 Metaheuristics for COVID-19 diagnosis

The metaheuristic techniques have been widely applied for performing the classification tasks of the COVID-19 infection.

Some of these techniques will be reviewed in the rest of this section. The Strength Pareto Evolutionary Algorithm was employed to adjust the hyperparameters of modified AlexNet for accurately and correctly classifying COVID-19 patients. The marine predators algorithm (MPA) modified using quantum computing was employed as a feature selection technique with DL techniques to automatically classify the patient infected with COVID-19 [12]. Binary variants of both particle swarm optimization and gray wolf optimization were used as feature selection techniques with DL for accurately diagnosing COVID-19-infected persons [13]. The arithmetic optimization algorithm was employed to adjust the hyperparameters of XGBoost for detecting COVID-19 disease in chest X-ray images [14]. This model had superior results compared to several rival techniques.

To segment the Covid-19 X-ray images, the slime mold algorithm (SMA) was effectively integrated with the whale optimization algorithm (WOA) for proposing a new variant called HSAM_WOA [15]. This strategy combined SMA with WOA to benefit from their complementary strengths and mitigate their individual drawbacks. Subsequently, 12 chest X-ray images were utilized to validate HSMA_WOA, and its results were compared to those of a variety of well-established rival algorithms to gage their efficacy. In conclusion, the experimental results demonstrate that the HSMA_WOA is the best option. Recently, a new metaheuristic technique has been presented for the segmentation of the COVID-19 X-ray images to reach similar regions that assist the machine learning and DL techniques to accurately predict and classify the persons infected with COVID-19 [16]. This technique improved the performance of MPA using the ranking-based strategy to improve the convergence speed of the algorithm for reaching better outcomes in smaller function evaluations. The experimental findings revealed the strong performance of this improved technique, which could come true strong outcomes for several metrics like PSNR, standard deviation, UQI, SSIM, and fitness values. An image segmentation technique, namely XMACO, was proposed for the segmentation of the COVID-19 chest images [17]. This technique was based on improving the ant colony optimization algorithm using two effective mechanisms, namely, the directional mutation (DM) and crossover (DX). The DX mechanism strives to enhance the convergence speed of the algorithm by enhancing the population quality during the whole optimization process. On the other side, the DM strategy improves the population diversity to avert falling into local optima.

9.4 Metaheuristics-assisted deep neural network for COVID-19 diagnosis

In this chapter, four metaheuristic algorithms, namely, NOA, LSO, DE, and TLBO, are employed to segment the homogenous regions in the chest X-ray images in an attempt to separate the background and the other undesirable regions to enable the DL models from detecting the COVID-19-infected persons correctly and accurately. These algorithms are first applied to segment the X-ray images. The segmented images are then broken down into training and testing datasets. The training dataset is used to train the DNN, and then the latter dataset is employed to observe the ability of this trained model to detect unseen data. Generally, the main steps of the studied algorithms are initialization, evaluation, building segmented images, and the proposed DNN. In this chapter, we will clarify the first four steps briefly because they are explained in detail in Chapter 5.

All the metaheuristic algorithms start with randomly distributing many solutions within the search space of the optimization problems. The image segmentation optimization problem is similar to the other optimization problems, where it has an upper bound and lower bound that are used in the initialization process to initialize the population individuals. Since the image intensities are ranging between 0 and 255, the upper bound and lower bound of any threshold value are 255 and 0, respectively. After the initialization process, the initial solutions are converted into integers as clarified in Chapter 5 to make them applicable for tackling the image segmentation. These converted solutions are evaluated using Kapur's entropy as an objective function, and the solution with the highest objective value is considered the best solution used within the optimization process for searching for better solutions. Following that, the optimization process is started to update these initial solutions in the hope of finding a better solution than the best solution achieved yet. After satisfying the termination condition of the optimization process, the best solution obtained yet is returned to construct the segmented images employed to train and test the DL neural network.

The DNN is composed of three components: an input layer, hidden layers, and an output layer. Before training the DNN, the input dataset is normalized between 0 and 1 to improve convergence during the training process. This normalized dataset is fed into the DNN, specifically into the input layer, which receives the data and passes it directly to each neuron in the first hidden layer. Each neuron multiplies the input data by its weights and sums the multiplied values. This sum is passed to the ReLU activation function, which returns the output of this neuron. These outputs are submitted to the subsequent hidden layers for further processing. The number of hidden layers and the number of neurons for each layer from those significantly affect the performance of the DNN, where using a large number of hidden layers more than a sufficient number of layers will cause two shortcomings. The first shortcoming is increasing the computational cost of the designed DNN during the training process. The second shortcoming is the overfitting problem. The same shortcomings are held true when using more neurons than required. Therefore, in the experiments section, we make extensive experiments to estimate the near-optimal value for those two hyperparameters. The resultant estimation of these experiments shows that using only three hidden layers will maximize the performance of the designed DNN, where these three hidden layers are composed of 4000, 3200, and 1000 neurons, respectively.

After further processing the input data by the hidden layers, the output of the last hidden layers is submitted to each neuron in the output layer that multiplies it with its weights. For each neuron, the summation of those multiplied values is computed and passed to the activation function called softmax to compute the final classification decision. The mathematical formula of the softmax activation function is expressed in the following formula:

$$\text{Softmax}(S_j) = \frac{e^{S_j}}{\sum_{j=1}^{C} e^{S_j}} \tag{9.1}$$

where S_j is the summation of the multiplied values for the jth neurons in the output layer. Several other activation functions could be used in the output layer, but the softmax is the most effective for the multiclass classification problems.

The DNN begins by arbitrarily initializing the weights of each connection between every two neurons and then seeks to precisely update these weights during the optimization process to estimate the optimal label of each input record in the dataset. This is an optimization process, so an objective function, also known as a loss function, is required to demonstrate the accuracy of the obtained weights during this optimization process. The most prevalent loss function is the categorical cross entropy (CCE), which has the following mathematical form:

$$\text{Minimize loss(CCE)} = -\sum_{i=1}^{M} y_i \cdot \log \check{y}_i \tag{9.2}$$

The notation $(\check{y}_i)$ denotes a vector containing the expected outputs of the training samples. As previously stated, the metaheuristic could be used to find the near-optimal weights that minimize this loss function to improve classification accuracy. However, one of the most significant drawbacks of these methods is that they require a large number of function evaluations to attain near-optimal weights. Therefore they are not the favored solution for this problem. Gradient-based algorithms are favored as a strong alternative for minimizing loss functions to obtain universal approximation. This is as a result of their ability to rapidly achieve near-optimal weights that minimize the loss function while requiring fewer computational resources. However, these methods are susceptible to falling into local minima due to the fact that the gradient of these solutions when the local minima is zero, preventing the updating of the current weights. There are a number of gradient-based optimizers, such as the stochastic gradient descent algorithm, the momentum gradient descent algorithm, the Adam optimizer, and the adaptive gradient (AdGrad) algorithm. In this chapter, the Adam optimizer is used to train the proposed DNN to search for near-optimal weights that could accurately classify the segmented chest X-ray images. Fig. 9.1 presents a general framework to clarify how to employ the metaheuristics algorithms for generating the segmented images that are used to train the designed DNN for identifying the COVID-19 infection.

In this figure, the input images are fed into the metaheuristic algorithms. These algorithms compute the histogram of these images, which is used to search for the optimal threshold values. Afterward, the algorithms generate N solutions, where each solution consists of d dimensions. In the image segmentation problem, these dimensions represent the threshold level, which is predefined to segment the images. Each dimension from those is randomly initialized within the search boundary discussed before. Then, each solution is evaluated based on Kapur's entropy, and the solution with the highest fitness value is considered the best-so-far solution. The optimization process of each algorithm is then started to update these initialized solutions to search for other solutions that could maximize the entropy between the segmented regions. During each iteration, the updated solutions are evaluated to measure their fitness values and update the best solution achieved yet. This process is continuing to satisfy the termination condition. The termination condition in this study is based on satisfying the maximum number of iterations. Ultimately, after reaching the maximum iteration, the best solution obtained even now is returned to generate the segmented images that are used to train the designed DNN.

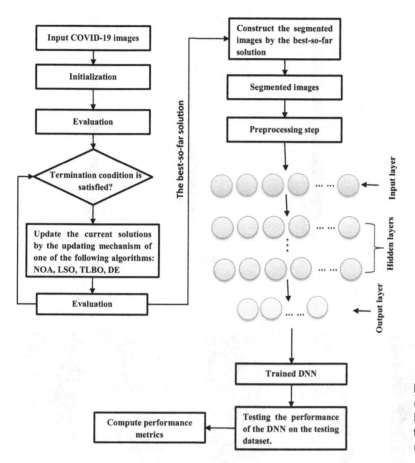

Figure 9.1 Framework of employing the metaheuristics-based image segmentation technique with the DNN for classifying COVID-19 infection.

9.5   Dataset description

Two publicly available datasets were combined to create the dataset used in this research. The chest X-ray images of the patients with proven instances of COVID-19 disease, common bacterial pneumonia, and normal are included in this dataset. This dataset is gathered from the study of Makris [18] and Kaggle's repository, where it includes 112 persons infected with COVID-19, 1575 normal persons, and 4265 persons infected with pneumonia. In brief, the dataset used in this investigation is composed of three groups (COVID-19, pneumonia, and normal), and its total number of cases is evenly distributed among those groups. Fig. 9.2 shows the total number of images in each category, whereas Fig. 9.3 shows examples of normal, pneumonia, and COVID X-rays.

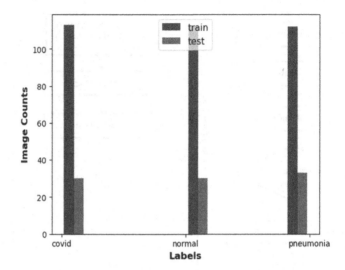

Figure 9.2 Depiction of three chest X-ray images belonging to different classes.

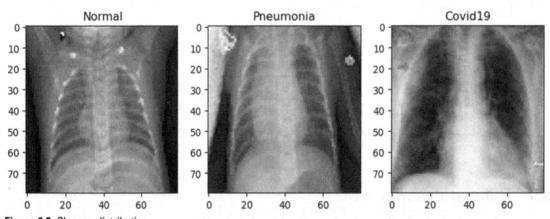

Figure 9.3 Classes distribution.

9.6   Preprocessing step

Before starting the training process, both training and testing datasets are normalized. Three normalization ways are classified either pixel-wise or dataset-wise [19]. The first way that is considered in this chapter is based on normalizing the intensities of the input images between 0 and 1 according to the following formula:

$$I' = I/255 \qquad (9.3)$$

where I' is the normalized image, I is the input image, and 255 represents the maximum intensity value for each pixel in the input image. The second normalization way normalizes the intensities between 1 and -1 as modeled in the following formula:

$$I' = \frac{I}{\left(\frac{255}{2}\right)} - 1 \qquad (9.4)$$

The last mechanism normalizes each image in the dataset based on the mean and standard deviation of this dataset. In this chapter, the first normalization mechanism that normalizes the pixel intensities between 0 and 1 is considered to be performed in the preprocessing step. This ensures that the intensities have a similar distribution, and subsequently, the convergence speed is significantly improved during the training process.

9.7 Experimental settings

The DNN has some hyperparameters that have to be accurately estimated to avoid both overfitting and underfitting problems. These parameters are the number of layers and the number of neurons for each layer. In the beginning, we design the DNN architecture with three hidden layers and strive to estimate the optimal value for the number of neurons in each layer from those. To do that, for the first layer, we conduct several experiments under various numbers of neurons, like 500, 1000, 2000, 3000, 4000, and 4500. After replicating the same experiments 30 independent times with the same number of neurons, the average accuracy on the test data is computed and presented in Fig. 9.4, which reveals that the near-optimal number of neurons for the first layer is 4000, while the worst number is 500. Likewise, for the second layer, several numbers of neurons ranging between 500 and 4000 are used to pick the best performing number. The average accuracy for each number of neurons utilized in the second hidden layer is reported in Fig. 9.5, which shows that the near-optimal number of neurons for this layer is 3200, while the worst number is 1500. The number of neurons for the third layer is estimated in the same way, which illustrates that the average accuracy of the testing data is maximized when the number of neurons is 1000.

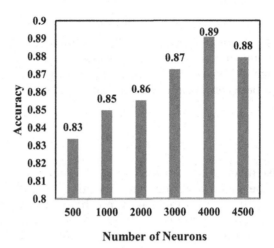

Figure 9.4 Observation of various neurons for the first layer.

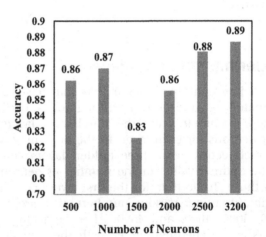

Figure 9.5 Observation of various neurons for the second layer.

Moreover, three additional hidden layers are added to observe whether the performance is improved by increasing the number of layers or not. After adding the fourth hidden layer, the DNN is trained, and the average accuracy on the testing dataset is computed and presented in Fig. 9.6. This figure shows that the highest accuracy value is achieved when the number of neurons is 200 or 600. When comparing the accuracy values after and before adding the fourth layer, we found that the performance of the DNN with only three layers is significantly better. To further confirm that, three additional layers are

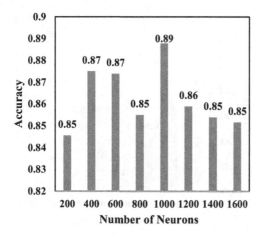

Figure 9.6 Observation of various neurons for the third layer.

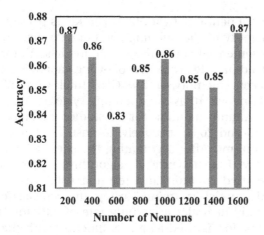

Figure 9.7 Observation of various neurons for the fourth layer.

added, and the average accuracies computed on the testing dataset after training the DNN is reported in Figs. 9.7, 9.8 and 9.9. These figures affirm that increasing the number of layers deteriorates the performance of the DNN. Therefore, in this chapter, the proposed DNN is composed of three hidden layers, where each layer has the number of neurons discussed before.

To construct and train the recommended DNN, the programming language Python, the Keras package, and a TensorFlow backend were utilized. Because the Keras package contains a neural network library that was built on top of Theano or TensorFlow, it makes it possible for researchers to

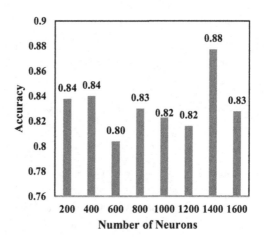

Figure 9.8 Observation of various neurons for the fifth layer.

easily design a neural network [20]. The Keras package provides the vast majority of the building components that are required to develop somewhat sophisticated DL models. All experiments are conducted on a PC with the following capabilities: 32 GB of random access memory, a 2.40 GHz Intel Core i7−4700MQ CPU, and Windows 10 as the operating system. The population size and maximum iteration for all studied metaheuristics are limited to 50 and 20, respectively, to ensure a fair comparison among algorithms. After segmenting the chest X-ray images by each employed metaheuristic algorithm, these segmented images are used to train and test the used DNN discussed before. This model is trained using the stochastic gradient descent algorithm under a learning rate of 0.01 for 10 epochs. The CCE function is used as a loss function with the DNN for measuring the difference between the true output and estimated output. The batch size is heuristically chosen from 32 for the training process.

9.8 Practical findings

In this section, the studied metaheuristic algorithms are employed to segment the chest X-ray images under different threshold levels (T-3, T-4, T-5, and T-10). The images segmented by each algorithm under each threshold level are used as training and testing datasets. The designed DNN is trained using the training images under a number of epochs up to 10. After the training process, the average accuracy and loss value on the

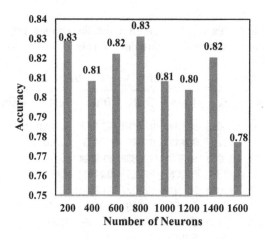

Figure 9.9 Observation of various neurons for the sixth layer.

testing dataset are computed and presented in Table 9.1. Also, this table contains the average accuracy and loss value on the training dataset to reveal whether the model suffers from the overfitting problem. This table shows that the images segmented by TLBO under the threshold levels, T-3 and T-4, could achieve better classification accuracy and loss value on the testing dataset. However, the classification accuracy and loss value achieved by TLBO under T-3 on the training dataset are slightly worse than those estimated by LSO. Despite that, under T-3, TLBO is considered the best segmentation technique because it could perform better on the unseen data and its segmented images assist the DNN in avoiding the overfitting problem. For the threshold level, T-4, TLBO is also the highest performing algorithm on the testing dataset, where it could achieve a classification accuracy of 94.66, and a loss value of 0.22, followed by LSO as the second best performing algorithm. Unfortunately, the performance of TLBO occupies the second rank after DE in terms of the best performing algorithm on the training dataset, where TLBO could achieve a classification accuracy of 90.68 and a loss value of 0.27, while DE could achieve a classification accuracy of 91.6024 and a loss value of 0.2420. However, the DNN trained using the images segmented by DE suffers from the overfitting problem since the classification accuracy on the training dataset is significantly higher than that of the testing dataset. From that, we can conclude that DNN with the TLBO could perform well on both training and testing datasets. Regarding the other threshold levels, the performance of the DNN with all algorithms is significantly deteriorated compared

Table 9.1 Classification accuracy and loss value obtained under the images segmented by each algorithm under various threshold levels.

T	Metrics	TLBO		NOA		LSO		DE		Normal	
		Train	Test	Train	Test	Train	Test	Train	Test	Train	Test
T-3	Accuracy	92.4332	**93.3333**	91.2463	91.0000	**92.9377**	92.4444	92.1068	85.0000	87.0238	88.3333
	Loss	0.2303	**0.2221**	0.2483	0.2526	**0.2411**	0.2306	0.2485	0.3767	0.3170	0.3375
T-4	Accuracy	90.6825	**94.6667**	91.0682	90.3333	90.3561	92.8889	**91.6024**	85.8667		
	Loss	0.2726	**0.2236**	0.2488	0.2491	0.2826	0.2369	**0.2420**	0.3522		
T-5	Accuracy	89.8022	65.1613	90.0495	**89.0000**	90.7418	88.2222	**91.2957**	85.8889		
	Loss	0.2854	0.9563	0.2803	**0.3048**	0.2665	0.3069	**0.2580**	0.3658		
T-10	Accuracy	87.0427	**90.5556**	86.4634	87.5555	**89.4512**	86.3333	86.0366	87.3333		
	Loss	0.3375	**0.2998**	0.3287	0.3305	**0.2919**	0.3498	0.3661	0.3277		

Bold values represent the best findings.

with both T-3 and T-4. In general, the DNN trained using the images segmented by TLBO under T-4 is a robust alternative for accurately detecting COVID-19 infection.

9.9 Chapter summary

This chapter investigates the performance of four metaheuristic algorithms, NOA, LSO, TLBO, and DE for accurately segmenting the chest X-ray images under different threshold levels, including T-3, T-4, T-5, and T-10. These segmented images are used to train a DNN for accurately and automatically identifying the COVID-19 infection. Increasing the used threshold level might negatively affect the quality of the segmented images, and hence the performance of the DL models might also deteriorate. Therefore several threshold levels are investigated to pick the most effective level that could produce segmented images able to improve the performance of the DNN for automatically and accurately detecting the COVID-19 infection. In addition, several experiments have been done to estimate the near-optimal number of hidden layers and their neurons for avoiding both overfitting and underfitting problems. The experimental findings reveal that the performance of the DNN significantly deteriorates when increasing the threshold levels used for segmented chest X-ray images. In addition, the DNN trained by the segmented images produced by TLBO under T-4 could achieve better classification accuracy and loss value on the testing dataset, and its performance on the training dataset is competitive with DE. However, DE suffers from the overfitting problem because its classification accuracy on the training dataset is so high compared to that obtained on the testing dataset. Therefore TLBO is considered the most effective image segmentation technique for producing segmented images that can accurately train the DNN for identifying the COVID-19 infection from the chest X-ray images.

References

[1] M. Riaz, M. Bashir, I. Younas, Metaheuristics based COVID-19 detection using medical images: A review, Computers in Biology and Medicine 144 (2022) 105344.

[2] M.S. Iraji, M.-R. Feizi-Derakhshi, J. Tanha, COVID-19 detection using deep convolutional neural networks and binary differential algorithm-based feature selection from X-ray images, Complexity 2021 (2021) 1–10.

[3] M. Kaur, et al., Metaheuristic-based deep COVID-19 screening model from chest X-ray images, Journal of Healthcare Engineering 2021 (2021) 8829829.

[4] X. Yu, et al., ResNet-SCDA-50 for breast abnormality classification, IEEE/ACM Transactions on Computational Biology and Bioinformatics 18 (1) (2020) 94–102.

[5] I.D. Apostolopoulos, T.A. Mpesiana, Covid-19: automatic detection from x-ray images utilizing transfer learning with convolutional neural networks, Physical and Engineering Sciences in Medicine 43 (2020) 635–640.

[6] T. Ozturk, et al., Automated detection of COVID-19 cases using deep neural networks with X-ray images, Computers in Biology and Medicine 121 (2020) 103792.

[7] M. Rahimzadeh, A. Attar, A modified deep convolutional neural network for detecting COVID-19 and pneumonia from chest X-ray images based on the concatenation of Xception and ResNet50V2, Informatics in Medicine Unlocked 19 (2020) 100360.

[8] C. Ouchicha, O. Ammor, M. Meknassi, CVDNet: A novel deep learning architecture for detection of coronavirus (Covid-19) from chest x-ray images, Chaos, Solitons, & Fractals 140 (2020) 110245.

[9] M. Heidari, et al., Improving the performance of CNN to predict the likelihood of COVID-19 using chest X-ray images with preprocessing algorithms, International Journal of Medical Informatics 144 (2020) 104284.

[10] S. Aslani, J. Jacob, Utilisation of deep learning for COVID-19 diagnosis, Clinical Radiology 78 (2) (2023) 150–157.

[11] A. Al-Waisy, et al., COVID-DeepNet: hybrid multimodal deep learning system for improving COVID-19 pneumonia detection in chest X-ray images, Computers, Materials & Continua 67 (2) (2021) 2409–2429.

[12] D.A. Torse, et al., Optimal feature selection for COVID-19 detection with CT images enabled by metaheuristic optimization and artificial intelligence, Multimedia Tools and Applications (2023) 1–31.

[13] M. Canayaz, MH-COVIDNet: Diagnosis of COVID-19 using deep neural networks and meta-heuristic-based feature selection on X-ray images, Biomedical Signal Processing and Control 64 (2021) 102257.

[14] M. Zivkovic, et al., Hybrid CNN and XGBoost Model Tuned by Modified Arithmetic Optimization Algorithm for COVID-19 Early Diagnostics from X-ray Images, Electronics 11 (22) (2022) 3798.

[15] M. Abdel-Basset, V. Chang, R. Mohamed, HSMA_WOA: A hybrid novel Slime mould algorithm with whale optimization algorithm for tackling the image segmentation problem of chest X-ray images, Applied Soft Computing 95 (2020) 106642.

[16] L. Liu, et al., An efficient multi-threshold image segmentation for skin cancer using boosting whale optimizer, Computers in Biology and Medicine 151 (2022) 106227.

[17] A. Qi, et al., Directional mutation and crossover boosted ant colony optimization with application to COVID-19 X-ray image segmentation, Computers in Biology and Medicine 148 (2022) 105810.

[18] Makris, A., I. Kontopoulos, and K. Tserpes. *COVID-19 detection from chest X-Ray images using Deep Learning and Convolutional Neural Networks.* 2020.

[19] L. Scime, et al., Layer-wise anomaly detection and classification for powder bed additive manufacturing processes: A machine-agnostic algorithm for real-time pixel-wise semantic segmentation, Additive Manufacturing 36 (2020) 101453.

[20] A. Gulli, S. Pal, Deep Learning With Keras, Packt Publishing Ltd., 2017.

10

Metaheuristic algorithms for multimodal image fusion of magnetic resonance and computed tomography brain tumor images: a comparative study

10.1 Introduction

Image fusion refers to the process of combining the key features of several different medical images into a single image with more information than any of the original images. Image fusion is particularly important because it improves the performance of object identification algorithms by merging images from several sources with other relevant data sets. In addition to this, it also helps to improve geometric corrections, sharpen the images, replace inaccurate data, enhance certain characteristics that are not obvious in either of the images, and contribute more data sets for better classification [1]. Multimodal medical fusion refers to the process of integrating the images that were produced by various imaging modalities into a single image [2]. There are several imaging modalities, including computed tomography (CT), positron emission tomography (PET), magnetic resonance imaging (MRI), and single-photon emission CT (SPECT), which were utilized to fuse functional and structural images [2]. In clinical applications, functional images are often mapped into structural images using fusion techniques [2]. Image fusion is most commonly used for three purposes, object recognition, classification, and change detection, which are extensively explained in the following list [1]:

- Object recognition: Image fusion could mix two or more images to produce a new detailed image. This detailed image improves the appearance of most useful objects found within it, and hence they could be easily identified.

Metaheuristics Algorithms for Medical Applications. DOI: https://doi.org/10.1016/B978-0-443-13314-5.00005-9

- Classification: Including data from several sources in the training dataset could improve the performance of the classifiers for achieving better classification accuracy.
- Change detection: Change detection refers to the process of identifying differences in an object observed at several periods. The results of observations for this object are compared to identify the difference between them. The detection of change is an essential step in monitoring and managing natural resources because it aids in analyzing the spatial distribution of the population of concern. In the field of medical diagnostics, the process of image fusion has been utilized for accurately detecting tumors, anomalies, and diseases.

Image fusion methods could be split into two groups: spatial domain and transform domain. The spatial domain approach manipulates the pixel values to achieve fusion between the images. Several image fusion techniques belong to this approach, some of which are hue intensity saturation-based methods, averaging, high-pass filtering (HPF)−based methods, principal component analysis, and the Brovey method [3]. In the transform-domain approach, the image is converted into a frequency domain that is manipulated using fusion operations to combine two or more images. Afterward, the inverse transform is performed on the fused domain to obtain the fused image [3].

The fusion of multimodal medical images is considered a significant step for combining the information obtained from various imaging modalities to obtain a single informative image. Image fusion techniques for multimodal images can be broken down into three categories: those that operate on the pixel level, those that operate on the feature level, and those that operate on the decision-making level. Pixel-level fusion is a processing method that works on the pixels of the source image while preserving practically all information from the original image. The attributes of the source images, like edges, textures, and fine details of the images, are taken into consideration by the feature-level technique. The decision-making level technique utilizes information that has been obtained via either pixel-level fusion or feature-level fusion to make the best decision possible to accomplish a given objective [4]. Over the last few years, multiscale transforms like discrete wavelet transform (DWT) and pyramid transform have been widely used for performing multimodal medical image fusion (MMIF) at the pixel level. DWT could perform better than the pyramid transform methods for image fusion [3]. There are several transform-based image fusion techniques, including contourlet, morphological wavelet, complex wavelet, curvelet, and multiwavelet. Among these techniques, the contourlet, complex wavelet, and curvelet techniques have better directional selectivity and shift-invariance property than the other techniques. Despite that, the DWT-based image fusion technique is still preferred for fusion because it requires less computational cost and could easily merge several images [3].

There are several transform-based techniques that were extensively used in the literature for MMIF. For example, fuzzy transform was used to improve the MMIF algorithm's performance [5]. This improved algorithm takes into account the error images obtained using fuzzy transform. Several other MMIF techniques use fuzzy transform to perform the fusion process in the medical field [6]. The DWT-based image fusion technique was extensively developed in the literature due to the merits described in the former. However, the main challenge of this technique is that it has some unknown parameters that need to be optimized for achieving a better fusion process. Due to the complexity of this problem, especially when increasing the source images, which results in increasing the number of parameters to be optimized, the metaheuristic algorithms were employed to search for the near-optimal values of those parameters for achieving better fusion performance, especially in the medical field. There are several metaheuristic algorithms that were adapted to estimate those parameters; some of them are described in the next paragraph.

The whale optimization algorithm was improved by the particle swarm optimization (PSO) algorithm to propose a new variant with better exploration and exploitation operators [3]; this variant was called HWFusion. It was applied to estimate the near-optimal values for the weighted coefficients using holo-entropy as an objective function to accurately fuse multimodal medical images. The experimental findings proved that HWFusion could achieve outstanding results compared to several other algorithms. In addition, the crow search algorithm was also adapted to estimate those parameters of the DWT to fuse multimodal medical images [1]. The PSO algorithm was adapted for estimating the unknown parameters of the DWT to fuse the images taken by various diagnostic tools such as MRI, CT, PET, and SPECT. The experimental results show that employing PSO with DWT could achieve superior outcomes compared to several other multimodal image fusion techniques. There are several other metaheuristic algorithms proposed for MMIF such as gray wolf optimizer enhanced using a chaotic map [7], hybrid metaheuristic algorithm based on the beetle swarm algorithm and salp swarm algorithm [8], world cup optimizer and shark smell optimizer [9], and equilibrium optimizer [10].

From these, the metaheuristic algorithms are considered an important technique for accurately fusing multimodal medical images. Therefore, in this chapter, we will investigate the performance of two different categories of metaheuristic algorithms: (1) the first category includes three recently published optimization algorithms such as NOA, LSO, and seagull optimization algorithm (SOA) and (2) the second category contains two well-established algorithms, namely differential evolution (DE) and teaching-learning-based optimization (TLBO). In addition, to further improve the fusion process for multimodal medical images, two additional variants are proposed in this chapter. The first variant is based on improving the performance of SOA to strengthen its exploitation operator in an attempt to move quickly in the right direction of the near-optimal solution; this variant is called improved SOA (ISOA). The second variant is based on further improving the exploitation operator of TLBO by integrating it with the first variant; this second variant was called TLSOA. All those algorithms are validated using five sets of MRI-CT images to reveal the ability of each algorithm for accurately fusing multimodal medical images. The experimental findings show that TLSOA shows superior performance for several performance metrics. This chapter is organized as follows:

- Section 10.2 explains extensively the DWT to show the unknown coefficients that need to be estimated by optimization techniques.
- Section 10.3 shows the image fusion rule used to combine two or more multimodal medical images.
- Section 10.4 describes the SOA's mathematical model and behaviors.
- Section 10.5 presents the main steps needed to adapt the metaheuristic for image fusion, in addition to describing two newly proposed variants (ISOA and TLSOA).
- Section 10.6 presents the performance metrics employed to observe the quality of fused images in comparison to the source images.
- Section 10.7 presents results and discussion to show the performance of each investigated metaheuristic algorithm.
- Section 10.8 presents a chapter summary.

10.2 Discrete wavelet transform

The WT has been demonstrated to be a more effective representative signal processing method in image processing than the

Fourier transform. In multiresolution signal processing, such as speech processing, subband coding, image compression, and other similar applications, it demonstrated its superiority over the Fourier transform. The DWT, which is the discrete variant of wavelet, is a better tool for the study of nonstationary data when it comes to image processing [1]. DWT decomposes the image using two levels. The first level is filtering under low-pass filtering (LPF) and HPF. The second level includes downsampling the output of the LPF. The vertical filtering and downsampling can split the image into four subimages: Approximation coefficient, including LL, and detailed coefficients, including HH, LH, and HL. In detail, the LL subimage represents the approximation coefficient, the HL subimage represents the vertical detail coefficients, the LH subimage stands for the horizontal detail coefficients, and the HH subimage stands for the diagonal detail coefficient. The LL subimage for image A could be computed by the convolution of both the LPF and low-frequency coefficient matrix using the following formula [3]:

$$A_x^{LL}(v_0, m, n) = \frac{1}{\sqrt{MN}} \sum_{i=0}^{M-1} \sum_{j=0}^{N-1} I^L(i,j) x^L(v_0, i, j) \qquad (10.1)$$

where $I^L(i,j)$ represents the coefficient matrix of low frequency, and $x^L(v_0, i, j)$ is an LPF function. The LH subimage for the same image could be generated according to the following mathematical equation:

$$A_x^{LH}(v_0, m, n) = \frac{1}{\sqrt{MN}} \sum_{i=0}^{M-1} \sum_{j=0}^{N-1} I^L(i,j) x^H(v_0, i, j) \qquad (10.2)$$

where $x^H(v_0, i, j)$ represents the HPF function. The HL subimage could be generated according to the following equation:

$$A_x^{HL}(v_0, m, n) = \frac{1}{\sqrt{MN}} \sum_{i=0}^{M-1} \sum_{j=0}^{N-1} I^H(i,j) x^L(v_0, i, j) \qquad (10.3)$$

where $I^H(i,j)$ indicates the high-frequency coefficient matrix. The HH subimage for image A could be estimated according to the following equation:

$$A_x^{HH}(v_0, m, n) = \frac{1}{\sqrt{MN}} \sum_{i=0}^{M-1} \sum_{j=0}^{N-1} I^H(i,j) x^H(v_0, i, j) \qquad (10.4)$$

The same previous four equations could be used to generate four subimages of the second image B, as defined in the following four equations:

$$B_x^{LL}(v_0, m, n) = \frac{1}{\sqrt{MN}} \sum_{i=0}^{M-1} \sum_{j=0}^{N-1} I^L(i,j) x^L(v_0, i, j) \tag{10.5}$$

$$B_x^{LH}(v_0, m, n) = \frac{1}{\sqrt{MN}} \sum_{i=0}^{M-1} \sum_{j=0}^{N-1} I^L(i,j) x^H(v_0, i, j) \tag{10.6}$$

$$B_x^{HL}(v_0, m, n) = \frac{1}{\sqrt{MN}} \sum_{i=0}^{M-1} \sum_{j=0}^{N-1} I^H(i,j) x^L(v_0, i, j) \tag{10.7}$$

$$B_x^{HH}(v_0, m, n) = \frac{1}{\sqrt{MN}} \sum_{i=0}^{M-1} \sum_{j=0}^{N-1} I^H(i,j) x^H(v_0, i, j) \tag{10.8}$$

10.3 Image fusion rule

After that, the detailed and approximation coefficients of both the source images that were decomposed utilizing the wavelet transform at two levels are fused utilizing the fusion rule that is described in the rest of this section [1]. In the fusion process, the approximation coefficient of the first image A is combined with the approximation coefficient of the second image B based on two different weighted variables to determine the weight of each coefficient in the fused image. Likewise, the detailed coefficients of the first image A are combined with those of the second image B based on different weighted variables to determine the weights of each coefficient in the fused image. To fuse the LL subimages of both A and B images, the following mathematical equation could be used:

$$F^{LL}(m, n) = \omega_1 A_x^{LL}(v_0, m, n) + \omega_2 B_x^{LL}(v_0, m, n) \tag{10.9}$$

where ω_1 and ω_2 are two unknown parameters that need to be accurately estimated for reaching the high-quality fused LL subimage. To combine the LH subimages, the fusion rule is stated by relating two different weighted coefficients, as defined in the following equation:

$$F^{LH}(m, n) = \omega_3 A_x^{LH}(v_0, m, n) + \omega_4 B_x^{LH}(v_0, m, n) \tag{10.10}$$

where ω_3 and ω_4 are two additional unknown parameters that need to be accurately estimated. In addition, the two functions to fuse the HL subimages and HL subimages of the source images are described as follows, respectively:

$$F^{HL}(m, n) = \omega_5 A_x^{HL}(v_0, m, n) + \omega_6 B_x^{HL}(v_0, m, n) \qquad (10.11)$$

$$F^{HH}(m, n) = \omega_7 A_x^{HH}(v_0, m, n) + \omega_8 B_x^{HH}(v_0, m, n) \qquad (10.12)$$

From the previous equations used to fuse the subimages of source images, there are eight unknown parameters (ω_1, ω_2, ω_3, ω_4, ω_5, ω_6, ω_7, and ω_8) that have to be accurately estimated to increase the fusion quality of two multimodal medical images. The estimation process of these parameters could be accurately estimated using the metaheuristic algorithms due to their ability to find outstanding results for several optimization problems. Therefore, in this chapter, we will propose a new metaheuristic algorithm based on improving the performance of the SOA for achieving a better fusion process for multimodal medical images. In addition, we investigate the performance of four well-known optimization algorithms described in detail in the first chapter. After estimating these parameters, the inverse wavelet transform is applied to the fused subimages to generate the fused image. Fig. 10.1 presents

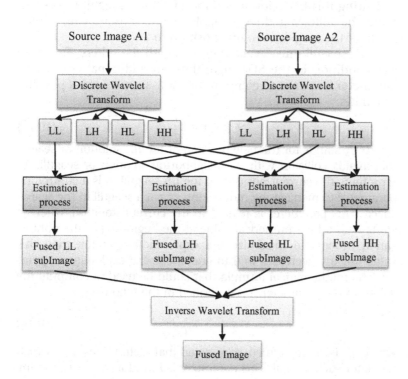

Figure 10.1 General framework of the multimodal medical image fusion.

the general framework of the MMIF under the wavelet transform and the estimation process for the unknown parameters conducted using metaheuristics.

10.4 Seagull optimization algorithm

Recently, Dhiman [11] presented a new nature-inspired metaheuristic algorithm, namely, the SOA, for finding near-optimal solutions to computationally intensive optimization issues. SOA was inspired by simulating the seagull's migration and attacking activities in nature. This algorithm could achieve outstanding results for a large number of optimization problems. This motivates us in this chapter to investigate its performance in estimating the coefficients of the DWT for achieving better fusion between two multimodal medical images. The behaviors of SOA, in addition to their mathematical models, are extensively presented in the rest of this section.

10.4.1 Migration behavior: exploration operator

During this behavior, it is important for a seagull to keep in mind the following three variables while it is moving with a group of the seagull from one position to another:

Each seagull must avoid collisions with the others: To satisfy this condition in the SOA algorithm, an additional controlling parameter A is used to compute the new search agent's position as follows:

$$\vec{C}_s = A \times \vec{X}_i^t \tag{10.13}$$

where $\vec{C}_s$ stands for the new position of the ith solution or seagull that avoids collision with the neighboring solution or seagull. $\vec{X}_i^t$ represents the current position of the ith seagull. A is a controlling parameter to manage the movements of each seagull in the search space. This parameter is related to the current iteration, where it starts with a high numerical value at the beginning of the optimization process to maximize the exploration operator, then this value linearly decreases to 0 to encourage the exploitation operator. The mathematical formula that could be used to compute the values of the parameter A is described in the following:

$$A = f_c - f_c \frac{t}{T_{\max}} \tag{10.14}$$

where f_c is a predefined parameter that determines the search range for each seagull. This parameter is introduced before starting the optimization process, and its value might differ from one optimization problem to another. In the classical SOA, the authors suggested setting the value of this parameter to 2, but this value does not hold true for all optimization problems in the real world.

Motion in the same direction as the best neighbor: After ensuring that there would be no collisions between neighbors, each solution should move in the direction of the best neighboring solution. The mathematical formula that could be used to simulate this behavior is presented in the following equation:

$$\vec{M}_s = B \times (\vec{X}^* - \vec{X}_i^t) \tag{10.15}$$

where $\vec{X}^*$ stands for the best solution achieved yet, and B is a factor that includes numeric values picked at random in the range $(0, 2A^2)$ to manage the equilibrium between the exploitation and exploration operators. This factor could be mathematically computed according to the following mathematical equation:

$$B = 2A^2 r \tag{10.16}$$

where r is a value chosen randomly in the range $(0, 1)$ according to the uniform distribution.

Stay near the best solution achieved yet: Lastly, each solution can generate its new position that could hold true this condition according to the following equation:

$$\vec{D}_s = \left| \vec{C}_s + \vec{M}_s \right| \tag{10.17}$$

10.4.2 Attacking behavior: exploitation operator

In this operator, the individuals in the population try to focus on the high-quality solutions obtained within the search process. During migration, seagulls are able to continuously adjust both their speed and the angle at which they attack their prey. Also, they are able to keep their height utilizing both their wings and their weight. During the attack process performed by each seagull to get the prey, the spiral behavior in the air in y, x, and z planes is followed by each seagull. This behavior could be mathematically defined using the following equations in y, x, and z planes:

$$\dot{x} = rd \times \cos(2r_2\pi) \tag{10.18}$$

$$\dot{y} = rd \times \cos(2r_2\pi) \tag{10.19}$$

$$\dot{z} = rd \times \cos(2r_2\pi) \tag{10.20}$$

where r_2 is a numerical value chosen randomly in the range (0, 1) by the uniform distribution. rd represents the radius of the spiral revolution and is calculated as follows:

$$rd = \mathcal{U} \times e^{\nu 2 r_2 \pi} \tag{10.21}$$

where $\mathcal{U}$ and ν are two constant numerical values to express the spiral shape. Finally, in each iteration, each individual or solution in the population is updated according to the following equation:

$$\vec{X}_i^{t+1} = \vec{X}^* + \left(\vec{D}_s \times \check{x} \times \check{y} \times \check{z} \right) \tag{10.22}$$

Finally, the SOA's pseudocode is listed in Algorithm 10.1.

Algorithm 10.1 SOA's pseudocode

Input: $\mathcal{U} = 1$, Maximum iteration T_{max}, Population size N, $f_c = 2$, and $\nu = 1$

1. Initialize N individuals within the search boundary, $\vec{X}_i (i \in N)$.
2. Evaluation and identifying the best solution achieved yet $\vec{X}$
3. Initialize the current iteration, t = 1;
4. **while** (t < T_{max})
5.   **for** each i individual
6.   r: pick a numerical value randomly in the range (0, 1)
7. r_2: Pick a numerical value randomly in the range (0, 1)
8.   Calculate rd according to Eq. (10.21)
9.   Compute $\vec{D}_s$ according to Eq. (10.17).
10.   Calculate $\check{x}$, $\check{y}$, and $\check{z}$ by Eqs. (10.18)–(10.20)
11.   Compute the new position of the ith solution according to Eq. (10.22)
12.   **end for**
13.   t++;
14. **end while**
Output: $\vec{X}^*$

10.5 Proposed algorithm for multimodal medical image fusion problem

In this chapter, we will investigate the performance of five metaheuristic algorithms, namely, NOA, LSO, DE, TLBO, and SOA, for tackling the medical image fusion problem. In addition, an additional algorithm, namely, TLSOA, based on hybridization between some SOA's merits and TLBO is herein proposed to present a new robust optimizer with strong exploration and exploitation operators for fusing the medical MRI brain images more accurately. This section is presented to show the main steps needed to adapt the metaheuristic algorithms for MMIF, in addition to extensively describing the proposed TLSOA.

10.5.1 Initialization

All the metaheuristic algorithms start their implementation by distributing N individuals at random within the lower and upper boundaries of each dimension in the optimization problems. The optimization problems investigated in this chapter aims at optimizing the fusion process between two or more medical images based on estimating the unknown parameters or coefficients that could accurately fuse the corresponding subimages of the source images. The upper and lower values for these parameters are 1 and 0, respectively. Therefore the metaheuristic algorithms start first with distributing N solutions, such that each solution consists of eight unknown parameters, within these boundaries to generate the initial population, as defined in Eq. (10.23). This population is then evaluated using the objective function described in the next section to determine the quality of each solution and extract the solution with the fittest objective value. Afterward, the optimization process is started to update the initial population in an attempt to search for a better solution.

$$\vec{X}_i = \vec{r} \qquad (10.23)$$

where $\vec{r}$ is a vector including numerical values picked at random in the interval (0, 1) according to the uniform distribution.

10.5.2 Root mean squared error

In this chapter, the root mean squared error (RMSE) between the source images and fused image are considered as an objective function to be employed with the metaheuristic algorithms for accurately fusing the medical images. First, RMSE is computed between the first source image A and the fused image F using the following mathematical equation:

$$RMSE^{(A,F)} = \sqrt{\frac{1}{MN} * \sum_{i=1}^{N} \sum_{j=1}^{M} (A(i,j) - F(i,j))^2} \qquad (10.24)$$

where $A(i,j)$ represents the intensity value of the ith row and jth column in the first source image, and M and N represent the number of columns and rows in the same image, respectively. Second, RMSE is computed between the second source image and the fused image using the same previous equation with using B instead of A, as defined in the following equation:

$$RMSE^{(B,F)} = \sqrt{\frac{1}{MN} * \sum_{i=1}^{N} \sum_{j=1}^{M} (B(i,j) - F(i,j))^2} \qquad (10.25)$$

Finally, the objective function could be formulated based on computing the average value of both $RMSE^{(A,F)}$ and $RMSE^{(B,F)}$, as defined in the following equation:

$$f(\vec{X}_i) = RMSE^{(A,F)} + RMSE^{(B,F)} \qquad (10.26)$$

This function needs to be minimized to achieve better-fused images from the given source images. Therefore, in this chapter, it is solved using five classical metaheuristic algorithms in addition to two newly presented algorithms to achieve an outstanding fusion process in the medical field.

10.5.3 Improved seagull optimization algorithm

It is obvious from the previous explanation of the classical SOA that it has a weak exploitation operator because it updates the current solution using two-step sizes, which might take the newly generated solution far away from the regions including the best-so-far solution. Therefore, in this chapter, we improve the performance of SOA by removing the $\vec{C}_s$ vector, which aims at avoiding the collision between the solutions within the search space, from Eq. (10.17). This strengthens the SOA's exploitation operator for reaching the intractable regions, which might include the near-optimal solution. This equation is reformulated as shown in the next equation:

$$\vec{D}_s = \left| \vec{M}_s \right| \qquad (10.27)$$

In addition, the spiral shape in SOA might also weaken its searchability because this shape is based on Euler's number, which has a fixed value of 2.71828 and might search in faraway regions from the best-so-far solution. Therefore, the spiral shape of SOA is defined in Eq. (10.21), which is also removed to improve its performance for tackling the optimization problems that need a strong exploitation operator for finding the near-optimal solution. Generally, the ISOA's pseudocode is defined in Algorithm 10.2 to clearly show its main steps.

Algorithm 10.2 ISOA's pseudocode

1. Initialization.
2. Evaluation and identifying the best solution $\vec{X}^*$
3. $t = 1$;
4. **while** $(t < T_{max})$
5.   **for** each i individual
6.   r: pick a numerical value randomly in the range (0, 1)
7. r_2: Pick a numerical value randomly in the range (0, 1)
8.   Compute $\vec{D}_s$ according to Eq. (10.27).
9.   Calculate x̌, y̌, and ž by Eqs. (10.18)–(10.20) with removing rd.
10.   Compute the new position of the ith solution according to Eq. (10.22)
11.   **end for**
12. $t++$;
13. **end while**

Output: $\vec{X}^*$

10.5.4 Hybridization between TLBO and ISOA

To further improve fusion performance in the medical field, we hybridize both ISOA and TLBO to present a new metaheuristic algorithm with better exploration and exploitation operators. TLBO enjoys a strong exploration operator that has enabled it to solve several optimization problems, but its exploitation operator still needs strong improvement to enhance its convergence speed and achieve better outcomes in fewer iterations. Therefore, it is integrated with ISOA, which has distinguishing exploitation operators, to present a new hybrid algorithm named TLSOA for fusing medical images more accurately. The TLSOA's pseudocode is described in Algorithm 10.3 to clearly show its main steps.

Algorithm 10.3 TLSOA

Output: $\vec{X}^*$

1. Initialize N solutions $\vec{X}_i, (i = 1, 2, 3, \ldots\ldots\ldots N)$
2. Compute the fitness value for each $\vec{X}_i$.
3. Extract the near-optimal solutions achieved yet $\vec{X}^*$ to represent the teacher
4. $t = 0$
5. **While** $(t < T_{\max})$
6.   Update $\vec{X}_{\text{mean}}$ using Eq. (10.21)
7.   Increment the current iteration, $t = t + 1$;
8.   ////teaching phase
9.   **for** each i solution
10.   Compute the new solution $\vec{X}_i^{t+1}$ according to Eq. (10.22)
11.   If $f\left(\vec{X}_i^{t+1}\right) < f(\vec{X}_i^t)$
12. $\vec{X}_i^t = \vec{X}_i^{t+1}$
13.   End if
14.   **End for**
15.   //learning phase
16.   **for** each i solution
17.   Compute the new solution $\vec{X}_i^{t+1}$ according to Eq. (10.23)
18.   If $f\left(\vec{X}_i^{t+1}\right) < f(\vec{X}_i^t)$
19. $\vec{X}_i^t = \vec{X}_i^{t+1}$
20.   End if
21.   **End for**
22.   //Improved SOA
23.   **for** each i solution
24.   r: pick a numerical value randomly in the range (0, 1)
25. r_2: Pick a numerical value randomly in the range (0, 1)
26.   Compute $\vec{D}_s$ according to Eq. (10.27).
27.   Calculate x̌, y̌, and ž by Eqs. (10.18)−(10.20) with removing rd.
28.   Compute the new solution $\vec{X}_i^{t+1}$ according to Eq. (10.22)
29.   If $f\left(\vec{X}_i^{t+1}\right) < f(\vec{X}_i^t)$
30. $\vec{X}_i^t = \vec{X}_i^{t+1}$
31.   End if
32.   **End for**
33.   Increment the current iteration, $t = t + 3$
34. **End while**

10.6 Performance metrics

Several performance measures have been used to show the quality of the fused images contrasted to the original images; these metrics are the peak signal-to-noise ratio (PSNR), the feature similarity index (FSIM), the structured similarity index metric (SSIM), mutual information (MI). In addition, the computational cost metric is used to show the speedup of each algorithm. More descriptions of each metric from those are presented in the following list:

- PSNR metric: PSNR [12] is a performance indicator based on calculating the error ratio between the fused image and source images individually. The PSNR's mathematical expression could be defined as follows:

$$\text{PSNR} = 10\left(\frac{255^2}{MSE}\right) \tag{10.28}$$

MSE represents the mean-squared error between each original image and the fused image:

$$\text{MSE} = \frac{\sum_{i=1}^{M}\sum_{j=1}^{N}|A(i,j) - S(i,j)|}{M*N} \tag{10.29}$$

where $A(i,j)$ is the intensity of the pixel in the ith row and jth column in the original image, and $S(i,j)$ is the fused image. M and N refer to the numbers of columns and rows in the given image, respectively. The PSNR metric between the fused image F and the source images A and B individually is computed using Eq. (10.28). Then, the average PSNR between them is computed to estimate the quality of the fused image, as defined in the following formula:

$$\text{PSNR} = PSNR(A, F) + PSNR(B, F) \tag{10.30}$$

where $PSNR(A,F)$ indicates the PSNR value between the first source image A and the fused image F, and $PSNR(B,F)$ represents the PSNR value between the second source image B and the fused image. The higher the PSNR value, the better the fused image is.

- SSIM: SSIM [12] is a performance metric intended to measure the contrast distortion, similarity, and brightness between two images. The mathematical formula of this metric is defined as follows:

$$\text{SSIM} = \frac{(2\mu_o\mu_s + a)(2\sigma_{os} + b)}{(\mu_o^2 + \mu_s^2 + a)(\sigma_o^2 + \sigma_s^2 + b)} \tag{10.31}$$

where μ_o is the average intensity of the original image and μ_s is the average intensity of the fused image. μ_o and μ_s represent the standard deviations of the fused and original images, respectively. μ_{os} represents the covariance between two images, whereas a and b are constants with values of 0.001 and 0.003, respectively. SSIM between each source image and the fused image is first computed. Then, the average SSIM value between the returned SSIM values is computed to show the quality of the fused image, as defined in the following formula:

$$SSIM = SSIM(A, F) + SSIM(B, F) \qquad (10.32)$$

where $SSIM(A, F)$ represents the SSIM value between the first source image A and the fused image F, and $SSIM(B, F)$ is the SSIM value between the second source image B and the fused image. The higher the SSIM value, the better the fused image is.

- FSIM: FSIM [13] is a metric for determining the similarity of features between the fused and original images. FSIM is mathematically defined according to the following mathematical formula:

$$FSIM = \frac{\sum_{X \in \Omega} S_T(X)^* PC_m(X)}{\sum_{X \in \Omega} PC_m(X)} \qquad (10.33)$$

where Ω represents the entire pixel domain of an image. $S_T(X)$ defines a similarity score. The phase consistency measure is denoted by $PC_m(X)$, which is expressed as:

$$PC_m(X) = \max(PC_1(X), PC_2(X)) \qquad (10.34)$$

where $PC_1(X)$ and $PC_2(X)$ describe the phase consistency of the two blocks, respectively:

$$S_T(X) = [S_{PC}(X)]^\alpha \cdot [S_G(X)]^\beta \qquad (10.35)$$

$$S_{PC}(X) = \frac{2PC_1(X) \times PC_2(X) + T_1}{PC_1^2(X) \times PC_2^2(X) + T_1} \qquad (10.36)$$

$$S_G(X) = \frac{2G_1(X) \times G_2(X) + T_2}{G_1^2(X) \times G_2^2(X) + T_2} \qquad (10.37)$$

where the similarity measure of phase consistency is denoted by $S_{PC}(X)$. The gradient magnitude of two areas $G_1(X)$ and $G_2(X)$ is denoted by $S_G(X)$. The constants, T_1, and T_2 are all present. The FSIM values between the source images individually and the fused image are first computed. Then, the average FSIM value of those values is computed to show the quality of the fused image, as illustrated mathematically in the following equation:

$$FSIM = FSIM(A, F) + FSIM(B, F) \qquad (10.38)$$

where $FSIM(A, F)$ stands for the FSIM value between the first source image A and the fused image F, and $FSIM(B, F)$ is the FSIM value between the second source image B and the fused image. The higher the FSIM value, the better the fused image is.

- MI: The last metric used in this chapter to measure the fused image's quality is MI, which is used to measure the amount of information that the fused image includes about source images A and B. A more detailed description of this metric is found in [14].
- Computational cost: Finally, some metaheuristic algorithms might have the ability to achieve competitive outcomes for several optimization problems. However, unfortunately, they may need high computational costs, especially for large-scale problems, to even reach the desired solution or satisfy the termination condition. Therefore, in this chapter, we investigate the performance of various algorithms in terms of the computational cost metric to show the algorithms that could achieve outstanding outcomes in an acceptable time.

10.7 Practical analysis

This section is presented to investigate the performance of five standard metaheuristics and two variants of the classical SOA for image fusion in the medical field. These algorithms are verified using five pairs of multimodal medical images, where two images in each pair are taken by CT and MRI diagnostic tools to investigate the ability of those algorithms to fuse accurately the multimodal medical images. Some of those images are depicted in Fig. 10.2. Those images are available online [15]. The controlling parameters for all algorithms are set as recommended in the classical papers, except the population size and the maximum number of iterations, which are set to 20 and 100, respectively, to ensure a fair comparison. All algorithms have been implemented using MATLAB R2019a on a device with the following properties: 32 gigabytes of random access memory, a Core i7 processor, and a Windows 10 operating system.

Under the objective function RMSE, all algorithms were executed 30 independent times on five sets of MRI-CT medical images, and the average values for various performance metrics were computed and are presented in Table 10.1. From this table, it is observed that TLSOA shows superior performance in all performance metrics employed to observe the quality of the

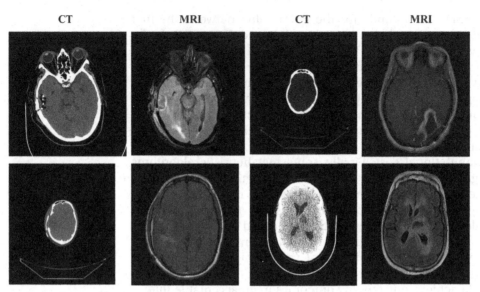

Figure 10.2 Some of the multimodal medical images used in our experiments.

Table 10.1 Comparison among algorithms under various performance metrics. (Bold values stand for the best outcomes)

Performance metrics	Algorithms						
	TLBO	LSO	NOA	DE	SOA	ISOA	TLSOA
RMSE	4.56541	4.45833	4.30379	4.28215	4.51054	4.42950	**4.11693**
PSNR	10.67279	10.90609	11.34020	11.43769	10.78427	11.02371	**11.86813**
SSIM	0.77324	0.78819	0.80872	0.81373	0.77939	0.79426	**0.83163**
FSIM	0.82142	0.82785	0.83825	0.84341	0.82360	0.83182	**0.84722**
MI	0.31435	0.32082	0.33337	0.33648	0.31736	0.32477	**0.34712**
CPU time	72.4790	72.8178	71.5695	73.9883	**71.5323**	71.6850	72.5698

fused images. In more detail, for the RMSE metric, TLSOA could come in at the first rank with an average RMSE of 4.11, followed by DE as the second best one, while TLBO is the worst performing algorithm. Regarding the SSIM metric, TLSOA ranks first with a value of 0.83, and DE comes after it with a value of 0.81, while TLBO is the worst algorithm. Likewise, for the other metrics, we can identify the best performing algorithm. From this, we can conclude that TLSOA is considered a strong alternative for accurately fusing multimodal medical images. Fig. 10.3 presents the source images and fused images obtained

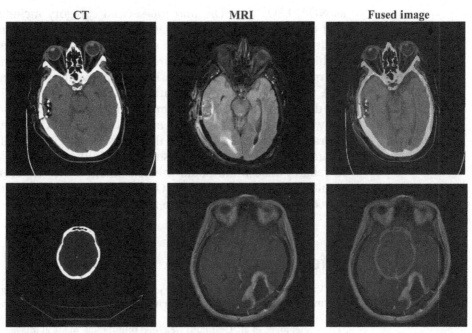

Figure 10.3 Comparison between the source images and the fused image.

by TLSOA as the best performing algorithm to show the difference before and after the fusion process. From this figure, it is obvious that TLSOA could significantly estimate the unknown parameters that could improve the performance of DWT for fusing multimodal medical images.

10.8 Chapter summary

Due to its simplicity and minimal computational cost, the DWT has garnered a great deal of interest in recent decades as a technique for image fusion. However, DWT has unidentified parameters that must be precisely optimized for a more efficient fusion procedure. In recent years, metaheuristic algorithms have been regarded as the most effective optimization strategies for addressing a variety of optimization issues. Therefore, this chapter is presented to disclose the performance of two distinct categories of metaheuristic algorithms to estimate those unknown coefficients for further improving image fusion of multimodal medical images. The first category includes three recently published optimization algorithms, such as NOA, LSO, and SOA, and the second category includes two well-established algorithms (DE and TLBO). In addition, two additional variants to further enhance the fusion process for multimodal medical images are presented. The first variant is referred to as ISOA and is based on improving the efficacy of SOA to strengthen its exploitation operator to move rapidly in the direction of the near-optimal solution. The second variant, known as TLSOA, is based on enhancing the TLBO exploitation operator by integrating it with the first variant. Five sets of MRI-CT images are used to demonstrate the ability of each algorithm to reliably fuse multimodal medical images. The experimental results demonstrate that TLSOA shows superior performance concerning many performance metrics.

References

[1] V.S. Parvathy, S. Pothiraj, Multi-modality medical image fusion using hybridization of binary crow search optimization, Health Care Management Science 23 (2020) 661–669.

[2] S. Shehanaz, et al., Optimum weighted multimodal medical image fusion using particle swarm optimization, Optik 231 (2021) 166413.

[3] P.H. Venkatrao, S.S. Damodar, HWFusion: Holoentropy and SP-Whale optimisation-based fusion model for magnetic resonance imaging multimodal image fusion, IET Image Processing 12 (4) (2018) 572–581.

[4] Z. Wang, et al., A comparative analysis of image fusion methods, IEEE Transactions on Geoscience and Remote Sensing 43 (6) (2005) 1391–1402.

[5] M. Manchanda, R. Sharma, An improved multimodal medical image fusion algorithm based on fuzzy transform, Journal of Visual Communication and Image Representation 51 (2018) 76–94.

[6] M. Manchanda, R. Sharma, A novel method of multimodal medical image fusion using fuzzy transform, Journal of Visual Communication and Image Representation 40 (2016) 197–217.

[7] C. Asha, et al., Multi-modal medical image fusion with adaptive weighted combination of NSST bands using chaotic grey wolf optimization, IEEE Access 7 (2019) 40782–40796.

[8] N.N. Kumar, T.J. Prasad, K.S. Prasad, Optimized dual-tree complex wavelet transform and fuzzy entropy for multi-modal medical image fusion: a hybrid meta-heuristic concept, Journal of Mechanics in Medicine and Biology 21 (03) (2021) 2150024.

[9] L. Xu, et al., Medical image fusion using a modified shark smell optimization algorithm and hybrid wavelet-homomorphic filter, Biomedical Signal Processing and Control 59 (2020) 101885.

[10] P.-H. Dinh, Combining gabor energy with equilibrium optimizer algorithm for multi-modality medical image fusion, Biomedical Signal Processing and Control 68 (2021) 102696.

[11] G. Dhiman, V. Kumar, Seagull optimization algorithm: Theory and its applications for large-scale industrial engineering problems, Knowledge-Based Systems 165 (2019) 169–196.

[12] Hore, A., & Ziou, D. (2010). *Image quality metrics: PSNR vs. SSIM*. In: *2010
      20th international conference on pattern recognition*. IEEE.
[13] L. Zhang, et al., FSIM: A feature similarity index for image quality
      assessment, IEEE Transactions on Image Processing 20 (8) (2011)
      2378–2386.
[14] N. Cvejic, C. Canagarajah, D.J.El Bull, Image fusion metric based on mutual
      information and Tsallis entropy, Electronics Letters 42 (11) (2006) 1.
[15] https://github.com/ashna111/multimodal-image-fusion-to-detect-brain-
      tumors. Accessed 30 Apr. 2023.

11

Metaheuristic algorithms for medical image registration: a comparative study

11.1 Introduction

Medical and scientific applications rely heavily on accurate image analysis, interpretation, and visualization [1]. Many of these applications need to compare, integrate, and fuse images captured at various periods by various imaging devices, or from various vantage points. Medical images have several uses, including but not limited to diagnosis, disease monitoring, intervention, and treatment planning, comparing patient data to anatomical atlases, assisted surgery, and anatomy segmentation. These images are typically obtained using a variety of tools, such as X-rays, positron emission tomography, ultrasound, magnetic resonance imaging, and computer tomography, at various times. Therefore misalignment between images is unavoidable, irrespective of whether they are of a single patient or several [1]. Image registration (IR) is, therefore, a crucial preprocessing operation in medical imaging, as it enables the alignment and integration of visual information acquired under varied situations. For this reason, IR attempts to calculate the best geometric transformation that overlays the shared area of the images. The goal of most IR methods is to adjust an input image so that its geometry matches that of a reference image. The similarity between the two images is calculated using a similarity metric after a spatial transformation is applied. In brief, the majority of IR techniques are composed of the following four steps [2]:

- Feature detection: In this step, the unique features, such as closed-boundary regions, edges, contours, line intersections, and corners, are automatically identified.
- Feature matching: This process involves matching up the features found in the sensed image with those found in the

Metaheuristics Algorithms for Medical Applications. DOI: https://doi.org/10.1016/B978-0-443-13314-5.00001-1

reference image. The spatial correlations between the features, a number of other feature descriptors, and similarity metrics are used for this aim.

- Transformation model estimation: This step involves estimating the type and parameters of the mapping functions that align the detected image with the reference image. An iterative optimization approach is applied to determine the best transformation by investigating all of the feasible transformations under the similarity metric, which is the topic of this chapter.
- Image resampling and transformation: Mapping functions are utilized to transform the detected image. The proper interpolation method is used to compute image values in noninteger coordinates.

In this chapter, some of the techniques proposed for IR are first discussed. Second, the mathematical models of two recently proposed metaheuristic algorithms, namely, marine predators algorithm (MPA) and artificial gorilla troops optimizer (GTO), are extensively explained. Third, the main steps for adapting the metaheuristics to tackle IR are presented. In addition, the convergence improvement strategy (CIS) used to improve the performance of the studied algorithms is described in detail. Afterward, some experiments are conducted to illustrate the performance of four metaheuristic algorithms, including NOA, MPA, GTO, and LSO, for IR in the medical field. Finally, the chapter summary is presented.

11.2 Techniques for image registration

There are two primary types of IR techniques: feature-based, in which just the most prominent or distinguishing features of the images are used for registration, and intensity-based, in which the entire image is taken into account during the alignment process. These two categories are described in detail next.

11.2.1 Feature-based image registration techniques

These methods involve extracting prominent structures or features, like lines, points, and regions, from the sensed and reference images that are used to perform the alignment process. The main advantage of these techniques is that they are significantly able to decrease the complexity of the IR problem because they use only parts of the images. However, these techniques' reliability is highly dependent on the feature extraction algorithm used to find the salient and distinctive features if the sensed and reference images have these features, which is the main limitation of these techniques. Several feature-based approaches have been proposed over the past few decades for performing the IR process. For example, a multimodal IR algorithm based on hierarchical feature extraction was proposed [3]. This algorithm is composed of two steps: feature extraction and geometric matching. The feature extraction step aims to extract hierarchically two types of features. An additional algorithm based on the fuzzy C-means (FCM) clustering for segmenting the images and the scale-invariant feature transform (SIFT) for matching the features in the segmented regions was proposed for solving the medical IR problem [4]. In this algorithm, FCM was applied on feature vectors that involve local information. This information is constant to the alterations in the scale, rotation, and illumination. Afterward, SIFT is applied to register the sensed and reference images. In addition, Gupta et al. [5] suggested an IR technique based on the FCM and speeded-up robust feature detectors to extract the salient and distinctive features and match them to perform the IR process.

11.2.2 Intensity-based image registration techniques

These techniques operate on images without making an effort to identify significant features; instead, they process a huge amount of data that significantly increases the computational cost. These approaches are more precise because they rely on the distribution of the intensity values to perform the alignment process. Unfortunately, they are affected by illumination changes and noise [1]. These techniques consider three important aspects of the IR process. The first aspect is the search domain, which involves a collection of the potential transformations that could be used to perform the alignment process of the images. The second aspect is the similarity metric used to measure the resemblance level between two images. There are several widely used similarity metrics, like the generalized correlation coefficient, the sum of squared intensity differences, Hausdorff distance, and information-theoretic measures [6]. The recent work pays attention to the mutual information (MI) as a similarity metric due to its ability to achieve a better IR process. The MI of two images measures the mutual dependency level between these images to maximize this level. Assuming that there are two images A and B, the MI for them can be computed as follows:

$$I(A,B) = H(A) + H(B) - H(A,B) \tag{11.1}$$

where H refers to the Shannon entropy, which is computed according to the following formula:

$$H(A) = - \sum_{i=1}^{M} p(i)\log(p(i)) \tag{11.2}$$

where M represents the maximum intensity value for image A, and $p(i)$ represents the occurrence likelihood of the intensity level i. $H(A,B)$ expresses the joint entropy between A and B using the following formula:

$$H(A,B) = - \sum_{i=1}^{M} \sum_{j=1}^{M} p(i,j)\log(p(i,j)) \tag{11.3}$$

where $p(i,j)$ is the likelihood of the intensity level i occurring in image A with the intensity level j in image B. However, the MI is sensitive to the partial overlap size between the images, which is its main drawback. Therefore, the normalized MI was presented to minimize this sensitivity for achieving a better IR process between images. The mathematical formula of the normalized MI can be expressed according to the following equation:

$$I_N(A,B) = \frac{H(A) + H(B)}{2H(A,B)} \tag{11.4}$$

Unfortunately, the normalized MI stills suffer from the same problem of MI. Therefore, the cross-cumulative residual entropy (CCRE), another better-performing similarity metric, was developed to present a smoother curve than the MI and the normalized MI in medical IR. CCRE is derived from CRE, which is comparable to other Shannon entropy-based similarity measures, and uses the cumulative distribution to determine the similarity measure of the uncertainty of discrete random variables. The CRE can be expressed as follows [7]:

$$\varepsilon(X) = - \sum_{u} (P(x > u)lb(x > u)) \tag{11.5}$$

where x and u are two independent random variables, and $P(x > u)$ represents the likelihood that the value of the variable

x is greater than that of the variable u. Based on this metric, the CCRE is defined as follows for reference image B and scene image A:

$$S_{CCRE}(A, B) = \varepsilon(A) - E(\varepsilon(A|B)) \qquad (11.6)$$

This equation can be extended as follows, according to Eq. (11.5) [7]:

$$S_{CCRE}(A, B) = \sum_{u \in A} \sum_{u \in B} \left(P(t > u, r = u) lb \left(\frac{P(t > u, r = u)}{P_A(t > u) P_B(r = u)} \right) \right)$$

$$(11.7)$$

The last aspect considered in these techniques is using the optimization algorithms with the similarity metric as an objective function to search for the best geometric transformation that could accurately align the scene and reference images. There are two strategies proposed to explore the geometrical transformation space for reaching the best transformation; they are the parameter-based techniques and matching-based techniques. In the former, the search process aims at estimating the optimal values of the transformation parameters. Those optimal values of the parameters could be estimated by optimization techniques like gradient-based optimization algorithms. In the latter, the search is performed in the space of the feature correspondences for reaching the matching features used to derive the transformation parameters by numerical techniques. These matching features could be estimated using the matching algorithms like iterative closest point.

11.3   Artificial gorilla troops optimizer

Recently, Abdollahzadeh proposed a new population-based optimization technique named GTO for solving global optimization and engineering design optimization problems [8]. GTO mimicked the social intelligence of the gorilla troops, which are divided into two main operators known as exploration and exploitation. In the former, GTO tries to attack the majority of regions within the search space as much as possible in the hope of finding the promising regions. Within the optimization process, those regions are exploited using the latter operator to move quickly toward the near-optimal solution. The mathematical model of GTO is described in the following sections, and its pseudocode is presented in Algorithm 11.1.

Algorithm 11.1 The steps of GTO

Output: X^*

1. Initializes randomly N individuals, $\vec{X}_i (i \in N)$.
2. Set β_1, W, and p.
3. Evaluate each $\vec{X}_i$
4. Identify the best solution achieved yet, X^*
5. $t = 0$; %% Initialize the current iteration
6. **while** ($t < t_{\max}$)
7.   **Update** C and L according to Eqs. (11.9) and (11.11), respectively.
8.   **// Exploration**
9. r: a numerical value selected at random in the interval (0, 1)
10.   **for** each i solution
11.   Update X_i using Eq. (11.8)
12.   Replace X_i with G_i if the objective value of the latter is better
13.   Replace X^* if there is better
14. $t++$;
15.   **End**
16.   **// Exploitation**
17.   **for** each i solution
18.   Update X_i using Eq. (11.20)
19.   Replace X_i with G_i if the objective value of the latter is better
20.   Replace X^* if there is better
21. $t++$;
22.   **End**
23. **End while**

11.3.1 Exploration operator

This operator encourages exploring the search space as possible for reaching the most effective regions that might involve near-optimal solutions. The weakness of this operator might cause falling into local minima and hence the algorithm could not reach these promising regions. Therefore the authors tried to design GTO with a strong exploration operator to diversify the search process for attacking the most possible solutions within the search space. This operator is mathematically described using the following formula:

$$\vec{G}_i(t+1) = \begin{cases} \vec{lb} + \left(\vec{ub} - \vec{lb}\right)*r & r_1 < p \\ (r_2 - C) \times \left(\vec{X}_r(t)\right) + \vec{H} \times L & r_1 \geq 0.5 \\ \vec{X}_i^t - L \times \left(L \times \left(\vec{X}_i^t - \vec{G}_r(t)\right) + r_3 \times \left(\vec{X}_i^t - \vec{G}_r^t\right)\right) & r_1 < 0.5 \end{cases}$$

$$(11.8)$$

$$C = F \times \left(1 - \frac{t}{T_{\max}}\right) \qquad (11.9)$$

$$F = \cos(2 \times r_4) + 1 \tag{11.10}$$

$$L = C \times l \tag{11.11}$$

$$\vec{H} = \vec{Z} \times \vec{X}_i(t) | Z = [-C, C] \tag{11.12}$$

where l is a controlling factor that includes numerical data generated randomly in the range $(-1, 1)$, $\vec{G}_i$ is a vector to include the newly generated positions of the ith solution, while $\vec{X}_i^t$ is a vector storing the current position of the same solution. $\vec{G}_r$ is a vector storing the positions of a solution chosen at random from the newly generated solutions, and $\vec{X}_r^t$ is a vector containing a solution chosen randomly from the individuals in the current population. p is a predefined controlling parameter at the interval of $(0, 1)$. $\vec{Z}$ represents a vector including numerical values randomly selected in the range $(-C, C)$. After that, $\vec{X}_i(t)$ is compared with the newly generated $\vec{G}_i(t+1)$; if the latter is better, it is set in the current population instead of the former.

11.3.2 Exploitation operator

In this operator, GTO simulates two behaviors: following the best-so-far solution and competing for adult females. The first behavior in GTO is mathematically formulated as follows:

$$\vec{G}_i(t+1) = L \times M \times \left(\vec{X}_i^t - \vec{X}^*\right) + \vec{X}_i^t \tag{11.13}$$

$$\vec{M} = \left(\left|\frac{1}{N}\sum_{i=0}^{N}\vec{G}_i(t)\right|^{g}\right)^{\frac{1}{g}} \tag{11.14}$$

$$g = 2^L \tag{11.15}$$

The second behavior is mathematically defined as follows:

$$\vec{G}_i(t+1) = -\left(Q \times \vec{X}_i^t - Q \times \vec{X}^*\right) \times A + \vec{X}^* \tag{11.16}$$

$$Q = 2 \times r_5 - 1 \tag{11.17}$$

$$A = E \times \beta_1 \tag{11.18}$$

$$\vec{E} = \begin{cases} \vec{N}_1, r_6 \geq 0.5 \\ \vec{N}_2, r_6 < 0.5 \end{cases} \tag{11.19}$$

The variables r_5 and r_6 were selected randomly from the interval between 0 and 1. The value of β_1 is predetermined prior to commencing the search process. Vector $\vec{N_1}$ comprises randomly generated values following the normal distribution, whereas $\vec{N_2}$ denotes a randomly assigned number conforming to the normal distribution. To alternate between the aforementioned behaviors, GTO utilizes a predetermined controlling parameter known as w and a factor denoted as C, as presented in the following equation:

$$\vec{G_i}(t+1) = \begin{cases} Eq\,(11.13) & \text{if} \quad C \geq w \\ Eq\,(11.16) & \text{if} \quad C < w \end{cases} \tag{11.20}$$

11.4 Marine predators algorithm

Faramarzi [9] presented the MPA as a novel nature-inspired algorithm for tackling continuous optimization problems. This algorithm attempts to imitate the way that predators behave when they attack their prey. When hunting their prey, predators specifically make a choice between Brownian strategy and Lévy's flight based on the relative speed of the prey and the predators. In general, the MPA can be mathematically represented in the following way:

Step 1: Building Elite (E) matrix

In this step, MPA considers the fittest solution obtained so-far as the top predator $\vec{A^I}$ in foraging and employed to create the *Elite(E)* matrix as follows:

$$E = \begin{bmatrix} A^I_{1,1} & A^I_{1,2} & \cdots & A^I_{1,d} \\ A^I_{2,1} & A^I_{2,2} & \cdots & A^I_{2,d} \\ \cdot & \cdot & \cdot & \cdot \\ A^I_{N,1} & A^I_{N,2} & \cdots & A^I_{N,d} \end{bmatrix}$$

where d represents the number of dimensions in the optimization problems. The positions of the prey individuals are created and initialized randomly within the search boundary of the tackled problem, as shown in the following two-dimensional array:

$$\vec{X} = \begin{bmatrix} x_{1,1} & x_{1,2} & \cdots & x_{1,d} \\ x_{2,1} & x_{2,2} & \cdots & x_{2,d} \\ \cdot & \cdot & \cdot & \cdot \\ x_{N,1} & x_{N,2} & \cdots & x_{N,d} \end{bmatrix}$$

It is vital to note that the previous two matrices are two extremely important features of the MPA that the optimization process relies on. During optimization, each prey's update will go through one of three phases based on its relative speed to the predators:

Step 2: High-velocity ratio

The velocity rate between the predators and prey in this phase is high, as the prey is moving quickly in search of food and the predators are tracking their motions. During this stage, the prey will come to the predators, eliminating the need for the predators to move for reaching the prey. This stage takes place at the beginning of the optimization process to search for a superior solution in every region within the problem's search space. This phase can be described using the following mathematical formula:

$$\text{while} \quad t < \frac{1}{3} \times T_{\max}$$

$$\vec{S}_i = \vec{R}_B \otimes \left(\vec{E}_i - \vec{R}_B \otimes \vec{X}_i \right) \tag{11.21}$$

$$\vec{X}_i = \vec{X}_i + P \times \vec{R} \otimes \vec{S}_i \tag{11.22}$$

where $\otimes$ represents the entry-wise multiplication, $\vec{R}_B$ is a vector to refer to the Brownian strategy and is randomly generated according to the normal distribution, P is a fixed numerical value and recommended 0.5 in the classical MPA, and $\vec{R}$ represents a vector including numerical values selected randomly in the interval (0, 1) according to the uniform distribution.

Step 3: Unit velocity ratio

After the first third of the optimization process, the exploration operation is gradually transited to the exploitation operation to zero in on the best solution obtained yet to accelerate the convergence speed toward the near-optimal solution. Therefore this stage is a combination of exploration and exploration. Based on this, the MPA splits the population into two equal parts: the first part is updated according to the exploration operator, while the rest of the solutions are updated according to the exploitation operators. Finally, the mathematical expression for this phase is as follows:

$$\text{while} \quad \frac{1}{3} \times T_{\max} \leq t < \frac{2}{3} \times T_{\max}$$

- For the first half

$$\vec{S}_i = \vec{R}_L \otimes \left(\vec{E}_i - \vec{R}_L \otimes \vec{X}_i \right) \tag{11.23}$$

$$\vec{X}_i = \vec{X}_i + P \times \vec{R} \otimes \vec{S}_i \qquad (11.24)$$

- For the second half

$$\vec{S}_i = \vec{R}_B \otimes \left(\vec{R}_B \otimes \vec{E}_i - \vec{X}_i \right) \qquad (11.25)$$

$$\vec{X}_i = \vec{E}_i + P \times CF \otimes \vec{S}_i \qquad (11.26)$$

where $\vec{R}_L$ is a vector storing numerical value randomly generated according to the levy flight, and CF is a phrase about an adaptive parameter presented to regulate the step size; it is derived according to the following mathematical formula:

$$CF = \left(1 - \frac{t}{T_{\max}} \right)^{\left(2\frac{t}{T_{\max}} \right)} \qquad (11.27)$$

Step 4: Low-velocity ratio

At this stage, specifically in the last third of the optimization process, the exploration capability is completely turned into the exploitation capability. In this stage, the predators use only the levy flight strategy to move faster than the prey. The mathematical formula to simulate this stage is as follows:

$$\text{while} \quad t \geq \frac{2}{3} \times T_{\max}$$

$$\vec{S}_i = \vec{R}_L \otimes \left(\vec{R}_L \otimes \vec{E}_i - \vec{X}_i \right) \qquad (11.28)$$

$$\vec{X}_i = \vec{E}_i + P \times CF \otimes \vec{S}_i \qquad (11.29)$$

Predator behavior can also be greatly influenced by other variables, such as fish aggregating devices (FADs) and eddy formulation. Some research indicates that, because of FADs, predators spend only 20% of their time investigating another environment in the hope of finding abundant prey, while the remaining 80% of their time is spent searching for a better position within the surrounding environment. The following formula can be used to mathematically simulate the FADs:

$$\vec{X}_i = \begin{cases} \vec{X}_i + CF \times [\vec{X}_{\min} + \vec{r}_2(\vec{X}_{\max} - \vec{X}_{\min})] \otimes \vec{U} & \text{if } r < \text{FADs} \\ \vec{X}_i + [\text{FADs}(1 - r) + r]\left(\vec{X}_a - \vec{X}_b \right) & \text{if } r \geq \text{FADs} \end{cases}$$

$$(11.30)$$

where $\vec{r}_2$ is a vector containing numerical values selected at random in the interval (0, 1). U is a vector including binary values (0, 1). FADs refer to the likelihood that FADs will influence the optimization process; this factor is recommended to be 0.2 in the classical MPA. a and b represent the indices of two solutions selected at random from the current population. After each process of updating, MPA makes a comparison between the objective values of the updated solutions and those of the current solutions to determine whether or not the positions have improved as a result of this update. If the updated position of each individual in the population is better than the current position of the same individual, it is recorded to be used in the next iteration instead of the current position; otherwise, the current position is continued to the next iteration. This behavior is referred to as memory saving. The steps of the MPA are listed in Algorithm 11.2.

Algorithm 11.2 MPA

1. Initialize $\vec{X}_i i = (1, 2, 3, \ldots\ldots\ldots, N)$, P = 0.5
2. **while** (t < T_{max})
3.   Compute the objective value for each solution
4.   Identify the best solution obtained yet X^*
5.   Apply the memory saving
6.   Update the elite matrix, E, if there is a solution better than the best solution obtained yet
7.   Compute the factor CF using Eq. (11.27)
8.   **for** each i solution
9.   *if* $\left(t < \frac{1}{3} {}^* T_{max}\right)$
10.   Update $\vec{X}_i$ according to Eq. (11.22)
11.   *Else if* $\left(\frac{1}{3} {}^* T_{max} < t < \frac{2}{3} {}^* T_{max}\right)$
12.   *If* $\left(i < \frac{1}{2} {}^* N\right)$
13.   Update $\vec{X}_i$ according to Eq. (11.24)
14.   *Else*
15.   Update $\vec{X}_i$ according to Eq. (11.26)
16.   *Else*
17.   Update $\vec{X}_i$ according to Eq. (11.29)
18.   **end for**
19.   Compute the objective value for each solution
20.   Update the elite matrix, E, if there is a solution better than the best solution obtained yet
21.   Implement the memory saving
22.   Apply the FADs according to Eq. (11.30)
23.   t++
24. **end while**
Output: Return X^*

11.5 Proposed algorithms for image registration

The IR as mentioned before needs an optimization algorithm with strong search abilities to find the best transformation for registration. Therefore, in this chapter, we will investigate the performance of four studied algorithms, NOA, LSO, MPA, and GTO, for this problem. In addition, to improve their performance for achieving better convergence speed, they have been integrated with an additional strategy, namely, CIS, to improve their exploration and exploitation capabilities for reaching the near-optimal registration parameters of the 2-D rigid geometric transformation under two different objective functions discussed below. The rigid transformation approach is used in our experiments due to its wide use as a registration strategy in clinical practice [8]. Three optimization parameters under this transformation have to be accurately estimated to register the scene ad reference images. These parameters include two translations and one rotation. Generally, the main steps of the studied algorithms to solve the IR problem are summarized as follows: Initialization, evaluation, improvement strategies, and pseudocode.

11.5.1 Initialization

To solve the IR problem using metaheuristics, there are a number of solutions that have to be generated at random within the search space before starting the optimization process to give these algorithms the starting points to search for the near-optimal solutions. As mentioned before, the IR problem under 2-D rigid transformation has three parameters: two translations ranging between -30 and 30 and one rotation angle ranging between 0 and 360. To find the optimal value within the range of each parameter, N solutions with three dimensions are randomly generated to determine the starting points of the metaheuristics. Due to the stochastic nature of the metaheuristics, the initial solutions in each independent run are different due to the randomization process employed to generate them. Sometimes, those start points might be local optima, which makes some algorithms unable to achieve better outcomes due to their weak local optimal avoidance capabilities. In brief, the more the start points cover the search space, the more the local minimum problem is significantly minimized, and hence the near-optimal solution might be achieved. In this chapter, the initialization stage generates these starting points within the search space according to the uniform distribution. Afterward, these points are evaluated as defined later to measure their quality and extract the best-so-far solution.

11.5.2 Evaluation step

In this chapter, two objective functions are employed with the studied algorithms to investigate if there are changes in the quality of the registered image or not. The first one is CCRE, and the second is the sum of mean squared errors (MSE) between the registered and reference images. The first objective function needs to be maximized for achieving better registration, while the second has to be minimized. The mathematical model of the first objective is explained in detail in the previous sections, while the mathematical model of MSE could be defined as follows:

$$\text{MSE} = \frac{1}{N_1 \times M} \sum_{n=0}^{N_1} \sum_{m=0}^{M} (R_{nm} - I_{nm}) \qquad (11.31)$$

where N_1 is the number of rows in the scene and original images, M represents the number of columns of the same images, and R_{nm} and I_{nm} are the intensity value in the nth row and mth coulmn within both the scene and referenced images.

11.5.3 Convergence improvement strategy

A novel strategy to enhance the convergence speed of the metaheuristics to reach the fittest values of the tackled optimization problems in a smaller number of iterations was presented [10]. This strategy is known as the CIS and is comprised of two parts: (1) The first fold uses levy flight to search around the best solution obtained yet while taking into consideration avoiding getting stagnation into local optima by strengthening the randomization search, as mathematically defined in Eq. (11.32); (2) the second fold strives to reduce the randomization process that was included in the first fold by updating $\vec{X}^*$ in the opposite direction of $\vec{X}_i$ as defined in Eq. (11.33):

$$\vec{X}_i^{t+1} = \vec{X}^* + \vec{L} \otimes \left(r \times \vec{X}^* - \vec{L} \otimes \vec{X}_i^t \right) \qquad (11.32)$$

where $\vec{L}$ represents a vector of numerical values created at random with the Levy flight method, and r is a value chosen at random between 0 and 1. As was previously stated, increasing randomization in search at the outset is intended to prevent the search from becoming trapped in local minima caused by repeatedly visiting locations close to the best solution achieved yet.

$$\vec{X}_i^{t+1} = \vec{X}^* + \vec{r}_1 \otimes \left(\vec{X}^* - \vec{X}_i^t \right) \qquad (11.33)$$

where $\vec{r}_1$ is an arbitrary numeric vector chosen at random from a uniform distribution between 0 and 1. The interchange between Eqs. (11.32) and (11.33) is determined by a predetermined probability, denoted as β, which is selected based on the inherent characteristics of the optimization problem. Finally, Algorithm 11.3 lists the steps of the CIS mechanism.

Algorithm 11.3 CIS strategy

Input: $\vec{X}_i(i = 1, 2, 3, .., N)$
1. *for $i = 1: N$*
2. r_3: A number value is chosen at random in the interval 0 and 1.
3.   *if $r_3 < \beta$*
4.   Update $\vec{X}_i$ according to Eq. (11.32)
5.   **Else**
6.   Update $\vec{X}_i$ according to Eq. (11.33)
7.   *End if*
8. *End for*

11.5.4 Pseudocode of a studied algorithm

The CIS is effectively integrated with the studied algorithms, LSO, GTO, MPA, and NOA, to propose new variants called ILSO, IGTO, IMPA, and INOA with better exploration and exploitation capabilities. In the beginning, for all studied algorithms, N solutions are first initialized at random within the search space of each dimension. These initial solutions are then evaluated using either the CCRE or MSE objective functions to determine the quality of each solution. The solution with either the lowest fitness value under the MSE objective function or the highest fitness value under the CCRE objective function is identified as the best-so-far solution. Afterward, the optimization process of each studied algorithm is called to update those initial solutions in an attempt to search for better solutions. Within the optimization process, specifically at the end of each iteration, the CIS strategy is applied to update the current solution in an attempt to improve the exploitation operator of each algorithm. The optimization process for each algorithm is continued until the termination condition is satisfied. In this chapter, the termination condition is based on reaching the maximum number of function evaluations. In Algorithm 11.4, we list the steps for adapting the MPA as an illustrative example for tackling the IR problem.

Algorithm 11.4 The steps of MPA for IR problems

1. Initialize $\vec{X}_i i = (1, 2, 3, \ldots\ldots, N)$, P = 0.5
2. **while** $(t < T_{max})$
3. Compute the objective value for each solution according to either Eq. (11.7) or Eq. (11.31)
4. Identify the best solution achieved yet X*
5. Apply the memory saving
6. Update the elite matrix, E, if there is a solution better than the best solution obtained yet
7. Compute the factor CF using Eq. (11.27)
8. **for** each i solution
9. *if* $\left(t < \frac{1}{3} * T_{max}\right)$
10. Update $\vec{X}_i$ according to Eq. (11.22)
11. *Else if* $\left(\frac{1}{3} * T_{max} < t < \frac{2}{3} * T_{max}\right)$
12. *If* $\left(i < \frac{1}{2} * N\right)$
13. Update $\vec{X}_i$ according to Eq. (11.24)
14. *Else*
15. Update $\vec{X}_i$ according to Eq. (11.26)
16. *Else*
17. Update $\vec{X}_i$ according to Eq. (11.29)
18. **end for**
19. Compute the objective value for each solution according to either Eq. (11.7) or Eq. (11.31)
20. Update the elite matrix, E, if there is a solution better than the best-so-far solution
21. Implement the memory saving
22. Apply the FADs according to Eq. (11.30)
23. Compute the objective value for each solution according to either Eq. (11.7) or Eq. (11.31)
24. Update the elite matrix, E, if there is a solution better than the best-so-far solution
25. Implement the memory saving
26. Apply the CIS using Algorithm 11.3
27. t++
28. **end while**
Output: Return X*

11.6 Practical analysis

This section is presented to investigate the performance of four standard metaheuristics, namely, MPA, GTO, NOA, and LSO, for tackling the IR problem. In addition, to enhance the performance of those classical algorithms, they are integrated with a novel strategy known as the CIS to enhance its exploitation operators for achieving better outcomes as quickly as possible. These improved algorithms are called INOA, ILSO, IMPA, and IGTO. Two different brain tumor images are used to assess the performance of these algorithms. Four performance metrics are used to compare their performance to determine which one is able to achieve a better registration process; these metrics include SSIM, PSNR, FSIM, and fitness value (F-value). All algorithms are implemented using MATLAB R2019a on a device with the following properties: 32 GB of random access memory, a Core i7 processor, and Windows 10 operating system. The maximum iteration and population size of 100 and 50 are set for all algorithms to achieve a fair comparison.

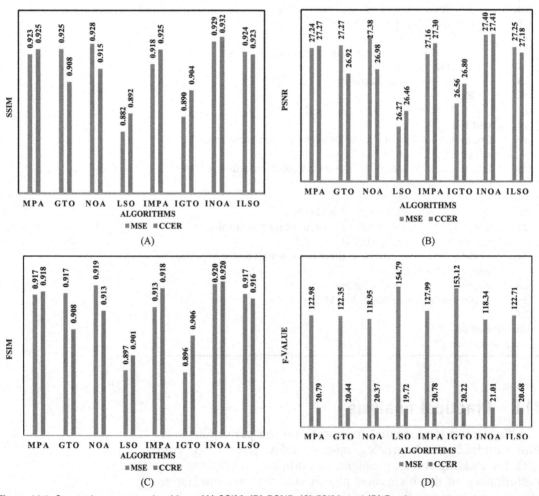

Figure 11.1 Comparison among algorithms: (A) SSIM; (B) PSNR; (C) FSIM; and (D) F-value.

Under both SSE and CCRE, all algorithms were executed 30 independent times on two medical images, and the average values for various performance metrics were computed and presented in Fig. 11.1, which illustrates that the quality of registered images relies on the employed optimization techniques more than the used objective function. For example, MPA with MSE could achieve better registration in comparison to employing CCER as an objective function, while IMPA with CCER performs better than IMPA with MSE. From that, we could conclude that the performance of the optimization process has the most effect on the registration process, not on the objective function. Among all the algorithms, INOA could perform better for all employed performance metrics. Therefore, it is the most alternative registration technique for finding the best transformation for two images in the medical field. Fig. 11.2 presents the scene and reference images before the registration process, in addition to presenting the registered image obtained under the INOA and the difference between the reference and registered images. From this figure, it is

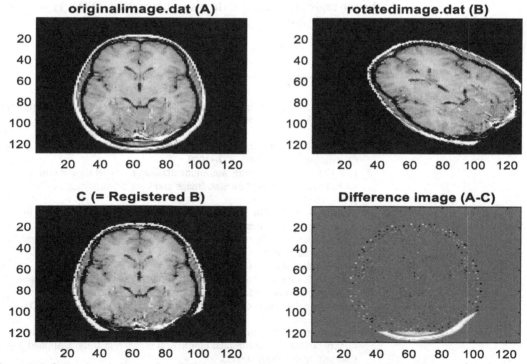

Figure 11.2 Comparison between the original and rotated images before and after registration.

obvious that the metaheuristic algorithms could significantly determine the best transformation which could effectively integrate two medical images.

11.7 Chapter summary

This chapter discusses the performance of some recently published and well-established metaheuristic algorithms with two distinct objective functions, namely, CCRE and the MSE, for solving the IR problem of medical brain magnetic resonance images. In addition, these algorithms were enhanced with a recently published technique known as the CIS to present new variants with better exploitation operators. Two magnetic resonance images of the brain were used to validate the traditional and enhanced algorithms. In terms of PSNR, SSIM, FSIM, and F-value, the algorithms were compared. The experimental results indicate that INOA performs better than all the others in terms of all the performance metrics. This shows that the CIS is a good way to improve the performance of metaheuristic algorithms to get better-registered images. It also shows that INOA is a strong alternative way to register images in the medical field.

References

[1] E. Bermejo, et al., Coral reef optimization with substrate layers for medical image registration, Swarm and Evolutionary Computation 42 (2018) 138−159.

[2] B. Zitova, J. Flusser, Image registration methods: a survey, Image and Vision Computing 21 (11) (2003) 977−1000.

[3] L.-Y. Hsu, M.H. Loew, Fully automatic 3D feature-based registration of multi-modality medical images, Image and Vision Computing 19 (1−2) (2001) 75−85.

[4] Mahmoud, H., Masulli, F., & Rovetta, S. (2013). Feature-based medical image registration using a fuzzy clustering segmentation approach. In: Computational intelligence methods for bioinformatics and biostatistics: 9th international meeting, CIBB 2012, Houston, TX, USA, July 12−14, 2012. Revised selected papers 9. Springer.

[5] S. Gupta, S. Chakarvarti, Zaheeruddin, Medical image registration based on fuzzy c-means clustering segmentation approach using SURF, International Journal of Biomedical Engineering and Technology 20 (1) (2016) 33−50.

[6] Y. Chen, et al., A full migration BBO algorithm with enhanced population quality bounds for multimodal biomedical image registration, Applied Soft Computing 93 (2020) 106335.

[7] P. Gui, et al., United equilibrium optimizer for solving multimodal image registration, Knowledge-Based Systems 233 (2021) 107552.

 [8] B. Abdollahzadeh, F. Soleimanian Gharehchopogh, S. Mirjalili, et al., Artificial gorilla troops optimizer: a new nature-inspired metaheuristic algorithm for global optimization problems, International Journal of Intelligent Systems 36 (10) (2021) 5887–5958.

 [9] A. Faramarzi, et al., Marine predators algorithm: A nature-inspired metaheuristic, Expert Systems with Applications (2020) 113377.

[10] M. Abdel-Basset, R. Mohamed, M. Abouhawwash, On the facile and accurate determination of the highly accurate recent methods to optimize the parameters of different fuel cells: Simulations and analysis, Energy (2023) 127083.

12

Challenges, opportunities, and future prospects

12.1 Introduction

The medical fields have several challenges that still need a solution through metaheuristic techniques, deep learning, or any other strategies. For example, there is a challenge in the medical field called the DNA fragment assembly problem (DFAP) that needs to be accurately tackled for reaching the original DNA from the given fragments [1]. In the fields of medicine and healthcare, one of the diagnostic tools that is utilized most frequently is the electrocardiogram (ECG). Using deep learning based on ECG data has several challenges, including interpretability, efficiency, integration with traditional methods, imbalanced datasets, and multimodal data [2]. Generally, in this chapter, we will extensively discuss the challenges and prospects in the medical field.

12.2 Challenges

Several challenges in the medical field are still open for researchers to search for solutions. For example, the segmentation of brain tumors has been widely recognized as a challenging issue within the realm of medical image analysis, owing to the unpredictable and variable shape and size of such tumors [3]. Several studies in the literature have been done to tackle this challenge, but they still suffer from a low quality of the final solution due to the heterogeneous nature of the tumor cells [4]. In addition, the classification of brain tumors has challenged researchers over the last few years to present robust deep learning techniques able to identify the tumor cells in the brain images due to their heterogeneous characteristics [4].

Humans express their sentiments through speech more than any other medium. Deep learning and machine learning methods are widely used for speech emotion recognition. Nonetheless, these techniques have a high computational cost, which is one of

Metaheuristics Algorithms for Medical Applications. DOI: https://doi.org/10.1016/B978-0-443-13314-5.00006-0

the greatest obstacles. This paves the way for researchers to propose a robust feature selection method capable of locating the near-optimal subset of features that can considerably reduce computational cost. In addition, the gradient-descent algorithms suffer from local minima/optima problems when applying to this problem as an additional challenge [4].

Technology and medicine are intimately tied to one another. The use of tomography or X-rays allows for the accurate detection and diagnosis of injuries sustained by humans as a result of accidents or other occurrences of a similar nature. The detection of edges plays an important part in the processing of medical images. Medical image edge detection is considered a challenging problem due to poor performance of classical algorithms [5].

Three main challenges have to be accurately tackled to improve the performance of the deep learning and machine learning techniques to achieve better accuracy for several medical classification/detection/recognition problems: hand vein recognition, diabetic detection and diagnosis, medical image segmentation and classification, Parkinson's disease diagnosis, heart disease prediction and diagnosis, breast cancer diagnosis, gene selection, brain tissue segmentation, human optic disk detection, malaria transmission detection, breast cancer classification, jaw fracture classification, brain tumor detection and classification, and iris recognition. These challenges include (1) reducing the computational cost, (2) avoiding overfitting and underfitting problems, and (3) getting rid of local minima problems, from which the gradient-descent algorithms suffer.

In the domains of machine learning and big data, incomplete data has become a significant challenge [6]. In the big data era, data extraction from disparate sources such as sensors, or systems is possible, but integrating this data remains a significant challenge. When developing a healthcare system for big data analytics, it is not sufficient to simply standardize the data formats that will be used; rather, we must also consider how to represent data that pertains to the same thing but is collected from various points within the system. This is because the data may be collected from different locations within the system. When the camera signals used to identify human position were altered, it became possible that additional signals from other sensors would be required to validate whether or not a bodily fall had occurred. For this reason, researchers must take into account information fusion problems while designing and implementing an efficient healthcare system, especially a smart home healthcare system [7].

Knowledge interpretation and presentation has always been crucial issue in the healthcare system. This is because physicians need to comprehend the findings of the system's analysis, carers need to be aware of the status of a patient's impairment, and people, in general, want to be aware of their current state of health. Providing a user-friendly interface, such as a dashboard, that visualizes relevant information is a natural approach. One approach is to utilize metaheuristics to simplify the insights gained through data analytics into a set of bullet points that the system's end user can quickly understand [7]. Since the majority of healthcare data are currently stored in a single system to improve the system's ability to analyze these data, the question of how to secure this data is more pressing now than ever. Most people feel that having cameras in their homes is an invasion of privacy, even if cameras can increase the reliability of analysis results in the healthcare system. One of the upcoming themes in healthcare data security research is figuring out how to employ metaheuristics. Another healthcare research topic will focus on improving device detection and prediction rates in the absence of cameras in the home by employing metaheuristics [7].

Parameter values used in mathematical models of drug delivery in living organisms sometimes are assumed to be constant across all individuals of a species or all humans, although these values actually fluctuate from one sample to the next. There is no need for high-risk and expensive laboratory methods when using inverse methods to estimate these parameters. Only by knowing the individual medication concentrations in tissue can the required property value be reached. Humans allow for the control of drug dosage and improved treatment procedures by adjusting the values of drug delivery qualities. Finding a reverse method based on highly performing metaheuristic algorithms for accurately estimating these parameters is a hard challenge [8].

The investigation of deoxyribonucleic acid (also known as DNA) is vitally important in a wide variety of disciplines, including zoology, medicine, biology, forensics, and agriculture. Due to the excessive length of a DNA sequence, it is common practice in many applications for DNA analysis to cut DNA strands into small fragments or segments. These smaller pieces then need to be rejoined after the analysis has been completed. This problem is called the DFAP. The DFAP is an example of an nondeterministic polynomial time-hard problem since its solution requires a nonspecific polynomial amount of time [9]. In the future, one of the challenges that need to be taken into consideration is how to find a new assembler that can be used to attack the DFAP using the overlap-layout-consensus approach. The nurse rostering problem (NRP) is a famous example of an NP-hard combinatorial optimization problem. It is still a hard challenge to allocate shift duties equitably among available nurses given the constraints of the real world [10].

Although it can be expensive, ensuring that hospitalized patients receive adequate nutrition is a crucial part of any competitive healthcare strategy. Providing a variety of diet menus for patients and correctly fulfilling physician orders for diet menus every day is a challenge for healthcare management and nutritionists. Meals for such a competitive system's patients must be meticulously coordinated to ensure that they contain the correct amounts of calories, protein, carbohydrates, fat, and so forth. For these reasons, it is common practice for hospitals to provide in-patients with set menu options. They are not concerned with providing their patients with optimal nutrition because doing so would present difficult managerial challenges, including the need for extensive preparation and costly expenditure [11]. Therefore finding a metaheuristic algorithm with strong characteristics to provide proper nutrition to patients is considered a hard challenge that has to be considered in future works.

Operating room surgery scheduling involves determining the start times of operations for surgeries that are currently being performed and assigning the necessary resources to the surgeries that are scheduled. This process takes into account a number of constraints to guarantee a continuous flow of surgeries, including the availability of resources as well as the specialties and qualifications of human resources. This activity is extremely important since it helps the hospital provide timely treatments for patients while also maintaining a healthy balance in its utilization of its resources [12]. This scheduling problem is considered an NP-hard combinatorial hard problem that needs a strong optimization technique to solve it. Therefore proposing a strong metaheuristic algorithm for overcoming this problem in a reasonable amount of time is considered a hard challenge that needs to be tackled in the future. Vehicle routing problems can be used to model the urgent problem of transferring biological samples from blood draw centers to a central laboratory. Periods and lifetime limitations are applied to this issue, allowing for transfers and multiple visits to certain nodes to lengthen the samples' lifetimes [13]. Proposing a metaheuristic-based technique for the biological sample transportation problems is considered a challenge that has to be tackled in the future.

In brief, the main challenges in the medical field, which need to be tackled by proposing new metaheuristic algorithms with strong exploration and exploitation operators for avoiding stuck into local optima and accelerating the convergence rate toward the near-optimal solutions, are listed in Fig. 12.1.

12.3 Future directions

Future work might involve investigating the performance of some recently proposed metaheuristic optimization algorithms for performing brain tumor segmentation for reaching the near-optimal region that might involve the tumor cells. Furthermore, the metaheuristics could be used for several challenges to improve the classification accuracy of brain tumors. For example, metaheuristics can be used as a feature selection technique with the deep learning model to select the near-optimal subset of features that have the highest influence on the performance of those models. Furthermore, they could be used as an optimizer instead of the gradient-descent algorithms to search for the near-optimal weights of the deep learning models, which

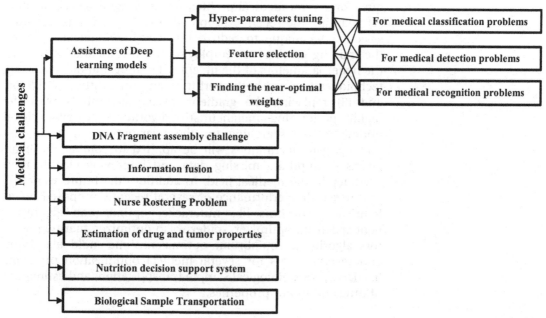

Figure 12.1 List of some challenges in the medical field.

could classify the brain tumor cells accurately. The deep learning models involve several hyperparameters like the number of layers, activation function, batch size, learning rate, and the number of neurons for each layer. Metaheuristic algorithms can be employed to estimate the aforementioned hyperparameters in order to optimize model performance and enhance classification accuracy for brain tumors.

Speech emotion recognition is a crucial problem that needs a strong feature selection technique to minimize the computational cost consumed by deep learning and machine learning to tackle it. Hence, the utilization of metaheuristic algorithms that have been recently proposed to address this challenge is deemed a promising avenue for future research. The following work could be performed to improve the quality and consistency of image edge detection [5]:

- Adapting and improving some of the recent metaheuristic techniques that have not been applied before to this problem.
- Integrating image segmentation with edge detection to obtain a more comprehensive edge.
- This challenge could also be improved by including a human in the loop.

To overcome three challenges discussed in the previous section that reduce the performance of the deep learning techniques for several medical problems, the future work will include (1) adapting the recently proposed metaheuristics as a feature selection technique to reduce the computational cost during the training process, (2) employing the metaheuristics to tune the hyperparameters of the machine learning and deep learning techniques to avoid both overfitting and underfitting problems, and (3) replacing the gradient-descent algorithms with the highly performing metaheuristic algorithms to avoid local optima during searching for the near-optimal weights. The metaheuristic techniques will be applied to combat the challenges of imputing missing data and improving classification accuracy in the medical field. In addition, the future work will also reveal the performance of several recently proposed metaheuristic algorithms like nutcracker optimization algorithm, light spectrum optimizer, spider wasp optimizer, marine predators algorithm, equilibrium optimizer, slime mold algorithm, and several others for several medical optimization problems like DFAP, NRP, biological sample transportation, and estimation of drug and tumor properties.

The classical metaheuristic algorithms have some shortcomings that prevent them from achieving near-optimal solutions for several medical optimization problems. These shortcomings are described in the following list:

- Stagnation into local optima that results from the weak exploration operator of these algorithms.
- Slow convergence speed as a result of the insufficiency of exploitation operators.
- High computational cost.

To overcome these shortcomings, in the future, these algorithms will be improved using some effective mechanisms, like quantum computing, levy flight, chaotic maps, and ranking-based strategy. Moreover, these shortcomings could be eliminated by hybridizing two or more algorithms together to propose a new variant combining the advantages of those algorithms.

References

[1] G. Minetti, G. Leguizamón, E. Alba, An improved trajectory-based hybrid metaheuristic applied to the noisy DNA fragment assembly problem, Information Sciences 277 (2014) 273–283.

[2] S. Hong, et al., Opportunities and challenges of deep learning methods for electrocardiogram data: a systematic review, Computers in Biology and Medicine 122 (2020) 103801.

[3] S.N. Shivhare, N. Kumar, Tumor bagging: a novel framework for brain tumor segmentation using metaheuristic optimization algorithms, Multimedia Tools and Applications 80 (17) (2021) 26969–26995.

[4] D.R. Nayak, et al., Brain tumour classification using noble deep learning approach with parametric optimization through metaheuristics approaches, Computers 11 (1) (2022) 10.

[5] C. Ticala, C.-M. Pintea, O. Matei, Sensitive ant algorithm for edge detection in medical images, Applied Sciences 11 (23) (2021) 11303.

[6] A. Garg, et al. DL-GSA: a deep learning metaheuristic approach to missing data imputation, in: Proceedings of the Ninth International Conference on Advances in Swarm Intelligence, ICSI 2018, 17–22 June 2018, Springer, Shanghai, China, Part II, 2018, p. 9.

[7] C.-W. Tsai, et al., Metaheuristic algorithms for healthcare: open issues and challenges, Computers and Electrical Engineering 53 (2016) 421–434.

[8] P. Mirchi, M. Soltani, Estimation of drug and tumor properties using novel hybrid meta-heuristic methods, Journal of Theoretical Biology 488 (2020) 110121.

[9] M. Abdel-Basset, et al., An efficient-assembler whale optimization algorithm for DNA fragment assembly problem: analysis and validations, IEEE Access 8 (2020) 222144–222167.

[10] A.M. Turhan, B. Bilgen, A hybrid fix-and-optimize and simulated annealing approaches for nurse rostering problem, Computers & Industrial Engineering 145 (2020) 106531.

[11] Y.Y. Ileri, M. Hacibeyoglu, Advancing competitive position in healthcare: a hybrid metaheuristic nutrition decision support system, International Journal of Machine Learning and Cybernetics 10 (2019) 1385–1398.

[12] W. Xiang, J. Yin, G. Lim, An ant colony optimization approach for solving an operating room surgery scheduling problem, Computers and Industrial Engineering 85 (2015) 335–345.

[13] M. Benini, P. Detti, G.Z.M. de Lara, Mathematical programming formulations and metaheuristics for biological sample transportation problems in healthcare, Computers and Operations Research 146 (2022) 105921.

Index

Note: Page numbers followed by "*f*," "*t*," and "*b*" refer to figures, tables, and boxes, respectively.

performance metrics, 39–40
practical analysis, 41–43
  comparison among
    algorithms over salt and
    pepper noise, 41*f*
wavelet denoising, 29–31
  depiction of three stages,
    31*f*
  principle of, 30–31
  wavelet transform, 29–30
WCA. *See* Water cycle algorithm
  (WCA)
Wearable devices, 47–48
Wearable sensors, 47–48, 106
Weighted KNN algorithm
  (wKNN algorithm),
  111–112

Whale optimization algorithm
  (WOA), 9, 165
Windows 10 operating system,
  156–157
wKNN algorithm. *See* Weighted
  KNN algorithm (wKNN
  algorithm)
WOA. *See* Whale optimization
  algorithm (WOA)
Wolf pack search algorithm
  (WPS), 9
WPS. *See* Wolf pack search
  algorithm (WPS)
Wrapper-based methods,
  125–126, 130–137,
  147–148

metaheuristic-based feature
  selection, 133–137
sequential selection
  algorithms, 131–133
wrapper-based feature
  selection techniques,
  131*f*
WSO. *See* Wasp swarm
  optimization (WSO)
WT. *See* Wavelet transform
  (WT)

X

X-rays, 161–162, 201–202, 222
Xception network, 162–163
XMACO, 165